The Glory Door

by B.J. Jones

God never gives us a dark so dark
that it cannot be brightened by the swish of
The White Mule's Tale.

author HOUSE®

AuthorHouse™ LLC
1663 Liberty Drive
Bloomington, IN 47403
www.authorhouse.com
Phone: 1-800-839-8640

Published by AuthorHouse   07/11/2013

ISBN: 978-1-4817-6046-1 (sc)
ISBN: 978-1-4817-6045-4 (hc)
ISBN: 978-1-4817-6044-7 (e)

Library of Congress Control Number: 2013910715

❦

*I dedicate this
book to God, who
is, like all I write,
the real author, and to
Ernest Holman McNabb, who
was my Uncle, my big brother,
my WW II hero and the last male
guardian of our McNabb name.
This is for you, Uncle Ernie.
May your memory and
your name last
forever.*

●

The
Senate Office buildings,
January 18, 2024
Capitol Hill, Washington, DC

❧

8:30 *A,M*

51 1/2 hours
before Inauguration:

The election had been monumental but it was over. He had won. Now Senator Ernest H. McNabb, President Elect to the Office of the 46th President of the United States of America sits in his current office on Capitol Hill, which still showed the evidence of the victory celebration that was held there a week ago. Bright colored confetti still decorated the nooks and crannies and about six dog-eared campaign posters stuck our from behind the door. He had his shoes off and his feet up on the desk watching a renegade helium filled balloon, sporting it's message "Trust in Ernest" dance about the ceiling. It was his way of enjoying his one whole day before session takes up again tomorrow morning.

It is a rare thing for him to have a day to himself, away from all the causes of the world, and get to use that twenty four hours any way he wants to and is now somewhere around eight hours and thirty two minutes of selfishly thinking about himself, and only himself, when the phone rings. Impulsively, he answers it after the second ring.

"Hello, this is Senator McNabb. How may I . . . uh, oh."

Before he even got the words out of his mouth, he knew he had done it again and looked around for Linda, his executive secretary and scheduler whose head had just popped through the door and was frowning at him.

It was a habit he had been unable to break throughout his entire growing up and political life. It started back on High Mountain, when he was twelve and his family had gotten their first telephone. It was a party line and their ring was supposed to be three rings, but Ernest always forgot and answered it after the second. Mrs. Tingsley, the mother of his best friend Trenton Tingsley, had the two ring signal but was used to Ernest's reactions and never got mad. When she knew Ernest was on the line, she would simply and quietly say, "Hello, Ernest . . . Goodbye Ernest" and Ernest would put his hand over his mouth and hang up.

Linda, who has been his secretary since he first entered the political world as Postmaster of the town of Sweetgum some twenty two years ago, was not that understanding, but tolerated him. He just plain old loved to talk to people and sometimes couldn't help himself. Politicos around the country predicted him to be the most story telling-ist president this country has ever had since Abraham Lincoln.

"Is this Senator McNabb?" The voice asked.

"Yes, this is he.

"Is it . . . President Elect Senator McNabb?

"Yes, to whom am I speaking?"

"Oh . . . I . . . well, I didn't . . ."

"You didn't what? . . . How may I help you?

"I . . . I didn't expect you to answer your own phone. I'm . . . I'm just a . . . I mean I'm Mary Jean Salt, my friends call me Pepper and I'm from the town of Sweetgum and I'm a reporter with the *Sweetgum Gazette* and I'm calling to see if I could schedule and interview with you, Sir."

"An interv . . . ? Young lady," Said Ernest, with a hint of impatience, "I, my family, my mother, my father and even Charlie, my dog have been interviewed up and down and inside and out by the Washington Post, The New York Herald, The Los Angeles Times, The New Orleans Picayune and others. And, if my memory doesn't fail me, I have already been interviewed by the Political Editor, the Fashion Editor, the Sports Editor and The Editor in Chief of the Sweetgum Gazette. I would think that through all those interviews you would have, by now, anything you need to know about me."

"That' all true, Sir. I've read them all and they are very complete . . . mostly."

"Mostly?"

"Yes Sir. I realize that you are, without a doubt, the busiest man in our country, but let me ask you Sir, could you possibly grant me a short interview if I promise . . . on the Bible, Sir . . . that I will only ask you one question?"

"One question? What is that?"

"Well, Sir, in the Washington Post interview, Jane Prentice, their Political Editor asked you what your top priority will be after you get to the Oval Office, and your answer was to *Make this nation's Glory shine again.*"

"Yes, I remember."

"Then in the Los Angeles Times, you referred to the War of 1812 as *The Glory Days* . . .and when you spoke at the National Headquarters of the Red Cross in Washington you said that *"Since 1915 The Red Cross has been bringing Glory to the Brave,* and after Iran attacked Israel, you referred to the craters left by their bombs as *Glory Holes.*"

"Well, as I think about it, I suppose all that is true," Said Ernest, "but . . ."

"And you nick-named Pennsylvania Avenue, leading to the white House as *The Glory Road,* and you called the re-building of the Trade Towers, their *Rising Glory,* and through your earlier years when you were campaigning in the Lucy-Mule Mobile, you called Lucy your *Shining Glory* and last September, talking to the House of Representatives in Washington you spoke of the importance of the Democrats and Republicans working together to *bring Glory back to our country.* Do you remember?"

"Well, yes, I did, but . . ."

"And, at the Convention for Human Relations, you said that we must strip away our prejudice and *Let our Glory shine through* and when Oprah asked you how you would describe the American People, you said *"The Glory-us!"*

"Yes, yes, yes, I recall *all* of that" Said Ernest, "Now, what is your one big question?"

"My question . . . my one big question is, *Who is Glory?*"

There was a long, uninterrupted silence. Pepper waited and waited and when she was afraid that she had lost her connection, called out, "Senator McNabb, are you there, Sir ?"

"Yes, young lady, I am here. I apologize for my silence, but . . . well, no one has ever asked me that question before."

"Oh? Then can I have the interview?"

"Yes," Said Ernest, "When can you be here?"

"Well, Sir, I don't want to be pushy . . . that is, pushier that I have already been, but I happen to be talking to you from my car parked on thirteenth street and Pennsyl . . . ." She paused. "I mean, I'm parked on thirteenth street and *The Glory Road.*"

Ernest laughed. "I see, then it shouldn't take you long to get here." He paused again, "The bigger issue, now that I think about your question is, how long can I take to answer?"

Chapter 1

"Lay the proud usurpers low!
Tyrants fall in every foe!
Liberty's in every blow!
Let us do, or die!"
ROBERT BURNS

It was the year of 1813, in the town of Edinburgh Scotland and Regimental Sergeant Hadwell Childers of the British Royal Army had just finished the most breathtakingly charged and dramatic marching order he had ever delivered to any group of conscripted new recruits and, looking at them now, he was quite proud of himself. They came in three months ago, an unruly mixture of homesick, clumsy farm lads and tousled-haired, overweight spoiled city kids who knew or cared nothing about war, and were now going out as a polished, in-step regiment of His Majesty's Soldiers of the Realm on their way to America to join in on the invasion of New Orleans.

As he watched them lining up at the gang plank of the H.M.T. Britannic, ready to board, he took a deep breath and silently congratulated himself with a rare bit of fatherly pride. "Not bad, Sergeant, if eh do hae tae say meself, laddie . . . Young they may be . . . but thanks to ye me boy, thay are READY!"

His moment of indulgent back patting was interrupted, however, as he heard a ruckus and loud laughter coming from the head of the line. He stepped up on an untended shipping trunk to get a better look and spied the unmistakable blond, curly hair of Privates Duncan and Fergus McNabb. It appeared to be a disagreement between the two brothers on the proper way to wear the uniform of The Royal Dublin Fusiliers. It seems that young Duncan had released the waistline button that held Fergus' kilt up and the whole squad was taking pleasure out of watching him juggle his musket, keep the tall bear-skin hat out of his eyes while protecting his *esprit de corps* all at the same time.

These two *full-of-the-divil* brothers were both tall, blond, muscular and had smiles that could melt the heart of a dragon. They had made his life interesting from the day he was ordered to drag them, kicking and screaming, down out of the Highlands to . . . *join their new comrades in the act of war.* For the boys, given their druthers, the last thing in the world the two of them could ever imagine, would be the idea of leaving their lofty, quiet little town of Grimsby and go fight in a war they knew nothing about.

"Napoleon, maybe, but America . . . whaur be that? Wha us?" Asked Fergus.

Sergeant Childers, who was then a Lance Sergeant, in charge of the squad of mounted Redcoats who trekked all the way up their mountain, just to pick up the two of them smiled.

"Didna ye hear, Laddie?" Said the Sergeant, as he escorted them to the wagon. "Tis an invite of the Crown . . . an His Majesty's invites canna be refused, didna ye know. Tis not polite."

Once they used up all their arguments, however, and seeing no way out, the two brothers accepted the inevitable and swore to each other a pledge to train harder, shoot straighter and charge in faster than their comrades, make short work of the rebelling colonist and be back home in three months.

When they informed the Sergeant of their plan, he looked at them out of the corner of his eye, removed the carved bulldog meerschaum from under his ample mustache and said, with as much sincerity as he could muster, "'Tis a guid plan, laddies an I bid ye guid luc, in the doing."

They had no way of knowing at the time, that their war would consist of exactly one battle, one charge and one well-aimed cannon ball and when mixed together, would mark the end of the McNabb brothers' military careers and the beginning of a whole and different life for them both.

———•———

The British troops sent to invade New Orleans were considered the best equipped and the best trained army in the world. Fresh from defeating Napoleon in France and greatly outnumbering the Americans, it was the opinion of the world that they could not be stopped.

The American's on the other hand didn't even have enough weapons to go around and were described as rag-tag, unshaven fighters with *dirty shirts*. What the world didn't know, however, was that the Americans were a magnificent combination of professional soldiers, Tennessee and Kentucky Militias, free blacks, Cajuns, Indians, farmers and shopkeepers who were, each and every one, expert marksmen who could bring down a squirrel from the highest tree with a single shot or a British red coat from behind that tree just as well.

———•———

It was a cold, foggy day-break on December 24, one day before Christmas on the east bank of the Mississippi river close to New Orleans, where over 3000 British soldiers covered their ears as their cannons pounded the heavily fortified earthwork on the opposite shore. The American fortification was nick-named *Line Jackson* in honor of it's famous leader, Major General Andrew Jackson.

After studying the defense, the British commanders agreed that the earthwork was indeed effective but far too short and left room on the southern end for them to take a division of fresh troops, go through the cypress swamp and hit the General from the back while he was busy fighting off the main force coming at his front.

The two pronged attack would have made short work of the famous general if it hadn't been for one man. Captain Jean LaFitte, the most infamous French privateer that ever sailed out of the Gulf of Mexico. He also saw the vulnerable left flank of the Americans and saw clearly that a second British force coming through the swamp could blind side the General, end the battle and be back aboard their ships sailing home in a matter of hours.

The privateer approached General Jackson with an introduction as well as an offer to bring his army of brigands and shore up the general's short end. General Jackson knew that it would give him over 800 men, many of which were the most accurate and devastating cannoneers the British army could ever face. His army now was made up mostly of local militiamen, free slaves and Choctaw tribesmen wrapped around a core of army regulars and were outnumbered more than ten to one. At first, he was a little hesitant but quickly saw the sense of it all and formed a battleground agreement with the famous pirate to cover the south end of Line Jackson. LaFitte knew the swamp like the back of his hand and it was an easy trick for him to secretly and quickly move his band through the murky mire, undercover of darkness, form their defense . . . and wait.

———•———

Privates Duncan and Fergus McNabb sat snuggly behind a huge great oak, draped with Spanish moss hanging down low enough to hide them from sight. There

4

was cannon fire all around and black powder smoke hung over the ground like a dense fog and it was bitter cold.

Their company was battle ready and awaiting orders. The brothers, on the other hand were battle ready and bored. At this particular moment, they were busy polishing their matching flintlock pistols, each with the "McNabb" crest beautifully carved in their cherry wood handles, which their "Dattie" gave to them on their sixteenth birthday along with a serious proclamation.

"Tis this day ye be a mon of the Clan McNabb, lads," He would say solemnly. "A bid ye to Cherish ye birthright un wi thae guns, protect it's honor."

Each took him seriously and did cherish those pistols, more than life itself and carried them in makeshift holsters sewn inside their red uniform jumpers where no officer could see them and maybe confiscate them as unissued weapons. When things got tense and they needed to get away from it all and find neutral ground, they would sneak away and find a private out-of-the-way spot to polish their guns and talk about home in the Highlands.

Unfortunately for the peace and quiet of their hiding place, their talks always seemed to get around to Bridget McDuffy, the freckled face daughter of Hamish McDuffy, Lord Mayor of their little hometown of Grimsby, whom they both loved. She was an unstoppable, red-headed flirt, one year older than Duncan and two years younger than Fergus. Tonight, however, they found that they could not *talk* to each other. Tonight, with the never ending boom of the cannons they *shouted* to each other and at times, they s*creamed.*

"AYE, TIS A BONNIE LASS WI HAIR O RED, she is, and . . . SHE PROMISED TO MARRY ME WHEN A GET BACK!" Screamed Duncan

"MARRY? YE?" Screamed Fergus. WHEN WE KISSED AT THE GANGPLANK, SHE SAY FOR ME

TA HURRY BACK SO'S THE TWO OF US CUD WED, she did!"

"WHAT?" Duncan screamed back. Then, before Fergus could answer and for no reason at all, the cannons stopped suddenly. "YOU GA IT ALL WRONG, YE NINNY!

Everybody in camp heard him.

"AHA," said a voice behind them. "There da two of ye are!" It was Master Sergeant Grantly Peacock looking down at the shiny pistols. "Put them things away afore the lieutenant sees em and grab your backpacks, bayonets and pull on your boots! We're forming up for a night march . . . through the swamp, we are."

"Through wha?" Asked Fergus.

"The swamp!" Answered the sergeant.

"You canna mean that, Sarge! You canna take the likes of me, Fergus McNabb, the creme of Scottish manhood and drag me handsome self through a muddy hell that stinks with bugs and crawls with snakes and be . . . for goodness sake, four feet below sea level! A'm a Highlander, A am! Ye canna do this!" Pleaded Fergus.

"Just watch me, laddie boy." Answered the sergeant. "Just watch me." And walked away.

Fergus looked at Duncan who was just sitting and staring into the night.

What be it Dunc?"

"It's be our first battle."

"Aye. What aboot it?"

"Tis in a bloody swamp!.

"So?" Said Fergus. "Wha da matter?"

"Tis in a bloody swamp! Das wha da matter!"

"So?"

"So . . ." Said Duncan, shaking his head. "Oor wee, nichtime attack wil nae go down in history as another *charge of the light brigade*, wi it now?"

Fergus smiled "Nae, Dunc, it won't"

6

Chapter 2

In 1814
we took a little trip
along with General Jackson
down the mighty Missisip,

We took a little bacon
and we took a little beans
and we fought the bloody British
near the town of New Orleans.

We fired our guns
and the British kept a coming
but there wasn't nigh as many
as there was a while ago.

Then we fired once more and
the British started running
down the mighty Mississippi
to the of Gulf of Mexico
(FOLK SONG)

British General Edward Pakenham's forces slogged through the night and reached solid footing just before daybreak where they re-organized and once again became an unrelenting, red-coated war machine, over 8000 strong and headed straight for General Jackson in a three pronged assault. Privates Duncan and Fergus McNabb were two rows back from the front line with chin straps in place and marching stiffly to a drum beat with muskets and bayonets at ready. The *sure-of-himself* General smiled as he watched their advance. "There was no way the famous Jackson can stand up under this."

What General Pakenham did not know, was the fact that Captain Jean LaFitte and his army of battle tested warriors and his awesome brigade of cannoneers were waiting five miles south of New Orleans and were dug in.

Packenham's forces charged and when they did, American cannons opened up. Scores of redcoats fell screaming. As they got into rifle shot range, rank after rank of American and pirate muskets alike, fired in unison.

Private Duncan McNabb was among the front ranks now, running as fast as he could. He looked over at Fergus running beside him. He had never seen his brother so magnificent. All of a sudden, a loud, unmistakable scream of a cannon ball was getting louder and louder overhead. Duncan, realizing there was no way to escape it, instinctively, without losing a step, held his rifle in one hand and pushed Fergus to the right so hard he fell into a crater hole, just as the ball exploded. That was all Duncan knew. Everything went black.

The battle lasted throughout the day and night with the British losing at every turn. At daybreak, under a dense fog, they started a retreat. By mid-morning, they had collected their wounded, including Private Fergus McNabb and retreated toward their ships. On that day, over 2000 British soldiers were killed, captured or wounded. The Americans lost only 7 with 6 wounded. From start to finish, throughout the whole three-pronged invasion, the Americans only lost 333 fighting men.

Cheers rang out. Jackson had held! Union forces and pirates alike jumped for joy. Malaki Messer, a young, black African who served as Captain Jean LaFitte's personal servant and bodyguard went wild. His big, brown eyes sparkled as he ran and jumped a-straddle of his friend *Hog Breath Hanratty*.

"We done it, Hog! We won! We done sent that General Pakenham a packing!"

Hog, who was dabbing at a big knot on his forehead, broke into a big smile that went from ear to ear and showed one front tooth missing. "He be called ole General *Smokin'* ham now, I reckon, won't he, Mal?" And cackled.

This major victory ended the War of 1812.

Chapter 3

After any major battle, the ground on which it was fought is never a pretty sight to see. Malaki, Messer, who had been with Captain LaFitte for twelve years now, knew that only too well. He was a six year old Gullah captive on a slave ship in the Caribbean, headed for the new world, when they were spotted and boarded by LaFitte and his band of privateers. After a short, but bloody battle, the terrified natives were released from their chains and brought top-side. When he asked if anyone spoke English, the young boy stepped forward. He had lived with a missionary family since his mother and father were killed by another tribe and it was they who taught him about God and enough English to get by.

Through the boy, LaFitte explained that all the slavers had been killed and that the ship was to be scuttled. He said that they would be released on one of the Sea Islands tomorrow and wished them well.

When they reached the once Spanish held island called Little Majorca, the largest and outermost island of the group, the frightened, but grateful natives were put ashore. When they were making ready to sail again, Captain LaFitte was surprised to find the young boy still aboard.

"What's this?" Said Captain LaFitte, "Why are you still aboard? Didn't I say . . ."

"I want to go with you." The young boy interrupted.

Captain LaFitte laughed. "Ha, maybe when you grow up, mate, but I . . ."

"I was the best fighter in our tribe." Said the boy, flatly.

"So?" Said LaFitte, in a disinterested way.

The boy took a spear that he had fashioned out of the handle of a deck swab and the broken blade of a hunting knife and said, "Do you see that man with the tall hat by the cabin?"

LaFitte looked around and saw Hog Breath Hanratty standing there looking hungry, as always, in his old beaten-up sombrero he took from a rich Mexican.,

"I see him. So what?"

"He should take his hat off in the presence of his Captain, don't you think?"

"Huh? What do you mean, boy. Hey! What are you doing? Stop! . . ."

Just then, the boy threw the spear. It sailed straight for Hog Breath, and before he could move, pinned his sombrero to the galley door.

Hog Breath took a long curved dagger from his sash and started for the boy.

"Belay that, you lubber!" Yelled LaFitte. "He meant ye no harm."

Hog Breath removed his hat and walked away, mumbling to himself.

"He could have killed you!" Said LaFitte, "Why did you do that?"

"To show you how I fight," said the boy.

The Captain looked into his large, unusually green eyes full of adventure and saw an African version of himself at six years of age. "What's ye name, mate?"

"I am called Adebowale Simballe," said the boy.

"Ade . . . bow . . . ? That's a problem." Said Captain LeFitte, rubbing the bristle on his chin. "If ye are going to be one of us, I can't go around calling you . . . Adabo Simba, or . . . what ever you said." He stopped, looked up at the jolly roger atop the main mast and curled his mustache. "I think I'll call you Malaki."

"Mal-ak-i?" Said the boy.

"Yep, Malaki . . . Malaki Messer. He was the best cook this scow ever had. He got himself killed two weeks ago when a cannonball off HMS London crashed through the galley bulkhead . . . I miss him, so I'll give you his name."

"Mali . . . Malaki Messer." The boy smiled. "I will do honor to that name."

"Good," said LaFitte. "Go report to Hog Breath in the galley. He's the mate who owned the hat ye just speared. He's gonna love you."

—◦—

In the next two years, Malaki grew by at least two inches and became an expert with a biscuit cutter as well as a saber and flintlock. His course, black hair grew into a great ball, two times the size of his head and his muscular body defined itself like a statue chisled in black marble and when he smiled, like all the time, his green eyes sparkled.

In the worst of storms, he could shinny up the main mast and lash off the giant canvass like the best of them. Captain LaFitte was so impressed, he decided to keep him as his personal servant because it would keep him out of the heavy fighting and more importantly, he liked having him around to talk to in the evenings.

Malaki was now a privateer without commission from any sovereign nation. He fought when he had to and laughed when he wanted to and, in time, became well liked by all hands . . . even *Hog Breath Hanratty*.

He never thought twice about going into battle, he just jumped into the thick of it all with sword in hand and only one thought in mind, "God of the Missionaries, if ye are there n' if ye can hear me, keep me in the right and, if it pleases ye God, keep me alive."

—————•—————

Today, as he walked and looked over the gore of the muddy, pitted battleground, he had other things on his mind. He was puzzled.

"It don't figure," He said to himself out loud. "Jes wat do them Gennals think they doing? I mean, that Gennul Packenham, he take thousands 'n thousands o young lads n' puts fancy red coats on em n' teach em how to shoot and march. Den that American General Jackson, he take thousands 'n thousands of his boys n' puts blue coats on em' n' teaches 'em how to shoot 'n march. Den, while them gennals sit back on the poop deck, shy of grapeshot and safe as a play-dead possum, points them lads face-to-face against each others bullets and then waits to see what crawls out of the bung hole!! And they do all that just for the love of their country! What kind of a bloody fight is that! Nobody gets nothin' out of it atall, 'cept dead."

However, he was not out this evening walking through a rainy, foggy, dead-silent battleground, to solve the unsolvable problems of the world. His motive this night was much simpler than that. He was out to see if one of them lifeless figures layin' out there might like to donate a gold pocket watch to an enterprising privateer who never knows what time it is. As he walked further out, the stench got worse and the oozing, muddy earth swallowed his feet with every step he took. He had about come to the end of his conviction.

He sat down on a half-buried forty pounder to light his pipe. The eerie silence prompted him to squint to see if he could see the other side. It was vast and it went from grey to dark grey to black. He was beginning to wonder if a gold watch was worth all this effort and started to turn back when he thought he saw something. He stood up on top of the forty pounder to get a better look. It was a light or a glow, away back in the darkness and it was moving. At first, he thought it might be somebody holding a lantern but as he got closer, the white glow got bigger. Now it was too big and too white to be just a lantern.

"Now, what n' whales belly could that be?" He said as he quickened his pace to get around a cluster of extra deep cannon holes. He squinted again. "It looks like an animal of sorts" he said to himself. "Least be, it's got mor'n two legs." As it got closer, he started to back up. It *was* an animal of some sorts. It looked like a horse, only it was shining so bright, he couldn't tell. Then he heard something. It was talking, only it's mouth was not moving.

"I am Glory. I light the way to the man who seeks himself." Said the vision and took two steps closer.

When Malaki heard what he thought he heard and caught sight of her big ears, he started backing up without looking and fell off the rim into a very deep and very dark crater. It was about four feet deeper than he was tall and when he looked up and saw the glow getting brighter and brighter along the rim, he tried to crawl up the other side but it was no use. He turned just as the animal's head popped clear.

"Well I'll be the devils digger if it ain't a horse! Least ways, it looks like a horse but I ain't never seen a horse the size of that n' with ears the size of them! Not here . . . not in Africa . . . not nowhere!"

"I am Glory. I light the way to the man who seeks himself." The vision repeated.

"I hear you, Mate!" He called. "But t'wood be the Angel's deed if you could lend me a han . . . er . . . a hoof and get me out of here!" The animal came closer, as if answering him and made another sound. It was sort of a snicker, only different. "Don't sound like a horse, neither," thought Malaki. "What was Capn' LaFitte telling me bout that General up Vinginy way . . . what was his name . . . Oh yeh! Washington! That was his name. He said he was cross breedin' horses with donkeys, or burros or something and gettin' bigger n' stronger animals than all git-out. What was it he called em . . . , Mules! That's it! I've think I maybe done met me my first mule! Ahoy, Lady!"

He stood up to reach and tripped over something. The mule made that strange noise again and leaned over the rim and stomped her hoof three times. Jessie looked down at his feet. It was a body, most buried in the mud. The snickering continued.

"Hold yer horse-s, lady or what ever it is a mule like ye holds, and let me look here." Jessie crouched over the body. "Looks to me like this bloke is 'bout dead as yesterday's rum keg. There ain't nothin' I can . . ." The mule stomped her hoof three more times and her ears went straight up. Malaki didn't realize it, but while he was talking to the mule, he still had hold of the body's hand . . . and it twitched.

"No, wait! This maté's still with us, I think. We're gonna need to get him out of all this mud to tell."

The mule's great, white head was not moving. Her eyes just stared at the body. She was motionless.

"Ok, ok . . . we need a rope . . ." He thought. "Me sash! That's it!" Malaki wore an extra long sash, wound around and around his middle to keep warm at night. He unwound it all, tied a fragment of iron to it's tassel and flung it up toward the lady mule. She stomped on it like it was something she did every day. Encouraged, Mal passed the other end under the arms of the unconscious body and waved his hand at the big animal to pull back. Sure enough, the vision had the scarf in her mouth and started back. Malaki watched in amazement as the body started to inch up toward the rim of the hole, little by little. When it cleared the top, Mal couldn't see anything, so he waited . . . and waited. Soon, the mule returned with one end of the sash in her mouth and nuzzled the free end back down. Mal found a bayonet under the mud and started digging footholds in the crater wall. Holding onto the sash, he made it more than half way up when the sash pulled out of the mule's mouth. His footholds were starting to give way and he was preparing to hit bottom again when he looked up and noticed that the mule had turned around and had lowered her tail down toward him. He reached, but his arms were too short and her tail was not long enough. It hung just inches from his outstretched fingers. He took a deep breath and in one great stretch, further that he ever stretched before, and caught hold, and three mule steps later, Mal, too was at the rim. As he cleared the mud off his face, he looked up.

"How come it is, Miss Mule, that I got mud on me so thick I look like a snappin' turtle, and you've been wallering out here as much as me and you ain't got nary a spot on ye. He cleaned some of the mud off of the motionless body and saw that it was a young lad no more that sixteen or seventeen. He was a Brit, wearing what was left of his red tunic and he had a death grip on something under it. He showed no signs of life. He was cold to the touch and when Mal tried to pry his hand loose from whatever he was holding, he would not let it go. He looked up into the big, brown eyes of his new friend. "Sorry, m'lady but I'm afeered he ain't no longer with us," and started to stand up.

When he did, the magnificent animal went to her knees. "What's this?" Said Mal, "Ain't no sense toting' a daid body, specially a red coat, clean back to the ship to bury. Might jes as well do it here and he started to get up. The mule wouldn't budge. Mal tried to pull her up onto her feet with no success. She turned her head to Mal and snickered again. Mal reached down to took hold of the clutching hand and pulled back when it twitched again.

"Uh-oh!" Said Mal, startled. "OK, m'lady . . . We'll do it your way. If there's any life left in this boy atall, the *Fixer* can tell us." With that, he planted his boots on the most solid ground he could find, put the soldier's right arm around his own neck and lifted the limp body out of the mud and over the Mule's back. She didn't move until he crawled on behind and the instant he did, she started to move. Jessie could feel her powerful muscles take hold as she rose, like she was taking a walk in the park on a sunny day.

The trip back to the ship took about an hour and they pulled up in front of a makeshift tent on the dock with wounded men in beds and cots. There was a hand-painted sign on the front of the tent which read " *The Fixer.*" Malaki slid down and draped the body over his shoulder, like he had done with comrades in so many battles, and entered the tent where a harried man in a bloody apron was tending a fallen mate. He looked up.

"Ahoy Doc!" Mal waved. "Got a customer fer ye . . . . I think."

Doc, The Fixer, was stitching a saber wound on the head of a young man who probably hadn't seen his twentieth birthday yet, and motioned toward an empty table in the rear. "Put him there. I'll get to him."

"Ye got it, Doc. I don't know jes how much life is left in this one but his big friend outside and I think that maybe, it might be worth a look."

Doc stood up. He was a tall, slender man in his late forties or early fifties. He was bald on top but had long white hair and sideburns around, with a full mustache and goatee. You could tell just by looking that he was an educated gentleman and at one time, was an upstanding physician back in London or Paris or somewhere.

His clear, blue eyes showed no emotion as they moved from Malaki's face to the muddy form laying on the table, brushed some mud off his chest and looked back to Malaki.

"This man's a Brit, and he's hurt bad"

"Thas what we figered, but we . . ."

"Since when have we been in the business of treating the very ones we set out to kill?"

"I know. I hear ye, Doc," said Jessie. "As a matter of fact, I said the same thing to me self when I first stumbled over him. I was jes gonna re-lieve the bloke of his pocket watch 'n go on me way, but he had this . . . well I guess you'd call her a friend standing there beside him and . . . well . . . she sorta convinced me different and we come here."

"What kind of a friend?" Asked Doc.

"I was afeared ye might ask me that, Doc, and I'll answer ye right out, but you gotta know that I ain't been hittin' the rum ration or nothing"

"Well?"

"Well," Said Malaki, looking down at the floor and mumbling, "She's a shining, white horse with big . . ."

"Malaki!" Doc said suddenly, "Look up here. I can't hear you. It sounded like you said she was a shining, white horse??"

Mal looked up into Doc's eyes. "I knew ye wouldn't believe me Doc, but that's the truth. She's a shining, white horse with ears as big as an angels wing and a nose to match . . ."

"You mean, like a mule?" Doc interrupted.

"Ye, that's it . . . a mule."

"And you found her where? On the battlefield?"

"Yep," said Mal. "Standing guard over the lad, like an Angel or something. If he lives . . . she's the one what saved his life. I would have walked right on by and never seen him, but she wuz shinin' like a star."

"Hm-m-m," said Doc, cleaning mud off the young soldiers face. "I've heard a lot about divine intervention from the hurt and dying, but this is the first time I . . ."

"De-vine what . . . ?" Asked Mal.

"You know, golden angels over head, bright lights shining in the darkness, voices from Heaven and such, but this is the first time I've ever heard of a mule from there. I didn't know you were such a church goer.

"Well, that's where I think Glory come from." Said Malaki defiantly n' I ain't been to church since neigh-on to never.

"Glory?" Mused Doc. "That's a good name. How did you think of it?"

"I didn't," Said Malaki, "She told me!"

"She told you?"

"Yep, she told me . . . I think. What was it she said?" Mal asked himself, "Oh yeah, she said something like . . . '*I am Glory. I light ye way to the lad who seeks hisself.*' Is that English, Doc? What does it mean?"

Doc stopped what he was doing and looked up, rubbing his chin. "*A lad who seeks himself?* I'm afraid I don't know."

"Well, anyhow, I got to figuring." Said Mal, rubbing the stubble on his chin, "If you'd fought a battle like that boy done 'n you found yourself all blowed up and left for dead in a muddy cannonball hole and ye wuz a man of God, the natural thing to do would be to pray for help and when God hears de prayer, He look down and see dat boy laying in a dark hole on a dark night and a dark pirate man frum Africa walkin' by and God knows, 'cause God knows everything, that one black man ain't gonna be able to hoist a body out of that muddy hole and carry him out of dat battlefield all by himself, so He lit up a mule like a light house, knowing that I would walk straight to it. Then, when I got up close, there she stood . . . in all her shining . . . ."

"Glory?" Said Doc without looking up.

"Ye got it, Doc . . . Ye got it!"

Doc stood up. "And just where is this . . . Shining Glory now?"

Oh," said Jessie, "she's tied up outside. Ye gotta see her, Doc!! I never seen the likes of such a be-au ti . . ."

Doc pulled back the tent flaps and stepped out with Malaki on his heels and looked around.

"Where, Mal?"

Chapter 4

🪆

"Watch out, Ferg! Run! Charge! Don look back, laddie! Are ye hit, lad? Listen! What's that? Oh me God! Go! Ferg! Go!!!"

For ten days, the tortured young soldier re-lived his battle all over again and mumbled and screamed throughout the nights. No matter which way he moved, he hurt,

"Am I home?" He thought to himself. "The noise has stopped. No more explosions. It's over! Is it over? Did we win?"

His hand automatically moved down his right leg. "It's gone! It's nae there!" He panicked. "What's nae there?" His mind was whirling but it wouldn't or couldn't stop on any particular subject long enough to form a complete thought. "That smell . . . It be alcohol . . . I think. Can't see. Are me eyes open? What be tha bloody ringing in me ears. Someone's talking! Who be talking?

I must open me eyes."

———•———

"Can you hear me, mate?" The Fixer's voice was calm and soothing. "Are you ready to come out and play with the rest of us?" He gently touched the young man's shoulder.

———•———

"It is a voice." The boy thought. "Some one is talking to me. I must concentrate." He gave it everything he had . . . and slowly . . . ever so slowly his eyes began to open.

———•———

"There you are, my boy. We were beginning to wonder. It's been ten days now. Can you talk? How're ye feeling?"

"Where . . . am . . . I?" He mumbled.

"You're in the hands of The Fixer." Doc said. "My name's DuPhol, Doctor Drey DuPhol, Least-wise it was before I took to the high seas. Now I'm just known as The Fixer. How ye feeling? I have to say, you're a tough one, you are, for a Brit. What's your name?"

"Brit?"

"Beg pardon?"

"Brit . . . Am I British ye say?"

"Well, considering what's left of your uniform, I'd say so?"

He thought, raised his head off the pillow. "It's . . . Me name is . . ." His head plopped back on the pillow. "I don't . . . know."

"*I am Glory. I light the way to the man who seeks himself.*" Doc remembered Malaki's words. He put his hand on the boy's shoulder.

"It's OK, my boy but if you're going to hang out with us, we have to call you something. What would you like us to call you?"

He closed his eyes and put a closed fist to his forehead. His eyes popped open, in alarm.

"I . . . don't . . . know,!.I don't know me name!" He kept repeating.

"Now, just take it easy," said Doc as he wrote *The Brit* on the case file. "We're glad to meet you anyway. Don't worry, it will all come back to you soon".

"How did I get here?"

"You were carried over here ten days ago by Malaki Messer, on the back of Glory Mule and you were beat up pretty bad. We thought you . . ."

"Glory Mule? Who is that?

"That mysterious white mule of yours that Malaki said . . ."

"I have nae mule." Interrupted the soldier.

"Well," said Doc, "I knew you'd say that to me, but be careful how you say it to Malaki. There are folks around here that are already saying he went daft from all the shooting and he's pretty sensitive about . . ."

"Who is Malaki?" Asked the soldier, weakly.

"Malaki? I would say, Malaki Messer is the man who, with Glory, saved your life. If we hadn't gotten to you when we did, I don't know if . . ."

Be I hurt bad, Doctor . . ." He looked up at the sign. ". . . Fixer?"

"Just Doc will do," said Doc. "Well, you're better now but when they brought you in, you looked like you were holding onto your life with one hand and your leg with the other. Do you remember that?"

"Me leg?" Said the young man.

"Yep, you had an iron grip on something sewn into what was left of that red tunic of yours and it took me two hours and three ice packs to get you to let go."

"What was it ?"

Doc went over to a locked cabinet and took out a package wrapped in oilcloth and brought it to him. "It was this. I don't normally allow weapons in the sick bay, but the way you were holding on to this one, I figured it must be special."

The young soldier untied the hemp cord and folded back the wrappings. He gasped. It was a flintlock pistol with a cherry wood stock and handle. Somehow, he knew it was his and he knew it was special, but he couldn't remember why. For the first time, in spite of all that had happened to him, he panicked and a tear rolled out of the corner of his eye and down his cheek.

"It may give us a clue to your name," said Doc. "Look at the handle."

The boy pulled his bandage up enough to peek out from under it with one eye and looked closely. Part of it was broken off, like it had been hit by a mini ball or something, but the intricate carving was intact. It was a coat of arms that looked familiar, with a pendant above it and a pendant below it. The one above, in Latin, said: "timor omnis abesto" and in the one below was the word *"McNabb"* with part of the second "b" missing. "If I remember my College of Medicine Latin, the upper pendant says *'Let Fear Be Far From All'* and the name below just might be your family name, *McNabb*, I think."

"Tis a familiar weapon, it be . . ." Said the soldier, "Cudd ye tell me once again the laddies name what saved me?"

"Laddie?" Thought Doc, scrunching up his mouth and rolling his eyes up. That accent, is not . . . Brit! Hm-m-m . . . McNabb? Of course, it all fits!" He jumped to his feet and said excitedly, "You're Scottish!"

"A am?"

"Yes, and I can call you Scotty!"

Once more the tent flap burst open. "Now what?" Cried Doc.

"You're awake!"

The young soldier looked up at a tall, impressive man, about his age and couldn't help letting his eyes roll up to the huge round mass of jet-black hair surrounding two glistening green eyes and a sea of white teeth so bright it made him squint when he smiled.

The young soldier liked him immediately.

"Ahoy friend. Glad to see you alive!"

Doc stood up. "Of course he's alive!" He said impatiently. "This . . . my newfound Scottish friend, is your savior from the other side, Master Malaki Messer . . . fighter, hero and an all-around soft-hearted pirate. Malaki, meet Scotty."

"Ahoy, mate." Said Malaki, "It does me ole heart good to see ye looking so good. We been waiting and waiting'. What's your name?"

"Well," Said the young man, "Tha doctor, A mean Doc said tha . . ."

"I just told you." Said Doc. "It's Scotty."

Malaki looked to Doc with a sneer. "That's it?"

"Scotty McNabb." Said Doc pointing to the gun handle.

"Mc . . . Nabb," Malaki read. "That sounds good for a last name, maybe, but Scotty ain't no first name for a man! It might be for a puppy dog but it ain't no man's name."

"It ain't . . . I mean isn't?" Asked Doc.

"No, I been thinkin' about it. I think we should call him Jesse Lafayette McNabb!"

"Jesse Lafayette McNabb?" Asked Doc, 'Who is Jesse Lafayette?'.

"He's the one what saved my life so's I could be here talking to ye today . . . that's who! Said Malaki. "Back when I was . . . nine or ten, we were doing battle with that big man of war HMS Cambridge and Capn' La Fitte had torn out a hole on her port side and figured that he 'bout had her licked, but that weren't so. Her capn' dropped their anchor right in the thick of things and did a hard-to-starboard maneuver and come around all of a sudden and when she did, I found meself looking' smack in the face of a broadside . . . I was standing midships looking straight down the barrels of forty cannons all being lit at once. I would of been kilt then and there, had it not been for Jesse Lafayette who swung down on a line and plucked me up to the poop deck just before he got his head blowed off by a cannonball. He saved my life by giving up his . . . so . . . . I figure that since he don't need his name no longer, we could save it by giving it to our new friend here What ye think?"

"Jesse Lafayette McNabb. It is a good name and that was a beautiful . . . er . . . story, Malaki but you can't just go around giving people names!" Said Doc

"I don't know why not." Said Malaki, with a wide-eyed look of surprise on his face. "When I needed a name, Captain LaFitte give me one that he respected. Now I'm giving Mr. McNabb a name to be proud of. What's wrong with that?"

"Well," said Doc, "he can't go anywhere without a name."

"Jesse Lafayette McNabb," The young soldier said to himself,. "A like it."

"OK, that does it." Said Doc, scratching out *The Brit* on his record and writing 'Jesse' over it, "Jesse Lafayette it is. Now if you two will allow me, I can get back to tending to all these other brave men who need me."

"OK, Doc," Said Mal, "But did you tell him about Glory?"

"You mean the imaginary *Glory Mule* you've been raving about?"

"Imaginary? Doc you got to believe that . . ."

"Er, gentlemen, when the war department fashioned these functional beds, someone had the forethought to put wheels on them. May I suggest that we roll Mr . . . Jesse Lafayette McNabb out on the dock in the sunlight where you two can visit and not disturb these other brave gentlemen who do not have a *Glory Mule*, even an imaginary one to help them and they must depend on the likes of me . . . plain old mortal me to give them strength."

The whole sick bay broke into cheers and whistles.

Malaki's big eyes rolled up and his cheeks puffed out as he exhaled. There was nothing more that he could say that would prove that there really was a glowing, white mule and decided there was no future in even trying.

As the weeks rolled on, the whole legend started to fade away. Every so often some of the blokes from the ship would walk by and give out a big "Hee Haw!" for Malaki's benefit but even that faded out after a while.

Jesse and Malaki became very close. Since Jesse couldn't remember his own life, he lived through someone else's and he was fascinated that Malaki was once a slave, rescued by a pirate and roamed the high seas until fate brought them together, on different sides, at the battle of New Orleans.

"It surely is a shame ye leg is still so beat up," Said Mal. We could be over to the Hog N' Whistle right now, sipping rum".

"A don't know about rum," Said Jesse, squinting his eyes and licking his lips but I sure have a taste for something sweet to eat right now. A love Doc, but the food here is nae gud."

"Sweet! Said Mal, "Funny ye mention that. I jes met somebody that invented that word." "and if Doc will lend me that ole mare again, I'll be back before sundown with sweet like ye never tasted in your whole life, laddie, . . . wherever that was."

"Hm-m-m," Said Jesse. "Hurry"

Chapter 5

The Old River Road running out along "plantation row" is always beautiful but, today, with the warm sun, the smell of honeysuckle vines and the thought of Leolla Thornberry on his mind, this morning out-did itself.

This was the second time Malaki had been out this far, being a seafaring man by trade, but he was too much a romantic not to notice again, just how beautiful it was. Then, right in the middle of it all, he thought of Hog Breath Hanratty and laughed to himself. "Why would I think of Hog right now?" But he knew. Hog was the main reason he had to come out Old River Road in the first place. Hog and them sweetater pies.

He looked down at Sally, Doc's ole mare and giggled out loud. "I tell you, girl, there ain't none other like him "That front tooth he lost was not his sweet tooth, that's for sure. I'd bet you a gold dollar that if somebody dropped a sugar cube in the middle of a tea house in China, it wouldn't matter a-tall whether Hog Breath Hanratty was sound asleep or smack in the middle of a rum-house melee, he'd be all over that sugar cube like a blue-tail fly."

It was Hog Breath that first introduced Malaki to the pies and it was those pies that introduced him to Leolla Thornberry.

It seems, that he was having a "Green Fairy Special," over to the Absinthe House when a pretty little missy came in with a basket full of sweetater pies and Hog Breath smelled 'em right off and bought one. When he first bit into it, he realized that it was, without a doubt, the most bodacious sweetater pie he'd ever had in his entire lifetime, so he bought the whole basket full and came back to the ship raving about them. Unfortunately, by the time he got there, he only had one left, which he broke in half and reluctantly shared with Mal.

Malaki, who had heard many "Hog Breath stories" bit into it with little interest. Then it hit him. It was a sweetness like he had never tasted before. It went far beyond just sweet, it was almost unnatural and sent waves of good up and down his spine. He wanted another. He had to hear more about the pretty little *missy* and he sat Hog Breath down and stood on his foot until he told Mal everything about her.

Hog said that she was a free lady of color who helped out with the laundry and such on The Blandshard Plantation and Misses Blandshard said that if she provided all the fixings, she would let the little missy bake in their kitchen.

He decided to see for himself and borrowed Doc's ole mare to do it.

It took him awhile and he got lost a couple of times, but his first sight of The Blanshard Plantation made everything worth it. It was a sight to behold. It's tiled, multi-gabled roof sat atop six massive white columns. The main entrance was at the center of a circular roadway and featured two great oaken doors with oil-burning *welcome* lamps on either side and a lavish porch that ran completely around the front and both sides with ornamental ironwork railings and all kinds of rocking chairs to suit the sitter.

Malaki wasn't sure just who might be watching him and urged Sally off the roadway and went around back. Plantation kitchens were almost always detached from the main house at the end of a breezeway. The Blandshard kitchen was no exception. He knocked at the kitchen door, removed his watch cap, smoothed his hair and waited. What happened next was his start to a new life.

The door opened and he found himself staring into two of the biggest, most penetrating brown eyes he'd ever looked into. They were bottomless and he was speechless.

"Yes?" She said.

"Yes!"

"Yes what?

"Oh" Said Malaki. "Yes, I am . . . Malaki Messer and I think . . ."

"You think what . . . Mr, er, Messer?"

"I think you are the most beautiful creature I have ever seen in my entire life and I want to buy a pie."

Her brilliant red lips parted and worked in harmony with her white teeth and haunting eyes to create a smile that rendered Malaki into a pile of mush.

"You're kinda pretty yourself, Mr Malaki Messer and I got pies to sell . . . Come in."

He did, and got his first complete look at the "pretty little missy" that *Hog* talked about. His cocky, self-sure manner abandoned him altogether. He was putty in her hands.

"I'm Leolla Thornberry," She said, "Where did you hear about my pies?"

Mal could do nothing but stare.

"Hello . . . are you in there, pretty boy?"

"What, oh, Hog Breath Hanratty told me and I . . ."

"Hog Breath who?" She said. "He doesn't sound very pretty."

"Hanratty and he's not . . . you know, it don't seem quite right for a woman like yourself to go around calling men pretty."

"You do if the man you are looking at *is,* but maybe we should get on a first name basis first. My name is Leolla Thornberry. I'm a Gullah from Little Majorca Island and . . ."

"Gullah?" Mal butted in. "That's the same tribe I was born into many years ago in Africa. I didn't know there was anyone from my tribe around. Are there others?"

"A whole island full." Said Leolla. Little Majorca. My father is Reverend Moses Thornberry. He's sort of the leader there and heads up the Gullah Sunshine Church and Genealogy Center. Are your folks living?"

"No" Said Mal, "They were killed many years ago when I was just little and I was raised by the missionaries, but I never lost hope that a friend or a distant relative might show up."

"Maybe my daddy could help. Little Majorca is one of the Sea Islands off the shore of the Quabalaka Mountain Range and most all Gullah records that exist are stored there. I hope to be going over there soon. Daddy wants me to help him. He's translating the Old and New Testament into a Gullah bible. Do you speak Gullah?"

"Ha," Said Mal, "If it hadn't been for the missionaries who raised me, I'd be lucky jes to speak English and I ain't been in no church since then. What is it . . . exactly?"

"The Gullah language is actually a form of English and African mixed together," Said Leolla, "And by the time it got blended with a southern accent . . . well, let's just say that only another Gullah could ever hope to understand it, so you can see why we need our own bible. But, that's not why you came here . . . You said something about a pie?"

"A pie? Oh yes, Hog Breath . . . er, I mean my friend brought one home yesterday and I have never tasted anything like it. What in dis world did you do to it to get so sweet?"

"Well, I really shouldn't give away my professional secrets but you don't look like the type that would . . . how do you say it, kiss and tell, so I will." Said Leolla,

"As you know, the Gullahs are people of the earth. We love and study growing things and one day when I was planting some sweet potato slips along with some sugar beet seeds, I started thinking how good it would be if a body could marry the two together and, just for the fun of it, I started experimenting and one day, I carefully dug a batch of my new sweet potatoes out of the ground and saw that they were a different color. They were sort of orange instead of brown. Then, when I tasted one, it was sweeter, a lot sweeter. Then I mashed some and fried them into pies and they got even sweeter. The rest is history. I make a batch every day and I sell every one I fry."

Malaki looked at his old busted pocket watch. "If you can excuse me, Miss Leolla, and I shorely would like to stay n' talk some more, but I see it's gettin' late and Sally and me have to get back. If I could buy a batch of them pies now, I could get 'em back to the ship by chow time."

"Ah, who is Sally, and what ship are you talking about and who's a chow time?" Asked Leolla.

"Oh, Sally's a horse and the ship is . . . ." He paused. "You know what, Miss Leolla, that's another story for another time, which brings me to a very important question. I was just going to ask if I might be so lucky as to . . . well . . . see you again?"

"If you hadn't asked" Said Leolla, "I was going to." She took his hand. "Come with me Mr Malaki Messer, I have a batch cooling on the porch of the main house. The Blanchards are not home and I'll give you a quick tour on your way out."

Now, two days later, he is on his way to see her again. Not that it was important, or anything like that, mind you, it's just that if he had to wait another day, he would have killed himself, or something. For two days and two nights, he walked around trying to think of some reason, any reason, to go back and see her and when Jesse said he craved something sweet . . . Bang! . . . That was it. Now he's almost there.

Nothing like this had ever happened to Malaki. He had met a lot of women in all the ports and rum halls along the way, but nobody like Leolla Thornberry. She had become the most important thing in his life. More important than the war with the British or pirate ships or white mules or sweetater pies or even Jesse. he had fallen in love with Leolla Thornberry and he's only seen her once.

He pulled Sally up to the big swinging gate with the letter "B" framed in wrought iron and looked up. His heart skipped a couple of beats and he took a deep breath. He was here, but was he ready for it? The reality of seeing her again hit suddenly. He closed his eyes and bowed his head.

"Lord, I can't nary remember when it was that we last spoke. I hope you don't feel the less for me and I am real sorry Lord, but if it's your will for Leolla and me to be together, would you put a good word for me in her heart before I get there? Thank ye kindly, Lord."

They went down the carriage road and started around back. The more he thought to himself, the more doubts popped up. "What if she *ain't* been thinking about me? After all, we've only seen each other one time. Why should she be interested in me? I'm a nobody. I'm a pirate, for crum sake. How can I tell her? What should I say? How should I act?"

When they came up in front of the kitchen, he spotted her looking out through the curtains. He jumped down and rang the little bell hanging on the door. When the door opened, it hit Mal again. She really was the most beautiful thing he could imagine. He better be more polite-like.

"Hello, Mr Messer," She said pleasantly.

"How nice to see you again, Leol . . . Miss Thornberry." Said Mal.

"It is me you came to see again, is it not?" Said Leolla

"Yes, well, the pies didn't last long, you know and . . ."

"But you really came to see me again, didn't you?" Insisted Leolla.

"Oh, for sure." Said Malaki nervously. "You see, I got this buddy named Jesse that was wounded in the invasion and he had a powerful craving for something sweet and I was telling him about your pies and he said he would love you forever if you would bake one for him and then Hog Breath Hanratty said . . ."

HOG BREATH HANRATTY! Screamed Leolla. Are you blind? Don't you know? Can you possibly imagine just how miserable I've been since you left. For some reason, you were all I could think about and I have been counting the seconds until you would ring that doorbell again and now you have and all you have to talk about is your buddy and HOG BREATH HANRATTY?"

Mal was dead silent. "Excuse me," He said, and slowly backed out of the doorway and closed it. Under his breath, he counted to ten, smoothed his bushy hair and rang the doorbell again. When the door opened, he stepped through and, with a little-boy look on his face, said. "What I was trying to say, Leolla Thornberry was, I think . . ."

"Yes . . . You think what?"

"I think . . . how can I say it? I think . . . I just fell in love."

Leolla's eyes slowly went from furious to friendly to kind a sleepy-like. She parted he red lips ever so slightly and whispered. "That's nice, I hope you didn't hurt yourself." And moved in closer, tilted her head up and closed her eyes. Her kiss was hearts, stars, and church bells ringing all at the same time and every nerve in his body twanged like a Spanish Guitar.

Finally, she slowly opened her eyes, took his arms from around her waist, stepped back and said, "Now, if you will excuse me and make yourself comfortable, it is now my turn" and, with that, disappeared into the scullery room.

In the time Leolla was gone, which to Mal, seemed and eternity, he heard her clanking pans and rustling paper and singing little songs. When she re-emerged, she was holding a big box with a ribbon around it and a big heart drawn on the side with red lipstick and under the heart were the words "HELLO TO JESSE".

"In case you got the wrong idea, I did remember his name and I want you to know that I'm anxious to meet him," she said coyly, "But I want him to like me too, so I'm baking him his *own* batch of pies to eat."

"You did?, You are? That's great, honey. He'll love' em. Did you autograph the box?"

"I'll have you know, I not only signed it, I wrote him a poem. Would you like to hear it?"

"A poem? My, I didn't know you had such talent. Of course I want to hear."

Leolla opened the lid of the box and took out a pink, sweet smelling envelope, opened it and read.

To Jesse

"I am a friend of your friend,
Malaki.
He says you're a regular guy.
So here's something sweet,

To eat, till we meet,
By and by.

Love,
Leolla,
The "Sweet Lady

Mal swept her off her feet and twirled he around. "He will love it!" He said, "And, he will immediately fall in love with you . . . too. Now I think I'm jealous."

Mal stayed for supper and afterwards, sat on the hearth of the giant cooking fireplace watching, while Leolla fried the new batch of pies. "That sounds . . . and smells mighty fine. What do you call them?"

"What do I call 'em? Why, *Leolla Thornberry's Sweetater Pies.* I reckon."

"Hm-m-m," Said Mal looking out of the corner of his eye, "Maybe someday, who knows . . . They might be known as *Leolla Messer's Sweetater Pies.* What ye think about that, my gorgeous, Gullah girly?"

She giggled and rolled her big, brown eyes back at him without moving her head. "Are you proposing to me, Malaki Messer?"

Mal, scrunched up his face and propped his head on his folded hands like he was thinking. "Well, maybe not yet, but I'm a-quivering."

He insisted that they both go back to deliver Jesse his *"Present From the Sweet Lady"* and after packing two dozen pies in a linen bag and putting them in the box and hanging it over the saddle horn, Leolla gave Sally a kiss on her nose and climbed up behind Mal.

They sang songs and laughed all the way back.

Just as Mal predicted, Jesse fell in love with Leolla the minute he met her. He not only loved her pies, but her style and her sense of color, not to mention her happy disposition.

"Miss Thornberry," He said, "Since my past only began when I woke up in Doc's office, I don't have a lovely lady like you in there. You are the first and I just want to say that you are a most welcome first addition.

From that time on, the three of them became close friends. They laughed at each other's jokes, dared each other's dares and treasured each other's treasures. Right now, Jesse was happy. He put his past out of his mind, for now.

Chapter 6

Somewhere
Over the rainbow
Skies are blue.
And the dreams
That you dare to dream
Really do come true.

Someday I'll wish upon a star
And wake up where the clouds are far
Behind me.
Where troubles melt like lemon drops
Away above the chimney tops
That's where you'll find me

Somewhere
Over the rainbow
Blue birds fly.
Birds fly over the rainbow
Why then, oh why can't I?

Several weeks later, Jesse and Malaki were just killing time sitting on the aft deck of "The Pride," the frigate that Captain LaFitte acquired back in the nineties from the British. Jesse was staring out at the horizon. He hadn't said a word in the last half hour.

"Where be ye Jesse lad. Don't ye feel like talking no more ?"

"Oh, it's not that, Malaki, A was . . . A was just thinking."

"About what?"

"Well, the war be over, right?"

"Right . . . And?"

"And it looks like, A be fit as, wah ye call it, a fiddle soon and A have to decide what A are going to be when A grow up."

"That's true," said Mal "Things can't stay like this forever, we're too happy."

"An, it seems like Captain LaFitte is nae going to be a pirate . . . er privateer anymore and ye will probably be hanging up ye cutlass soon n', who knows, ye and Leolla might get married and A was just wondering . . . wha about me?"

"Well, that's a rub." Said Malaki "When you get right down to the short hair of it all, they did send ye over here to fight agin us."

"Aye, I know," said Jesse and A sure hope you don't . . ."

"And we won!" Mal interrupted. "Not only the battle, but the whole dang war and it pert near got you kilt!" He paused, "But . . . they didn't and even though there ain't no war going on right now, I reckon they still think of you as . . . a prisoner."

"What do ye think they will do when they catch up with me?" Asked Jesse.

"I been thinking about that me self," said Mal, squinting his eyes and rubbing his stubble chin again. "Ye may be a prisoner of war, but I don't think ole General Jackson knows a dang thing about it!"

"Ye don't?" Said Jesse.

"No, you don't remember nothin' about it, but when we de-livered you to The Fixer's hotel, he was too busy to have you sign in on the guest book and as far as I know, folks done forgot that ye was wearing what was left of a red coat and if that ain't enough to throw 'em off the trail, you even got a brand new name to go by. "

"Ye're right, but where do A go from here," asked Jesse?

"Glad you asked that," said Mal. "Here's the good part. I just heard that the Captain's going to break sail next week n' head over to Bull Island, one of them little islands off the coast of the Quabalaka Mountain Range and it lays just seaward of Little Majorca. That's where Leolla is from and her daddy is the preacher there. He wants her to come home and help him with a Gullah bible he's printing and I was talking to her last night and she likes the idea a lot."

"What idea?" Asked Jesse.

"What idea? Why the idea of you two coming along when the Captain sails, of course."

"Us? Coming along? How be tha? Said Jesse.

"I got it all figured out!" Said Mal. "Leolla could legally come along as a passenger, with her daddy living there n' all. Nobody would ever question that."

"That sounds good so far, but . . ."

"I know," interrupted Mal. "What about me!" He mocked. I got that all figured out too. If I were to get ye a big sash, like mine, and some bell bottoms n' a watch cap to cover up all that yeller hair of yours and you slip that fancy pistol down in that sash so's the handle shows, I don't think no man jack among 'em would ever notice ye was not one of us. And, what if they do?" He said, thinking. "There ain't a soul on that crew that has a background clean enough to tattle-tale on ye. What ye say to that plan, maté?"

When Jesse heard the words "Mountain Range", for some reason, a chill went up his back. "What would A do there," he said.

"Don't rightly know," said Jess "but least-wise ye wouldn't be a prisoner of war!" He opened one eye. "Would ye now?"

———•———

Everything went just as Malaki planned it. Jesse, in his bell bottoms, watch cap and a sneer on his face made a better pirate than most pirates.

They were better than two weeks at sea before Jesse caught sight of the mysterious port Malaki called "Bull Island" It meant going down river into the Gulf of Mexico, around the tip of Florida and north into the Atlantic to a little group of islands just off the mainland near Fort Beula at the mouth of the mighty Quabalaka River. Jesse had borrowed a telescope from one of the officers and was fascinated with what he saw. The islands were beautiful, all clumped together with forests and waterfalls, rocky cliffs and endless beaches. Then he raised his glass slightly and spotted the misty peaks of the mountains far, far off on the horizon beyond the islands. That same chill went up his spine. He couldn't explain it. It had to be something out of his past, but what? He wondered if he would ever be able to put it all together again or would all the new experiences that were coming at him like cannonballs, crowd out all traces of who he was before . . . .

"Ahoy there maté . . . Hello-o-o! . . . Anybody home!"

Jesse looked around. It was Malaki, who evidently had been trying to get his attention for some time now. "Oh, begging yer pardon, mate," Jesse said mockingly. "What be's on your horizon this fine day?"

Mal ignored Jesse's bad imitation and said with some authority. "You best be getting below decks now, mate. We'll be dropping anchor soon and . . . well, you're standing on it."

Jesse looked down and then back up again. "Anchor? We not be to the islands yet."

"That's the truth, my Captain, Malaki said with humility and pointed starboard, "but we'll not be sailing The Pride into them shores. Not even Captain LaFitte could do that without ripping out her bottom side on the rocks n' reefs that's guarding them fine, white beaches. So go wrap anything you don't want wet in oilcloth n' stow em in boxes that float, cause we'll be taking that little steamer you see coming up on the port side the rest of the way in and," he took Jesse's scope and struck a pose, "just by looking at that surf, I'd say that them beaches don't want to have no part of us. Hope ye can swim, mate."

Chapter 7

❧

Amazing Grace,
How sweet the sound,
That saved a wretch like me.
I once was lost but now am found,
Was blind, but now I see.

JOHN NEWTON

1725-1807

It only took Jesse three months or so to decide that
Little Majorca Island was created by God, just for him.
It had become his home . . . his only home. As he stood
before the mirror in his soft, Majorcan leather boots that
came up over his knees, his striped silk pirate shirt with
full pleated sleeves gathered at the wrist, a slightly curved
saber dangling from a leather sash worn over one shoulder
and topped off with a broad brimmed hat, pulled up on
one side and pinned with a ample, white plume he said to
himself, "If I'm going to spend the rest of me life seeking
meself, I best look the part."

All the girls giggled and crowded around when he
came into the market place. His long blond hair had
grown down to his shoulders now, his deep tan, and his
newly grown mustache and goatee were adding quite a
touch of *dash* to the boys on the wharf. He carried his tall,
muscular body and blue eyes like a cat that was ready to
pounce. He loved life.

If a body watched him real close, they might detect
a very slight limp and although he still hadn't regained
his memory, it didn't seem to matter so much any more.
He was happy and as far as he was concerned, his life
started two years ago when he first opened his eyes in a
bed somewhere and met a doctor and a pirate who nursed
him back to health and, in turn, introduced him to the
only lady in his life, so far. A beautiful Gullah maiden
whom he loved dearly but Malaki loved more. They were
family and whatever happened from here on out, nothing
could ever change that. All he wanted to do now was to go
forward. He knew there was no turning back.

He reasoned that Bull Island and Little Majorca,
because of their history as pirate havens and considering
the role Jean LaFitte played in winning the war of 1812,
would be a safe place for him and hoped that the U.S.
government would find it the better part of discretion
to look the other way when they were searching for

criminals, deserters and especially prisoners of war. Even if someone did come, Jesse wasn't too worried. No one ever questioned, or even seemed interested in what their citizens look like, sounded like or how they make their living. He was secure. If anything, he might be a tinge on the bored side because, on Little Majorca, if a body didn't have a war to fight or ships to plunder and didn't grow corn or tobacco, there just wasn't an awful lot to do.

. With Malaki and Leolla, however, it was another story. Leolla took them to Gullah town the day after they arrived and when Malaki rounded the bend and got his first look, he had to stop and rub his eyes to believe what he was seeing. There was a wide-wide main street running from where he was standing to a big church down at the other end with bright red doors and a whiter than white steeple with a purple bell in it. A little cemetery laid off to one side with a carved picket fence around all the graves that faced east, so the spirits of the slaves could find their way home to Africa after they died.

It was a busy place and the stores and businesses were located back behind the church, with multi-colored signs that were not just informative, they were also works of art and the houses down the street were all built just alike, but different. That is, each one was painted different colors which gave them different personalities. A green house might very well have a purple door and a red house might very well have a green tin roof. They all had fences to keep the free-roaming cattle out of the okra 'n peas 'n such, but even so, as they walked along, Malaki caught glimpse of a wild turkey ever so often, skittering through the oleanders at the edge of the yards.

Of all slaves everywhere, the Gullah-Geechee were, sure enough, the keepers of the culture. They were great folk artist, story tellers, carvers, potters, unique chefs, experimental gardeners and exploiters of color and fashions that made their white owners sit up and look. As a matter of fact, most of the Goullahs were free slaves and kept their massa's family name out of sheer respect.

Then she introduced them both to Reverend Moses Thornberry, her daddy. He was a great barrel-chested man with a chin that jutted out beyond his nose with a two inch pure white beard on the end of it. He also had two matching white eyebrows that curled out over his dark, golden brown skin, and when he laughed, which he did a lot, they danced up and down like little white caps on the ocean. He always wore a black cotton shirt with the sleeves cut off and a white "parsons" collar showing around the neck and a big floppy hat.

They hit it off immediately and the good Reverend couldn't wait to introduce them to his congregation at the Sunshine Church, come Sunday.

In the meantime, he fixed up a room for Mal and Jesse in the back of the rectory with a back door that opened right out on a patio with an old fashioned "crank-up" well and benches where they could sit and watch the fishermen below.

The next morning the sun peeked over the horizon just like it always did, on it's way to another perfect day in paradise and Jesse was out back with his telescope, watching two fishermen pull in a net full of fish bigger than their boat and Malaki was in a chair, leaning back against the barn having a cup of coffee. He hadn't said two words all morning.

Leolla came bounding through the screen door with a happy "good morning" to Jesse and a kiss on the forehead for Mal. He smiled, and leaned back on the barn again.

"Well, aren't you a jolly ray of sunshine this morning? Should I go away and come back again, or do you always whoop it up like this when a pretty girl gives you a kiss? Maybe I'll have better luck with Jesse. Good morning, Jesse, "And gave him a kiss on the cheek. "My, don't you look stunning this . . ."

"I'm sorry, honey," Mal interrupted. "I guess I just have something on my mind and it's got me worried. Maybe we should talk."

"That sounds like a good idea," Said Jesse. "Why don't the two of you walk down on the beach, pull up a palmetto tree, and visit?"

As they walked, Leolla did all the talking about the weather n' such and when they crossed over the wetland they found a little spot down on the water that looked right and spread a blanket.

"Ok, Mr Sunshine . . . What's on your mind? Chirped Leolla.

"Honey," Said Mal, "I hope you know that I love you more than anything or anybody on God's good earth."

"And I love you, Malaki Messer . . . so?"

"Well, that's just it . . ."

"What is?" Said Leolla, puzzled.

"It's God's good earth . . . and sometimes I feel like I ain't fit to live on it."

"What do you mean, honey?"

"I been thinking for weeks now how to ask you . . . to . . ."

"Oh-o-o-o. Is that all it is?" Cooed Leolla and took a small compact out of her purse and opened it. "Just a minute." She looked at herself in the mirror, pursed her lip, smoothed her hair, closed it and looked back at Mal with a big smile on her face. "Ok, I'm ready now. What do you want to ask me?"

"Don't mess around," Mal said, trying not to laugh. "When two people get married, they do it in front of God."

"Yes . . . so . . ."

"Don't you understand? Before I met you, I was a pirate. I roamed the seas like the rest of 'em and . . . I've looted, I've stole and pillaged . . . I've even killed people."

"But you don't do that anymore."

"No, but I did, and I don't think God is ever going to let me forget it. That's no way to start a marriage. You deserve somebody better than me."

Leolla saw how serious he was. Her heart suddenly opened up for him but she didn't know what to say. She loved him more now than she ever and in her heart, knew that if he keeps feeling like this, she'll lose him and never get him back. Then she got a thought.

"Malaki," She took his head in her hands and looked deep into his eyes. "Would you say to Daddy . . . what you just said to me?"

"Well, I don't kn . . ."

"He is the closest person to God that I know," She said quickly, And it is He that has to answer your questions and you can speak to Him through daddy. He will know what you should do."

———•———

Leolla dropped Mal off in front of the church, kissed him and said "Whatever happens, Malaki Messer, know that I love you more than I ever thought I could love anyone, anywhere. You Trust daddy now, you hear?"

Mal was just about to ring the bell when Pastor Moses opened the door. "Come in, my boy. I understand that you need to talk to us. God's waiting in the kitchen."

All of a sudden, Mal couldn't hold it back any longer. Tears flowed from his eyes and he was speechless. They went back and sat at his big, round table in the kitchen. Moses poured coffee and sat quietly until Mal controlled himself and apologized.

"That's OK," Said the pastor. There seems to be something powerful big on your mind, what is it?"

Mal took some deep breaths and cleared his throat. "Well, you probably wonder, like Leolla wonders, why I ain't never asked her to marry me?"

"It did cross my mind," Said Moses, "You love her don't you?"

"More than anything in the world! God knows that! "So?"

"Well, God does know that, but I know He's up there saying Leolla can't marry up with the likes of me.

"Oh?" Said Moses, "Just what is the 'likes of you?'

Mal looked up into Moses' eyes. "Pastor, since I wuz jes a boy, I was a pirate. I wuz responsible for the de-mise of many of my fellow human beings. Capn' LaFitte told me that it wuz ok 'cause they wuz my enemies and if I didn't kill them, they would kill me and I didn't think too much about it at the time, but now I don't know what to do. The missionaries told me that the Bible sez 'thou shall not kill and Pastor Mose . . . I done *done* it!"

He put his head down into his hands. Then he raised up quickly. "Pastor, I wants to marry up with Leolla more than anything in the world and I knows that to do that you have to go before God 'n promise him to have 'n to hold 'n all that stuff and . . . I don't know who I'm talkin' to, pastor. I ain't got no God!"

"Yes you do, Malaki. My God is your God . . . but let's go all the way back to Africa and the missionaries. How did it start?"

Malaki went into detail about everything he could remember about his life since he was taken by the slavers to the rescue by Captain LaFitte and all the encounters since. He spoke about how he killed without thinking about it because it was self defence. It was the pirate's way and he thought nothing about it."

"And when did things start to change, Mal?" Asked Moses.

"Change? . . . Well . . ." Malaki then told Mose about the night he rescued a wounded British soldier on the battlefield and how scared he was when he first saw the light coming through the darkness and the encounter with a white mule from somewhere else. He described how he and the mule seemed to understand each other without words and how she would not leave until he loaded the wounded soldier on her back and found him safety. Then he described their trip back to the ship and how he, for the first time since he was a baby living with missionaries, thought of God. He even told the funny little story of how he named the mule *Mercy*. Then he told how the mule disappeared later and no one has ever seen her since. "That was when things started to change, Pastor."

Moses listened without speaking a word and then took out his bible and started leafing through it and looked up.

Let me ask you something, son, did you hate the people you killed?"

"Hate them Pastor?" Said Mal looking out into space, "I don't think I stopped long enough to think 'bout dem 'cause, like I said, they wuz gonna kill me."

"But," Said Moses, "If somehow, you saw them again, do you think you could forgive them for that?"

Mal closed his eyes and pondered that question for quite a while. "If it was me *then* . . . ,I don't know. But, if it is me *now* . . . I shorely could. You see, Pastor, I'm different than I was then. Something come over me and I feel different about things now. I mean, you take Jesse Lafayette McNabb out there, He *was* that British soldier that was sent over here to kill me and I might likely have killed him too, if we had met in battle but when that white mule come down and introduced us, that soldier was half dead in a cannonball hole. But, when I held his hand and it twitched, it shorely wern't hate I felt.

"What did you feel, Mal?" Asked Pastor M.

"Well, I was mighty *sorry* that he was hurt . . . pity, maybe."

"Pity . . . ?"

"Yes, but that wern't the all of it though. I wanted to take away his hurt, somehow and I wanted to save his life because I felt . . . ?

"Love?" Asked Moses.

"Maybe it was." Said Mal. All I know is that I love him now like a brother and if the time ever come when he was in danger again, I would likely risk my own life to save his and I bet he would say the same thing about me!"

Pastor Moses put his hand on Mal's shoulder, "Know this, my son, it was the devil who led you to take a life and feel nothing, but it was God that sent you the means to save a life and cherish him as a friend. Have you thought about that?"

Malaki looked straight at Moses. "But that was only one man. Tell me this, Pastor, do you think God could ever forgive me for *all* the bad things I done?"

"Yes. You need to be baptized, Mal. It is God's way to wash away all your sins so He can forgive you."

"You mean, that there's a chance that God would take me up to His heaven when I die, like He do with all them people who ain't never killed nobody?"

"That's what I mean."

"Malaki beamed.

"And about the white mule?" Said Mose, "I don't doubt at all that the good Lord sends angels of all shapes and forms to keep us out of trouble.

Mal sat silent with his eyes closed. Finally he looked up. "If I asked Leolla to marry me and she said yes, would you be happy?"

Pastor Mose put his arm around Mal. "If you truly do repent, He will forgive all . . . and . . . so would I. I would be proud to have you in our family. Baptism first and Marriage second. Yes?"

"You got it, Pastor Mose!" Said Mal, "You got it!"

———•———

The next morning, Mal was himself again. Leolla could hardly keep up with him as he rushed around buying a new white shirt and trying on black pants which he needed for the ceremony and Jesse couldn't stop laughing at Mal's shameless flirting with Leolla while she was trying to get his mass of bushy hair trimmed down to a manageable size. Mal was now getting up earlier than anyone else and was the last to go to bed at night, mainly because he insisted on sitting out by the well and jawing with all the workers coming down off the slope. He was a self-appointed bundle of good.

Reverend Thornberry realized, however, that if they were going to make it until Sunday they needed something else to occupy their minds and told Leolla and Malaki that they were thinking about doing a little painting over at the Praise House and wondered if they could lend a hand. They said yes and as they were going out the door, Jesse said that he was going to explore the area and would see them both back at the house that night.

Jesse was fascinated with the island. He packed a lunch, borrowed a burro and went from one end of the island to the other. On Friday, at low tide, he crossed over the saltwater swamp that divided the island from the mainland and headed toward the mountains. They were too far away really see, of course, but he did reach a couple of foothills about two hours in. When he climbed to the top of the first one, that strange feeling ran up his spine again.

That night when Mal got back from The Praise House, he was going to tell him what he saw but he made the mistake of asking how the painting went.

"Painting? Oh great. Leolla and I painted the whole Praise House *Haant Blue.*"

Jesse asked him what *Haant blue* was and Malaki said it was really sky blue. So then, Jesse asked why they call it *Haant blue* and Malaki says, getting a little impatient, "That's because it scares off *haants.*" So then Jesse asked him if that was really true and Malaki just about bit his head off. "Sure do! I just told ye, that it's the color of Heaven and everybody knows that them evil *haants* don't have nothing to do with Heaven! Don't you know nothing, boy?"

That night, they all ate around the big table in the kitchen and after supper, Reverend Thornberry gave Jesse and Mal one of those pipes that he carves out of meerschaum and they all went out on the porch where the rocking chairs were, lit up and listened to Moses tell stories.

Besides being God's messenger and the foremost authority on the bible in his part of the world, Pastor Mose is also known as the best story teller that ever came out of these parts. He's famous for his *Brer Rabbit* stories and all the messes that rascal gets into and stories about huntin' dogs, bears, talking catfish, squirrels and . . . well it went on forever. He had them laughing so much, by the time they finally got to bed, they were worn out.

Chapter 8

Saturday morning, Jesse found himself alone again while Mal and Leolla finished their *haant paintin'* and he found a comfortable spot on a bale of cotton down on the dock. The sun was warm and there was a cool breeze coming out of the north and he took a deep breath, closed his eyes and decided that there was no place better on this earth, for him to be, for the next hour or so, than right there. Then he smelled a familiar smell and heard a familiar voice coming from somewhere. He raised up and looked around, and to his surprise, discovered that it was Reverend Thornberry still puffing his pipe and still telling stories.

It appeared that he was *wettin' a line* with a group of Gullahs who were paying no attention atall to their bobbers, in that Moses was telling a huntin' dog story and had their complete attention. They didn't want to miss a word. Jesse figured that since nobody had noticed him sitting there, he might just as well listen in.

"Last week end," Pastor M said, "I didn't have much to do, 'cause Leolla was over to Rachel's house helping' her put up a batch of t'maters, so I decides to go over and say howdy to ole Rufe Franklin. You boys remember Rufe, don't you? He's got to be the best dog hunter on the island"

There were several nodding heads.

"Well I heard Rufe had been feelin' poorly and thought he might like a bit of company." He took a few puffs off his carved eagle head pipe, closed his eyes and let the smoke out real slow and when every one of the boys were leaning in to catch the next word, his eyes popped wide all of a sudden.

"When I got there, . . ." He said, pointing his pipe at *Birdsong* Bevens, who was about the color of a tarnished penny due to a healthy dose of Cherokee on his momma's side and who was listening harder than anybody else,

"Rufe was jes settin' out on his porch, not moving and enjoying the day, and beside him was . . . ." *Birdsong* leaned forward. "The purtiest redbone hound I ever laid my eyes on, all stretched out beside him, sound asleep.

"So I walk up and sez 'howdy, Rufe, that shorely is a handsome redbone you got there,' and I started to reach down n' pet him . . . but then I thought better of it and I looked up at Rufe and said.

"Your dog don't bite, do he?"

And ole Rufe, who had his chin buried in his hands, looked up with jes one eye, to see who's talking, and sez . . . nope.'

So I reached down to pet that dog and when I did, he 'bout took off my thumb and I quick-like yanked back my hand and I sez to Rufe,

"I THOUGHT YOU SAID YOUR DOG DON'T BITE!!"

Rufe looked over at him and closed his eye again. He don't . . ." He says,

"But that ain't my dog . . .'

Birdsong threw up his arms and fell off the dock, laughing. Jesse had heard that one before and was still giggling when he heard cannon fire. Three shots evenly spaced, a pause and three more. He sat up just as Reverend Thornberry came off the dock.

"Hello, Reverend. Did ye hear that? It sounded like it came from Bull Island."

"It did," Said Pastor Mose. "Three shots and then three shots. It's the pirate warning signal that a danger or trouble is approaching the island."

"What ye think it is? Said Jesse, starting to get that funny feeling again.

"Not sure. They'll be people from Bull Island at the baptism in the morning. Maybe we can find out what's happening then.

—•—

Word of Malaki's baptism had gotten around. The story of the handsome bad man and the beautiful, preacher's daughter had covered the island like a blanket and everybody wanted to meet him. The church was full, long before the service started and extra chairs had to be set up in the back and down the aisles while Clara and Louise Underhill's sister-blending voices, brought tears to many an eye with their presentation of *Amazing Grace*.

Reverend Thornberry paused to let some of the more emotional parishioners collect themselves before he launched himself into a long but good sermon on the subject of sin and how it is not the end of your world and how forgiveness is always there for you, if you repent.

"Amen."

Then, he mopped his brow and looked out at the congregation. "As you all know, and for anyone who might have been on the other side of the world for the last month, this is the time God has chosen for the baptism of Mr Malaki Messer and I invite all who wish to attend to meet around *The Lord's Lagoon* in ten minutes.

It was not easy, but amidst the rumble of voices, the rattle of chairs and much laughter, the entire congregation managed to find a place to sit and stand and ogle around the pretty little pond behind the church where two white swans, Mark and Lukee made their home and gracefully swam from side to side listening to the harmony of the Underhill sisters who were out doing themselves with the blues'y African song, *Take me to the Water*.

> "*Take me to the water.*
> *Take me to the water.*
> *Take me to the water,*
> *To be baptized.*"

Pastor Mose, who was already waist deep, motioned for the ushers to lead Malaki out. Mal wasn't quite sure of this part. He was a man who roamed the high seas most of his life and rode out many a storm with waves as high as the masts themselves, but these little church ponds can get pretty tricky sometimes and he didn't swim just all that well. But . . . he made it and Pastor Moses smiled when he arrived. He put his left hand behind Mal's neck and held a white linen cloth in his right hand, "It was John who said, If we confess our sins, He is faithful and just to forgive us and cleanse us from all unrighteousness.

So, Malaki Messer, having heard your confessions, I Baptize you in the name of The Father, The Son and The Holy Ghost." Then he gently covered Mal's nose and mouth and lowered him under the water's surface. When he came up, he sputtered a little, opened one eye . . . and then the other, looked around at all the people and smiled bigger than he knew he could. The result was a mixture of laughter, applause as six more cannon shots resounding in the Heavens.

After the ceremony, everyone left but Pastor Mose, Mayor Franklin Witherspoon, George Blandshard and Frank Blacky Yocum who commands the harbor patrol. Frank said that the first cannon signal sounded when Dutch Harry Van Dych spotted the sails of the USS Yorktown off Point Mallard, Florida on a course directly into Bull Island Sound and they were picked up off Norris Point and relayed the canon fire to Bull Island who in turn alerted their own citizens.

The Yorktown is a four masted schooner known for it's speed and is used primarily to transport high ranking military personnel and government officials. They also carry small steam driven personnel boats that can navigate the natural obstacles blocking tight harbors and are capable of transporting a full squad of marine rangers. The second cannon report heard this morning was to verify the fact that they are an estimated five days out and that any unauthorized or questionable ships in the area should consider sailing to international waters until the Yorktown's purpose is announced.

———

Mal had just changed into dry clothes and he and Jesse were listening quietly from the back. Malaki knew that he and Leolla had good reason to be there and papers to prove it and were convinced that no one could possibly know about Jesse. They didn't know what he looked like, what his name was or where he went.

"How could they, Jesse?" Said Mal, "Doc is the only living human being that knows you are here and we know he would be the last person on earth that would ever tell them. Whoever these people are, they have to be after someone else!"

"I guess you're right, Mal but I . . . ."

Young Lemar Tyrone, a boy from the village, rushed up all out of breath.

"Hey, Lamar, what's up.

Lemar leaned against the railing for a moment to catch his breath and looked up.

"They's a man coming up to see you, Mr. Mal!"

"Oh?" Said Mal. "Who is it?"

"I don't rightly know, Mr Mal. He was on the dock and said he would give me a gold piece if I could tell him where you and Mr. Jesse is and I told him I don't know nothin' 'bout that, but then, that dumb ole Mary Lou Lewis pointed up the hill and said you was up behind the church there, gettin' baptied. I thought I better run up here and tell you personal like.

Mal reached into his pocket and pulled out a shiny coin. "Here, buddy. You did good. I'll go see who it is.

Lamar went skipping off and Mal joined Jesse on the front steps.

"Whoever it is, ain't from around here." Said Mal. It would have to be an outsider to offer a boy a gold piece just to tell where you were Jesse, but who?"

"Thas him! There he be!" Said Lamar, running out and pointing down to a dark figure coming up through a bunch of church people going the other way.

As he got closer, they saw that he was a tall, lanky seaman in a black p-coat and watch cap carrying a duffle bag over his shoulder. He had a familiar walk but was still too far away to see. He was walking over the rough pathway and had his head down and as he got closer, he looked up.

"It be Doc!" Said Jesse. "Doc, 'The Fixer' DuPhol!" He yelled. "Doc! Up here, Doc! How, in this world be ye?"

"Jesse boy!" Doc held him out at arms length. "I don' think I would have recognized you, lad. You sure look different than when you left. That's good!" Then he looked around at Mal to see if anyone else was listening. "If you two could break loose from your . . . er . . . . friends here, we need to go find a place to talk."

The smile went off Jesse's face and he led them to a table and chairs on the church patio. Jesse noticed that Doc was distracted and more serious than normal.

"What be it, Doc," said Jesse.

"Well," said Doc, "I best start with you, Malaki."

"Me Doc? What did I do?"

"You didn't do anything but good, Mal. It's just that I saw . . . I . . ." Doc stuttered. "I owe you an apology, Mal."

"What for, Doc. What did you see?"

GLORY!" Doc blurted out.

"You saw GLORY?" Said Jesse. "When?, Where?

"I'll tell you, but let me start at the beginning." Doc sat down and mopped his brow.

"It was about two weeks ago, I was working late trying to put a cap on the whole battle of New Orleans. Andy Jackson had given me thirty days to have a completely documented case file to him prior to his meeting with president Monroe and the British ambassador on the subject of espionage. It seems that two British spies were caught and executed down in Florida trying to stir up trouble with the US and the Indians, and President Monroe ordered a complete sweep of the southern states to make sure there weren't any more walking around like them and gave that job to General Jackson."

"Spies?" Asked Jesse. "Dae thay think that A . . . How could A be a spy. Me life didna even start until A met ye!"

"I know that and you know that but that didn't stop a big blue-coated colonel from barging into my tent with two armed soldiers. He flashed his badge and introduced himself as Colonel Nicholas Walton, USDNS. That's the Department of National Security."

"What were they after?" Asked Mal.

"I didn't know," Said Doc. "The Colonel asked if I had ever treated any British wounded and I told him that I had helped out over at the prisoner of war clinic but I didn't know any of their names and while we were talking, these other two soldiers were searching my files and making a mess out of my workplace. I told him that they couldn't do that without a warrant, and he recites some law that stated that if it's a US government file, it's the property of the Government and, unless I had something to hide, I shouldn't worry about it."

"Did thay say who thay wis looking for?" Asked Jesse.

"No, just more suspicious people, I reckon. Anyhow, before I had a chance to say anything, one of the soldiers hands the Colonel a file. I couldn't see what it was but the Colonel stops talking and examines it. Then he closed it and looked back at me and squinted his eyes sort a funny-like and says. 'So, Doctor, you said that, to your knowledge, that the only British casualties you tended were at the prison?" And I said correct. There is no name on any of my files that identifies the injured as being British. Then he handed me the file."

"What was it?" Said Malaki.

"It was that file that had the word *Brit* crossed out across the front and the word *Jesse* written over it. Remember?"

"Uh oh . . ." Said Jesse.

"I know," Said Doc. "The Colonel didn't let me say anything before he went on and said 'According to this file, Doctor, you not only had a *Brit* here, but his name was *Jesse*, whom ever that might be. How do you explain that?' And I said I didn't know and that we had some pretty bad cases and that this one must have died before we identified him."

"Did he believe that?" Asked Mal.

"Who knows. He didn't say anything. He just unbuttoned his frock coat and slipped the file inside and said, 'You'll be hearing from us . . . Doctor."

"Did ye?" Asked Jesse.

"No, but I did hear from someone else, the very next day."

"Who?" Asked Mal.

"I'm getting to that." Said Doc. I was looking for my notebook to see if I could remember what was in the file they took, when the tent flaps flew open and I looked and there stood . . ."

"Who?" Said Mal and Jesse, together.

"Glory, and she had this in her mouth." Doc handed them the file. It had Brit written on it with Jesse scribbled over.

"The file!" Said Mal. "How did she get it?"

"I don't know," Said Doc, impatiently, "Glory said nothing, and I didn't know if the Colonel had missed the file yet either. All I could think of, Mal, was what you told me about Glory and how dedicated she seemed be to Jesse and how she always knew when he was in danger."

"Do ye think she wa asking ye to find me?", Said Jesse.

I know she was. Even though she never changed her expression or moved her mouth, the words *'I am Glory. Warn the Man Who Seeks Himself.* That you, Jesse! She wanted me to find you and get you to safety. Can you believe that?"

Jesse just sat there and didn't answer.

"Did you hear, Jesse? I said can you be . . . ."

"I heard ye, Doc" Jesse interrupted. "A was just thinking . . ."

"Thinking what?" Asked Doc.

"All this talk about Glory. How she first met Mal on the battlefield and helped him pull me oot of the hole and she and Mal carried me over to ye, Doc and ye fixed me up. Now, ye saying ye saw her nose to nose when she brought back tha file that could harm me."

"Yes . . . so?"

"Why?" Said Jesse, "She's done all this to help me and . . . now, out of the three of us, A'm the only one that's never seen her."

"That's the truth," Said Mal. Did anyone else at sick bay see her?"

"I don't think so," Said Doc. "I asked the boys in the next tent if they had seen any mules lately and they just laughed and said no but if they see one, they will be sure to send her over. So I started to ask around and discovered that Union Army Intelligence officers were all over the place, asking everybody if they knew anyone called Jesse. They got no leads until they questioned that young man I was working on when you came in, Mal. Remember? He had a saber cut on his head and . . ."

"I remember." Said Mal. "What did he say?"

"Well, when I asked him, he said he told them that he remembered some pirate bloke carrying in a bloke that was half dead and put him on the table in the back and just before I put that bandage over his eye, he thought he saw a piece of a red coat, but because he was so muddy, he didn't know for sure."

"Uh-oh," Said Mal.

"I know, he also told them that when he came back a week later to get his bandage changed he asked me whatever happened to that guy the pirate carried in with the mud all over him. At first, I couldn't remember, then I said 'Oh, you probably mean *Jesse?*"

"You did?" Said Mal?"

"Yes, but he also said it could have been J*ackie*, he didn't know. Needless to say, the government boys jumped all over that. Then they deduced that the last time this *Jesse* was ever heard of was the same day that Jean LaFitte's frigate *The Pride*, with thirty seven crew members and two passengers sailed for the Sea Islands. Then they checked previous rosters and discovered that Jean LaFitte's crew never had thirty seven seamen, they always sailed with a crew of thirty six!"

"They know you're here, Jesse! Said Mal.

"And they're coming," Said Doc. "They'll be here in five days. Jackson smells blood. Suspected spies are being tried left and right and some are being sent to prison for years or life. A few are even being hung. We can't let them catch you, Jesse. That's why I've come. I had to warn you . . . You must go."

Jesse stood up and put his arms around his new-found family. "Maybe A don know who A am, people, but A certainly know who A'm not. A'm not a spy!"

"We know that, Jesse, but . . ."

Mal, ye are my brother, ye are. Ye, and someone or something called Glory Mule saved me life and Doc, ye pulled me through and A lived. A love this country and A love ye guys and after all ye've done, I certainly can't let ye down now."

"Where do you think you can go?" Asked Doc.

"A'm not sure, Doc but ever dae tha we have been here in sight of those mountains, A've felt them calling. A dinna know why thay're calling, but since A have to go somewhare, A think A'll go an see who lives up there. Who, knows, maybe A'll even find me."

Chapter 9

Her name was *Winis Owi Iwi*, which is Cherokee for *Wings Of Ivy*, and in Running Deer's words, *"She was a gift of the forest."* Now, as she heard the drums and watched her beautiful daughter sway to their beat, wearing her crown of white dogwood blossoms, she couldn't have been prouder. Her *Wings of Ivy* was about to accept her passage into womanhood. It is a sacred ritual and is always held on the night of the first full moon when Mother Earth commanded the grass to grow and the trees to come forth with their greenery.

She loved her daughter very much and remembered only too well the day of eighteen moons past when she had gone to collect berries and nuts for her Red Feather to have when the time came for *Usdi*, their baby. It would be their first little one and she wanted everything to be as he would like it.

Her search had taken her beyond the great river and she was about to turn back when the skies darkened and a mighty storm broke out. By the time she had reached the bridge of stones where she had crossed, the waters had risen and turned white with rage and the rocks were gone. She had no choice but to find shelter and wait for the storm to stop. She climbed part way up the mountain until she found a rock cave where she could wait . . . and built a fire. The rain was cold and the fire was warm as she pulled her deerskin wrap around her shoulders, and fell asleep. When she woke, the storm was gone, the birds were singing and the sun was, once again, shining bright.

She was sure the river would be itself by now and was starting her trek back down the mountain when she felt the pain. She paid little attention to it at first and it went away only to return stronger than it was before. A fearful thought ran through her mind. Her *Usdi* should not arrive until the planting moon had passed but what if the Great Spirit sent it now? The pains persisted until she had no other choice. She must lay down and wait for the Great Spirit to guide her. But where? When she reached the valley below, she spotted a lush "Indian bed" growing around and up a giant sycamore tree. "Indian bed" was the name given a type of ivy that grew thick and lush like a bed and when the weary Indian laid down in it, he soon fell fast asleep.

Running Deer put her hands on her stomach and felt a kick. "I know, little princess, it looks good to me too. Perhaps this is where the Great Spirit has chosen for you to see your mother and for me to see my Princess for the first time.

With her head against the soft moss growing on the sycamore, she laid down in the lush foliage and waited. In time, a baby's cry joined the songs of the birds and the wisp of the wind. Running Deer delivered a beautiful baby girl, in the same manner her Cherokee ancestors had borne their children for generations past. She fed and wrapped her baby in the deerskin as the sun sent it's welcome rays down through the sycamore and formed a halo around the baby's face as if to say "You have done well, Running Deer." When she stood and looked down, what she saw was her angel . . . with wings of ivy.

———·———

Now, she watched as *Wings Of Ivy,* swayed back and forth to the chant sung for, and by all Cherokee maidens when they accept their rite of passage. Her father, Red Feather, was proud. He was now chief of the seven clans of Cherokee which made Wings Of Ivy a princess. The full moon was truly full and lit up her smiling face as she passed before him gracefully to the sound of the drums. Nothing could spoil the magic of this night. Then he frowned.

His thought was of Yellow Owl, a most holy man from the Wakona Knob Cherokee who arrived three hours past on this day to talk before the tribal council. He asked for a place at the council fire to talk of his visions. Red Feather knew it must be important because Yellow Owl had come to his village only once before and that was three suns before the big flood. The council was to take place at sunrise after rite of the first full moon. Then his smile returned. Tonight belonged to his princess as she takes her first step into womanhood.

At sunrise the next morning, a council of five, wearing breechcloths and leggings, arrived at the wattle of Red Feather and formed a circle around the center spot where the Holy Man would sit. The wattle, or house of the Chief was always in the center of the village and was twice as large as the individual wattles that formed the village itself. They were built of thick river cane walls covered with mud plaster and topped with weather-proof thatched roofs. When the deerskin curtain over the door was closed, it offered a private place.

When Yellow Owl arrived, he was pleased. All was in order. He squatted in the center and spread his medicine deerskin and prayed, saying that he came with humility to share a message from the Great Spirit with His people. He lit a pipe an handed it to Red Feather, who sucked the pipe, blew the smoke over the deerskin and handed it to the next council member who did the same. After all had smoked, they watched the smoke trails for a sign from the Gods and looked at Yellow Owl.

He spoke of two visions. The first was a sight of thousands upon thousands of white eyed warriors, all in coats of the blue jay, with long knives on sticks of thunder. They walked to the beat of drums and their numbers were so great, they reached to where the sun rises. "They circled the Cherokee, killing as they did. Those that were not killed, were collected in a great line and driven, like cattle, down the mountain and across the river of rock. The loud screams of the women and the cries of the men became faint and disappeared altogether by the time the sun came up."

"By Morning," He said, "All that could be seen were the tracks of moccasins going westward. It was clear that all Cherokee were gone, never to return."

The council was silent. Red Feather broke the silence. "What does the smoke tell you" What does it mean?"

"We have heard," said Yellow Owl, "Many tales of the white eye chief sending an army of blue coats to move entire tribes from their hunting grounds and sent to a place far in the west. They then take the land of the Indian and give it to the white man to live while the hunt for the yellow rock. If the Indians fight back, more blue coats will come, as many as the locust, and the Indian has but two ways to go, move . . . or die."

"But why us?" Interrupted Tall Trees, the youngest of the council. "Why the Cherokee? We have no yellow rock."

"Not that we know" said Yellow Owl, but the drums tell us that the white eyes are looking everywhere for it, and if it is discovered on the land of the Cherokee, there is a fear by many, that the chief of all white eyes in Washington will force us out of our sacred mountains and we too, will be sent west to live with our brothers."

"You spoke of two visions, Holy Man" Said Red Feather, "What was the second?"

"It was a more pleasant vision but contrary to the first. It raises many questions." Said Yellow Owl, "It began with some of our people who were hurt and bleeding, looking into the black of night for any sign from The Great Spirit. A light shone off in the distance going in and out of the trees. As it approached, it took the form of a great, white horse-like spirit with ears like the wings of Angels. There were three riders. Two had skin as dark as the walnut tree, and the other had golden hair, the color of the oak leaf on the last day of the full moon. The Great Horse vision spoke without speaking. It said to us:

"For many, the Cherokee way of life is not to be, but for those of you who will follow me and "Man Who Hunts Himself," the Cherokee way will be forever."

"Did they follow?" Asked Red Feather.

"Yes, in the vision, our people did so and she led them to the Sacred Wall of Stone that encircles the top of our mountain. The very wall that our prophets have always told us, is a wall the Great Spirit built between the world we live in and the world to which we go some day and is sacred to the Cherokee. We also know that the sheer face of the holy wall is not to be climbed and there is no doorway into it, yet, as we all saw in the vision, she walked through the stone without stopping. The Man Who Hunts Himself with yellow hair looked back and said

'Follow us, in this secret place, the Cherokee will find a new beginning."

Chapter 10

Jesse and Malaki knew that they had all of two days to decide what they were going to do. They sat with Doc and talked throughout the night.

"If you ask me," said Doc, "Andy Jackson has gotten to the end of his rope and he wants to put it around the neck of any bloke that even hints at working for the Brits. He will let nothing stand in his way to a bigger and greater America and if that mean his own private war against spies and deserters, then he will declare one. And, when he catches one, he'll hang 'em. He figures that's what you do in time of war with the likes of them."

"But A'm nae a spy, nor a deserter." Jesse insisted.

"Can you prove that?" Said Doc.

"A canna prove anything, Doc." Said Jesse. "A can only remember from the time A woke up in ye sick bay. "

"Then you've got to run Jesse! You've got to run! And, you too, Malaki."

"Me? No!" Said Malaki.

"No?" Said Jesse, "I just figured that you 'n me were . . . ."

"No!" Mal repeated, "I could never leave Leolla."

"But Mal," said Jesse, "They already know that it was you that brought me here. They will consider you just as guilty as me. I could never leave you alone to face that."

"That's right, Malaki. They will come after you special." Said Doc

"I can't go," said Mal, again, "I love her!"

"What do you think she would say if she knew this?" Asked Doc.

Malaki sat silent, staring at nothing. Finally he spoke. "Tell ye what," he said, "I'm meeting her and her daddy over at their house for breakfast in the morning. She fixing a batch of them sweetater pies that everybody's talkin' about and I, fer sure, don't wanna miss that and . . . I'll talk to them then. I don't rightly know what I'm gonna say, but I'll talk to 'em."

———•———

The next morning, Malaki put just a tad of sweet smelling pomade on his great mass of kinky-curly hair and decided to wear his new white shirt he was saving for some occasion. He didn't know what, but something.

Leolla met him at the door fifteen minutes early. She thought it strange. "Malaki Messer is never early! Late, maybe, but never early. What's he up to?"

Moses met him at the kitchen door with open arms. "Malaki, my boy! It's about time you got here. Leolla tells me, the only way I'm gonna get me one of them pies today, is to have breakfast with you. Let's get at it!" Malaki gave him a pirate hug and they sat down.

The kitchen smelled wonderful. The pies were sizzling and Leolla sat Malaki at Moses' right and looked at him . . . sniffed . . . and then, looked at him some more. With a slight smile of approval, she took a large linen napkin out of the bureau drawer and tucked it into the collar of his new white shirt.

"He's up to something," she thought. He don't slick down his hair and put on his new shirt just for nothing. What was it he said yesterday? Oh, yes. He said 'What do you think Moses would say if I told him that we wuz thinking 'bout gettin' married?' Don't that beat all? He's never asked me that, yet. Hm-m-m, what is he up to?"

She served the pies and they were gone in a matter of minutes. "Uh-uh!" Moses said. "I don't think I ever tasted nothing as good as that in my whole life." Leolla poured coffee and sat down.

"I agree," said Malaki, patting Leolla's folded hands, "Them pies is something else, and I'm surely glad to have a chance to sit down with the both of you this morning, 'cause I got something I need to talk about."

Leolla sat up straight in her chair, touched her napkin to her lips softly and brushed back a curl that had found it's way down onto her forehead and folded her hands again.

"Yes?" She purred, "What is that . . . ?"

Malaki started at the beginning when Doc arrived and didn't miss a thing about the fix they were in and how they've got just a little over four days to decide before the government ship gets in.

"What are you going to do?" Asked Pastor Mose.

"Jesse's answer," said Mal, "is to run to the mountains and start a new life up there somewhere and wants me to come with him."

"WHAT ? COME WITH HIM?" Leolla's eyes were spitting fire. "WHAT ABOUT ME?"

"Well, honey . . . I was just thinkin' . . . . what would make me happy would . . . ."

"And just what is that, pray-tell? Nobody here wants to step in front of what makes YOU happy. Tell us, Malaki Messer, just what would make . . . YOU happy?" Snapped Leolla.

"Well . . ." Mal starting slow but gaining momentum with every word, "What would make me the happiest man in the whole world would be, if you would come with me and we could start that new life together." He pulled the napkin from his collar and put his hand over his heart. I love you, Leolla. More than I ever thought I could love anyone in my whole life. Could you . . . . would you possibly come with me?"

Leolla melted. Her hand moved across the table to his and they both looked at Moses.

"We would need your blessing, Mr Mose, what are you thinking?" Said Malaki.

The old story-telling man of God sat quietly with his fingers forming a little steeple in front of his nose and said nothing. Then his eyes turned up to them.

"I think that it's the right thing to do."

"What is?" Said Leolla.

"I think that the two of you needs to run off together . . . and be happy."

"You do?" Said Leolla.

"You do?" Said Malaki.

"Yes, and even as I say it, I know that I will miss you both more than I will miss anyone in my whole life . . . but it's plain to see that you have found each other, you love each other, and you're in a powerful hurry. So, go."

Leolla's eyes got as big a saucers. "Daddy, I can't tell you how happy that . . . ."

"Right after . . ." Moses went on.

"Right after what?" Said Malaki, bending over.

"Right after you jump the broom."

"Jump the what, Daddy?" Said Leolla, also bending over.

"The broom . . . darlin' . . . the broom! I can't have you two running around up in those mountains if'n ye ain't married. Who knows, up on that mountain top you may not run into another preacher for ten years. We can't have that, now, can we?"

"No sir!" Said Malaki, "You mean that all we got to do is jump over a broom 'n we're married?"

"Well," Said Moses. "That ain't the whole of it. I still has to say my words, and that brings me to my surprise."

"Surprise, daddy?" Said Leolla.

68

"Yep. I finished it last night and I was waiting for just the right time to show it to you and this seems to be the right time if I ever seen a right time."

"What daddy?"

Moses went into the work room and came back with a square looking package wrapped in parchment paper. He turned his back while he unwrapped it and spun dramatically, holding a beautiful, leather-bound book with gilded pages and the words *"Holy Bible"* embossed in the black leather. Stamped under it in shining gold letters, read *The Gullah-Geeche Translation.*

"Your wedding will go down in history as the first Gullah to Gullah wedding ever performed, with this bible."

"Oh-o-o, It's beautiful", Said Leolla. "And look, Mal, It's autographed by the author!"

Mal flipped open the cover and on the parchment fly-sheet, written with a flourish, under a red heart, were the words, *God and I love you both with all our hearts. Don't ever forget. Rev. Moses Thornberry, Your Daddy.*

Leolla looked up as big tears welled up in her eye. "I love you, Daddy."

It took a lot of scurrying about, but by five o'clock that afternoon the praise house was fitted for a wedding. There is no occasion that brings out the Gullah in the Gullah, like a wedding. Chairs were set up in rows like magic. Little bouquets of camellias seemed to just happen at the end of each row and a dramatic aisle of white sand, trimmed with sea shells, flowed down the center. Reverend Thornberry moved his podium out from the praise house with a small carpeted box with white linen cloth for Leolla and Mal to kneel on.

Then, dramatically, off to the right, with lots of room in front for folks to crowd around, was another five foot square of white sand trimmed with sea shells and centered in that square of sand, with a bright red handle, was a broom, brought in directly . . . from the pantry.

By five-o-five, every chair was filled and the standing room only space . . . was already stood on. It seemed like every Gullah, Massa, Pirate, man, woman, dog, cat, sheep, pigs and horses were all there, in Sunday-go-to-meetin' clothes. These were the folks who knew how to put on a wedding. The same folks were landed on the desolate island of Little Majorca and made it a joyous and warm community.

Then, with the help of a slightly out of tune piano, a single violin and a flute, the song, that is sung at every Gullah wedding ever, filled the air.

> *Come to a wedding,*
> *Come to a blessing,*
> *Come on a day when happiness sings.*
> *Come rain or sun,*
> *Come winter or summer,*
> *Come celebrate love, and all that it brings.*
>
> *Love is the gift,*
> *And love is the giver,*
> *Love is the gold that makes the day shine,*
> *Love forgets self.*
> *To care for the other,*
> *Love changes life from water to wine.*

Malaki was already up front looking nervous. Jesse, his best man with his long golden hair and mustache shining in the late afternoon sun, was impressive, but not much help. He was paying more attention to a flirty young lady in a pink dress on the front row, than he was to his friend Malaki. As luck would have it, so far, Malaki had not gotten even one spot on his new white shirt.

When the rinky-tink piano played "Here comes the bride, Mal turned and the same jolt of electricity shot up his spine that hit him the first he ever laid eyes on her at The Blandshard Plantation and instantly fell in love all over again.

Moses walked out holding the beautiful, new bible in front of him. He nodded and the bride and groom knelt and he read some words from it. Malaki couldn't understand some of them, but what he did understand, did the job.

Then Reverend Thornberry looked out at all the faces. "We are gathered here today in the sight of God, angels and all of you to celebrate one of life's greatest moments.

The piano started a soft rift as Sue Bell Clauson sang a traditional African love song.

You are sweet,
O love, dear love,
You are soft as the nesting dove.
Come to my heart and bring it rest
As the bird flies home to it's
welcome nest

They said their "I do's", exchanged rings and Pastor Mose pronounced them man and wife and with a plethora of "Ooo-s and Ah-h-h-s", they kissed. Then Moses put his arms around them both and said, "Ladies and Gentlemen, I will present to you Mr. and Mrs Leolla and Malaki Messer . . . ." The congregation started to applaud and Mose held up his hand . . . . "right after . . . they jump the broom.

Everyone squealed and started crowding around the "broom site" Moses waited until things were quiet again, with his arms still around the bride and groom, said, in historical fashion.

"We end this ceremony with the African American tradition of jumping of the broom because slaves in this country were not permitted to marry, they jumped a broom as a way of ceremonially uniting. Today it represents great joy and at the same time serves as a reminder of the past and the pain of slavery. As they jump this broom, they physically and spiritually cross the threshold into the land of matrimony and mark the beginning of making a home together. Now, let's all rejoice as our bride and groom start their lives together with a . . . clean sweep.

The crowd parted. Malaki looked at Leolla and smiled confidently. Leolla looked into his eyes, wrinkled her nose playfully and hand-in-hand, they jumped over the broom to a new life and another roar of cheers and whistles.

Moses, with tears in his eyes, closed the Bible, tucked it under Malaki's arm. "This is for you, from the Gullah's God. Keep it always. There's lots of pages for you to write in the names of all your children . . . and my grandchildren, and watch for me when you get up there. God may just decide that you need a Gullah church on that mountain to baptize 'em in." He gave them both a hug.

Doc rushed up and gave Leolla a kiss, shook Mal's hand three times and said, "I don't mean to rush you love birds, but while you two were jumping brooms, some awful bad guys got another day's jump on you. Can we get you out of here . . . now!

Then he put his arm around Jesse's shoulder. "Goodbye, my friend. God's speed and when God brings your memories back to you, save room for ole Doc." Then he turned and walked away.

They had packed their belongings on the back of a burro named Clyde before the ceremony and at sunup, amid tears and great emotion, Pastor Mose led Clyde as

Jesse, Malaki and Leolla followed down off the slope and toward the wetland. It was dark by the time they finally made the crossing and got to the mainland. They said their good-byes to Pastor Mose and watched him disappear back into the dense undergrowth and headed into the forest in the general direction of the islands.

About a half mile in, the moon was mysteriously bright and dramatically lit up the entrance to a cozy little glen with a brook running through it.

"This looks like a good place to spend the first night of a honeymoon," Said Jesse. "What do you say?" Leolla and Malaki looked at each other and smiled. So did Jesse as he built a welcome fire, strung a rope between two trees in front of a big rock, hung a deer skin over it, made sure his flintlock was primed and laid down.

Mr and Mrs Malaki Messer spent the first night of their "honeymoon" on the other side of that rock under a colorful Gullah patchwork quilt by the fire . . . giggling.

The next morning, Jesse tied burlap bags around Clyde's hoofs while Malaki put out the fire and spread leaves and pine needles around the area while Leolla checked for any signs or tracks that would tell anyone that they had camped there. Satisfied, they started out on a deer path leading through the vast forest. Their only means of direction came from a pocket compass Malaki had in his knapsack, the telescope the Lieutenant gave Jesse before he left the *Pride* and Mother Nature herself. Malaki knew that moss always grew on the north side of a tree or hill or rock and the winds that pulled the tree tops back and thinned out the clouds enough to get a glimpse of High Mountain, looming above it all. Every time that would happen, Jesse would get the same jolt of excitement running up his spine.

Malaki and Leolla were no help. Even though the three of them had become very close, he was alone most of the time now. To them, the whole adventure was just an extended honeymoon. Jesse respected that, however, and walked ahead as they brought up the rear. He could hear them giggling and laughing over Clyde's clip-clop. Jesse fought back the dark feeling that was building up inside him. He couldn't help it, no matter how much he tried, he envied their happiness. A dark cloud of loneliness had formed over his head.

One night, after they had bedded down he closed his eyes. "Hello God. I can't remember when we last talked or who it was doing the talking and maybe I don't know who I am but you do and I pray you'll let me know when it is your will. I wish you could tell me God, why does the sight of that mountain affect me so? Why does it make me feel good and normal again? You know where I came from God but I don't. Was I good? Am I bad? Please help me to be worthy of your blessings."

Two days into their trek, they came across the only other human beings they had seen in over a week. After satisfying himself that they meant no harm, the man standing guard in front of a half built cabin laid down his musket and introduced himself as Ernest P. Holman. He was a settler building his sod home along a pretty little stream, named Yahoola Creek that wound down out of the foothills. He introduced his wife Melba and their three year old, blue-eyed blond daughter, Tricha, who did nothing but stare at Jesse.

You'll have to excuse the child, Mr . . . er . . . Mac. You be the only person she ever seed in her whole lifetime with hair as blond as hers. Jesse laughed and squatted down to say hello. Her blue eyes rolled up in amazement as she touched his thick, blond mustache with her little finger and giggled.

Melba had spread a cloth over some hand hewn boards on top of two tree stumps and invited them to supper. Jesse and Malaki put out some fresh straw and gave Clyde a bag of oats while Leolla helped Melba with the food.

"I hope you know, how good it is to have another woman around here, Leolla". Said Melba.

Leolla laughed. "As someone who has spent the last two weeks with nobody but two men and a donkey to talk to, I know what you mean.

Melba stopped what she was doing, turned and lightly touched Leolla's hair. "If I might say so, you is just about the most beautiful lady I ever seen."

Leolla, a bit embarrassed, did a mock curtsy and hugged her.

As they ate, they told stories about each other and laughed and Ernest, meaning to compliment his guests, said that they were head 'n shoulders more fun than that squad of soldier boys that come through last week.

Jesse and Malaki, together, sat straight up in their bent wood chairs.

"What soldiers?" They said at the same time.

"Oh," Said Ernest, a little surprised at their sudden interest. "They was United States Army folks who was looking fer some spies, or something. They weren't near as much fun as you folks.

"Last week, you say?" Said Jesse, "Where were they headed?"

"Well, they didn't rightly know. I told them that if they keeps going north up the hill, they will come to the town of Sideways and I warned them that Sideways is the only crossroad town they'll come to before they head on up to the top High Mountain."

"How did they get ahead of us?" Said Malaki.

"Thay probably rode throu tha night, thay did, whilst ye twa wis skinny-dippin' in tha pretty little loc we camped at last week." Said Jesse, shaking his head.

"Say," Says Ernest. "You folks ain't them spies they wuz loookin' fer . . . is ye"

"Nae!," Said Jesse. We be hamesteaders, jes like ye. We be trekin' up to the top of the high mountain to live."

75

"That's a comfort," Said Ernest, winking at Leolla. "Ye shorely don't look like no spies."

"When did they leave?" Asked Malaki.

"Well, let's see," Said Ernest, "They camped here for two days and then took off for Sideways. They purty much ought to be there by now.

"Which way do you go if you don't want to go through Sideways?" Blurted Malaki.

"What he means," Said Jesse, quickly. "Is there . . . er, another way we could go if we didn't want to go through a town?"

"Hm-m-m," Said Ernest, "from here, no matter where you're aiming to go, you almost has to go through Sideways to get there." Then he stopped to think. "I supposed, now that I think on it, you could go up through the Cherokee country, I reckon. I wouldn't advise it though."

"Why not?" Said Jesse.

"Well, first off, it's a straight up climb to get there and second, a body never knows what kind of a greeting you gonna get from them people when you do. I've heard stories . . ."

"How do we get there?" Malaki interrupted.

Ernest stopped and thought for a minute, slapped his knee and said, "Well sir, I'll tell you . . . when you go north for about six miles, you'll come to a fork in the road. The left fork, which is the main road, will take you around to the other side of the mountain to Sideways. The right fork, which ain't nothin' more 'n a deer path will take you up, straight up, to Cherokee country. Now, if I was you, I'd . . ."

"Thank you very much," Jesse interrupted, "And thank you for your hospitality and supper. We best be going now."

As quick as they could, they packed everything and left down the path. It was midnight before they came to the fork in the road, turned right and started up the hill. The moon lit their way up a deer-path trail for about two miles, and then went under a cloud. Since they couldn't see their hands in front of their faces, they stopped at a clearing under a rock cliff overhang, tied Furball to a tree, spread some hay and they all fell exhausted into a well earned sleep.

Chapter 11

The fire in their wattle house was warm and inviting. Running Deer was softly humming a lullaby as she knelt behind Ivy weaving bright colored beads into her long black braids. They watched the smoke rise gracefully and disappear through the dark opening in the roof. Both were silent. The prophet Yellow Owl's vision had brought unrest to the entire village. Finally, Ivy spoke.

"Mother, was I not born in this village?"

"You were," Said Running Deer, "Just as your father and your father's father were. But not in this wattle. You and The Great Spirit had other plans."

"Oh!" She said, playfully, "Tell me mother, what did I do? Was I naughty?"

"No," Said Running Deer, without looking up. "But you had a mind of your own. "You see, I wanted everything to be perfect for Red Feather during the time I knew I would not be able to tend him and went across the river of rocks to gather some berries and nuts for him to eat but I was not watching the skies and a great storm came up and the river swelled and became angry before I could return, so I sought shelter and slept the night.

The next morning, the sun was shining again and the river was flowing peacefully. Then, just as I was about to cross, a pain went through my body. At first I thought it was the effect of sleeping on the hard stones and paid little attention. Then it came again, only harder. That was when I realized that the Great Spirit had spoken and I started looking for a place to lie down."

"Where?" Said Ivy, "Where did you lie down? In the leaves?"

"No, it was a most beautiful little glen, all bright and green in the sunlight and I spotted an *Indian bed* of Ivy growing at the base of a mighty sycamore."

"And that was where I was born?"

"Yes, And at sun up, when her rays came down to greet you, I stood and looked at you asleep in the ivy and your name popped into my head."

"Wings of Ivy." Oh, mother, that is a beautiful story. Can I go see?"

"You want to go see the place where you were born?"

"Yes, may I, please?"

The next morning, Ivy was up with the sun and down by the brook admiring the bright red feather Running Deer had fastened to her head band. She had also packed a basket pouch with corn, beans and squash, known as "the three sisters" to the Indian, along with other fruits and nuts and walked down to the brook and hung it on the back of Furball, a burro and long time pet of Ivy's. "Good, daughter, Furball's back is far stronger than mine. We will get hungry along the way." Then she filled a water skin with fresh water and went to Red Feather.

"If we should not return before nightfall, my husband, do not worry. We will find shelter and return on the next sun."

"Be wary, woman, remember the visions of Yellow Owl. Watch carefully and do not take any risks." He warned, and bid her goodbye.

The sun was shining bright and the trees were full of nature's song as the two of them happily started their adventure.

As they walked along the deer path, Ivy was quiet. When her mother asked why, she said, "I was just thinking about Yellow Owl's visions. Do you think they will come true, mother?"

"If they do," Said Running Deer, "It will be the last of the Cherokee in this land."

"But he had a second vision, mother. The one about the shining white horse-creature with wings on his head who will lead us to a secret place where we could build a new life."

"Yes, A new beginning." Said Running Deer.

"But, Mother, would that not mean that our nation would end before we could have a new beginning . . . ?"

Running Deer frowned. "Hush child, we are approaching the river. Soon you will see where you began."

They reached the river, crossed on the stone bridge and walked along the shore for the better part of the morning until Running Deer saw the grassy slope she was looking for. They climbed up the embankment and when they reached the top, they got their first look into the glen. Ivy gasped.

"It is beautiful, Mother."

"Yes," Said Running Deer. It is a fitting place for a princess to be born. Now, it is a fitting place for a princess to eat." With that, she spread a grass-cloth across a low rock and used it as a table as they ate and talked the afternoon away with tales of Ivy when she was growing up.

When they finished, Ivy jumped up suddenly and said, "Now, Mother, Where?"

"Where?"

"Yes, where was I born?"

"There," She pointed." At the foot of that great sycamore, is where my eyes first beheld your beauty."

Ivy giggled. She couldn't wait and ran ahead to the spot where her mother pointed. The sycamore was large indeed and the thick blanket of Indian ivy was even more lush than Running Deer had remembered.

Ivy stopped, took it all in. "Where were you lying, Mother?"

Running Deer pointed to the exact spot in the center of the ivy patch.

Ivy waded out to the spot and looked up and closed her eyes as if she was hearing a voice. Then she raised her arms to the sky and started slowly turning around and around. Then, as if some spirit had taken her over, she started singing.

Running Deer recognized it immediately. It was a lullaby. The same lullaby that every Cherokee mother, since time began, sang to their little ones.

> *Ho, ho, what tay nay,*
> *Ho, ho, what tay nay,*
> *Ho, ho, what tay nay,*
> *Key, oh kay nah.*
> *Key, oh kay nah.*
>
> *Oh, oh, little one*
> *Oh, oh, little one*
> *Oh, oh, little one*
> *Now, go—to—sleep.*
> *Now, —go—to—sleep.*

As she sang, she bent over, lowered her head and slowly twirled closer and closer to the ground. When she reached it, she spread out flat and tucked her knees up under her chin, put her arms around them and closed her eyes . . . and giggled.

Running Deer had been watching her every move and when Ivy closed her eyes, she cheered and clapped her hands.

After the show, they spread out their blanket nearby and talked and laughed the day away. When Ivy looked up, the sun had already started to fall behind the tree tops and the dark shadows of nighttime were reaching down the mountainside to pull the cover of darkness up around it.

"Mother," Said Ivy, "look at where the sun has fallen. How will we ever get back to Red Feather before nightfall?"

Running Deer smiled in the same manner she always smiled when Ivy, or any child was being as a child who knows nothing.

"Be at peace, my daughter, I know you only too well and I took the precaution to let Red Feather know that we would likely stay through the night and return when the sun is high in the sky again."

"But where will we sleep?"

Running Deer smiled again in the same manner as before. "I know of a small cave in the rocks where I slept the night before you were born. I am sure it is still there. Come my Angel, Get Furball and let us go and see."

They climbed up the hillside until they found the rock cliffs Running Deer was looking for and located the narrow foot-hold path that led up to the cave. When they reached it, Ivy was dazed. It was like their own wattle house. They built a fire, spread grass for Furball and soon, were talking and singing non-stop. When they could hold their eyes open no longer, they slept.

When the fire went out, the cave was as black as black could be Ivy, heard a noise and her eyes snapped open. She heard it again. It sounded like a growl.

She groped until she felt her mother's shoulder. She shook it and put her hand over her mouth so she could not cry out.

"Did you hear that?" She whispered under her breath.

"Hear what?" She asked, pulling Ivy's hand from her mouth.

"It sounded like . . . ."

It came again, only this time, louder and more threatening.

Running Deer sat straight up.

"It sounds like a bear. Probably a momma bear with cubs. Wait here," She whispered, "I will make my way to the entrance and see.

The noise happened again. A growl mixed with the sound of rustling leaves.

"Not without me!" Said Ivy. What if she decides to come in?"

Slowly and quietly, the two of them inched their way to the front of the cave to see what they could see . . . or not see.

Chapter 12

❀

The black bear mother stood on her hind legs outside two leaning rocks that formed her winter hibernation home. She sniffed the air. She was well over eight feet tall standing up and she did just that when she wanted to get her nose up above all the other scents of the forest. Her two cubs were curious but careful as they hung onto her leg and peeked around.

It was the first night of the full moon and Mother Earth was commanding all things, plant and animal alike to come forth and grow. Her three cubs were no exception. They were born during her hibernation and she and her cubs were more than ready to meet the world again. They were going downhill to a small stream where she could show her cubs how to catch the small blue gill that swim there.

Normally, she walked behind them watching as they frolicked and rolled, one over the other down the hill, baby-growling and swatting each other.

When they would get too far away, Momma would do her fake-angry growl and show her teeth and the cubs would scurry back and nestle down behind her massive legs and peek out.

But now, something was bothering her. There was a smell in the air that she had never smelled before. She sniffed again. The scent was still there. It was similar to the smell of the red hunters, only different. She heard sounds coming from the old cave up in the rocks. She stepped in front of the cubs and growled again, only louder to see what would happen.

———•———

Jesse's eyes popped wide open. Malaki was already awake.

"What was that?" He whispered in Jesse's ear. "You got that gun of yours loaded?"

Jesse reached under his bedroll and grabbed his flint lock and double checked it's prime. "A hear it." He whispered back. "If it be a bear, me flintlock is nae going to be much help. Slip back to the pack and bring that old musket of ye and be quiet about it. Bears can hear night crawlers crawl from a hundred yards oot. If it be a bear, it be up there by that old cave. Maybe that be her den."

Malaki quietly got up, stepped over Jesse and landed his foot on a round rock and went head-over-hill down the slope. When he did, Leolla screamed.

The mother bear pushed her cubs behind the rock. "That was not the sound of a red hunter." She thought to herself. "That came from below, not above." She charged through the underbrush, stopped and reared up. She caught a glimpse of Jesse's blond hair and pulled a low-hanging branch out of her way to see better. She smelled danger and charged again, roaring as she went.

When she was no more than forty feet from Jesse, a rock rolled down off the bluff where Ivy and Running Bear were watching and distracted the momma bear and she whirled. That frightened Ivy who was leaning out of the cave and she jumped. The bear spotted her and the red feather against the dark entrance of the cave, stopped and started toward Ivy.

With her back feet on the bluff and her front claws pulling at a sapling the bear was within four feet of Ivy. Ivy screamed and Running Bear started throwing rocks and limbs down on the momma.

Jesse was relieved to see the bear go in another direction away from him, but was confused as to why she did it. Malaki returned with the musket and was loading it as fast as he could.

"Is it a bear?" He asked, out of breath. "Where is she?

"She's be away from us!" Said Jesse. "She be after something or someone else. See her? She's climbing up toward that cave up there on the bluff."

Then Jesse spotted the red feather. "Look Mal! There be someone up there!"

"I see em!" Said Mal. "It looks like two women!"

"Aye, Indian women. They're not armed."

The bear was just feet away from the cave. Running Deer had a burning stick from the fire trying to keep it away from Ivy. The bear raised her paw and knocked the stick out of Running Bear's hand. Ivy screamed and put her hands in front of her face. Jesse, without thinking ran straight for the bear with his flintlock in his hand, grabbed the sapling, shook it and shook it until the bear looked down and Jesse fired. The mini-ball grazed the bear's forehead and caused her to release the tree and fall down at Jesse's feet. Before he could re-load the bear came across and with a mighty swipe laid Jesse's chest open from shoulder to belt line. Jesse fell back on the jagged bluff and hit his head. Blood was puddling under his lifeless body.

Then, just as the bear was about to sink her teeth into Jesse's neck, Ivy jumped down and screamed at the bear and when she did, the whole area lit up like the sun had just come out and a piercing sound reverberated off the rocks and stopped all, man and animal alike, in their tracks.

"E-E-E-E-HA-A-A! . . . E-E-E-E-HA-A-A!"

The bushes parted and a brilliant white form came out, walked between the bear and Jesse and stopped still. Her eyes were locked on those of the bear. Neither made a sound.

Leolla buried her face in Malaki's chest. "What is it, Mal? What do I hear?"

"It's . . . No, it couldn't be.

"What?"

"It's so bright! I can't see, but I think it's . . ."

"What, Mal? I see nothing."

"It's Glory! O my God, it is . . . How in the world did . . . ?"

A silence fell over the entire scene. Ivy, who was now cradling Jesse's head in her lap watched as the bear stopped her attack, turned and with a trickle of blood running down her face, gathered her three cubs and went back into the forrest.

Malaki rushed out. The great mule looked. "Glory, you can't be here! You . . . ." He looked at Leolla. "Honey, this is Glory. She's the one I've been talking about.

Leolla was frozen. All she could see was Malaki. "Where?"

Mal looked down at Jesse. "Oh my, Jesse boy, can you hear me" He looked up at Ivy. What can we do Ma'am . . . we can't let him bleed to death!"

Before Ivy could speak, Glory made a whinny sound and Furball, the little burro walked out and lowered herself down to her knees and started to glow.

"I see'd that before!" said Malaki. "I know what she wants us to do." He looked at Ivy, who still had not said a word. Could you help me get em aboard? Who are you, anyhow?"

"I am called Wings Of Ivy," She said, in English, as they lifted Jesse onto the Furball's back. "And this," She nodded at her mother climbing down the bluff, "Is Running Deer. My mother. Our village is not far. We must take him there."

With Jesse aboard, Furball still did not get up. Ivy looked at Malaki and Malaki looked at Glory. "She wants you to ride on tha glowing donkey with him and hold him." He shrugged. "It's her way, I reckon."

Her mother, who was wrapping Jesse's chest in a soft deer skin, looked around and saw nothing. "Who, Daughter?"

"Never Mind, Mother. Can you walk beside us" Running Deer nodded.

Once Jesse and Ivy were on Furball's back, the little burro rose and immediately started down the hill toward the rock bridge. Ivy looked back. The white spirit horse was gone.

At the village, the dogs were barking and Red Feather went out to look. He saw a light glowing deep in the dark of the forest and grabbed his bow and ran across the stream that separated the village from the woods.

When they emerged, he couldn't believe what he was looking at. It was the burro Furball and she seemed to be glowing in the dark and Wings of Ivy was riding it. When he saw the limp body in front of her, he readied his bow and approached them very carefully. Running Deer, who was out in front, ran to meet him before he did something "war like" and let him know that there was no need for alarm. She promised to tell him all just as soon as they can get the yellow hair to Grey Wolf, the medicine man,.

"He was hurt, my husband, by the mother bear, while saving the life of your daughter,"

That was all Red Feather had to hear and called to a brave to run and alert Grey Wolf.

When they reached the wattle of Grey Wolf, Wings Of Ivy jumped down off the glowing burro and helped carry Jesse in.

Red Feather looked at Malaki and Leolla and said to Running Deer, "Show these people where they can rest." And went in with Wings Of Ivy.

After looking at Jesse's wounds, the medicine man said that he had lost much blood and must be sewn immediately and, with that, deftly took a bone needle and strips of tendon and sewed the large artery together and took a pillow of moss, mud and the juice of the elderberry and covered the head wound and covered him with a thick bear skin.

"He must be kept warm through the night." Said Grey Wolf, "If he lives until the sun rises, he will recover."

Ivy looked at her mother, "Mother, may I tend him tonight? I will move the hot stones close around and keep him warm.

Running Deer looked at Red Feather.

He smiled. "That is good, He said and started toward the flap that covered the entrance. "I must now see the burro of light that brought you here. In all my moons I have never seen . . ." When he looked out, Furball was standing in the dark, munching hay. Her light was not on.

Chapter 13
❧

Red Feather's story of the spirit that possessed the burro, Furball, spread throughout all the tribes. The visions of the prophet Yellow Owl were coming true. Red Feather was the target of most questions and all he could say was that he too saw the great light before it disappeared . . . he thinks. Did he actually see the glow, or was Ivy holding the yellow hair on a normal Indian burro? Could the twilight reflections have been playing tricks on him and he imagined the rest?

Jesse didn't regain consciousness for two days but was still too weak to talk and could only remember the bear attacking him. Too many things had happened to him that nearly killed him and, according to Malaki, they all involved a white mule or horse spirit that he had never seen. Malaki couldn't say where she came from or even if she was real, but as Jesse looked at his wounds, which were real for sure, and watched the most beautiful Indian maiden he had ever seen, go back and forth tending him, he was not going to start doubting it now.

On the third day after their dramatic appearance, Tsali, or prophet Yellow Owl returned to the village to hear for himself and Red Feather summoned Running Deer, Wings of Ivy, Leolla, and Malaki to join them at the council fire the next morning. All were excited and talking all at once when Red Feather held up his hand and called for silence. He looked at Wings of Ivy.

"Daughter, in your own words, tell this council and Yellow Owl what you saw three moons ago."

Ivy started her tale from the time she and Running Deer were awakened by a noise and slowly, but accurately related all that happened after that. How she saw the bear at the same time she saw the yellow hair and the two with dark skin. She dramatically described the bear climbing up the rocks to attack her while Running Deer tried to fight it off with a fire brand, and then how she heard the shot fired by the yellow hair that wounded the bear, and how the bear turned and attacked yellow hair instead.

"The bear slashed open the breast of yellow hair and was standing over him when we all saw a bright light coming out of the forest and when it made a strange and challenging cry, the bear turned, with her cubs and went away. I cannot say if it was the same as Yellow Owl's vision but it was real to us. She looked at Running Deer for conformation. "No one made a sound when Furball, the little burro came forward and knelt, but we somehow knew what to do. We put yellow hair across her back and when I mounted, she started to glow and led us all here."

Yellow Owl asked, "Did all the village see the little burro glow?"

Running Deer answered. "No, all were asleep" Then she paused, "Now that it's over, we even question ourselves. Did anyone ever really see a vision? Are visions not like smoke from the council fire, real until it floats into all that is around it and then disappears? The glowing spirit was real until it got us safely back among our people . . . then, the light disappeared."

"A wise and profound answer, Running Deer." Said Yellow Owl, "The Great Spirit lets us see his visions until there is no more need. Then He takes them away until they are needed again."

Red Feather agreed. "Let us welcome and tend to our new friends and put this all aside. Yellow Owl has other news."

Yellow Owl reported that a new leader for the "White Eye" has been elected. He has signed a paper that says that all Indian land here in our sacred hills will be taken and the Cherokee will be sent to other land west of the great river. It is said that our Choctaw and Chippewa brothers are already being moved as we speak and there are tales of cruelty and even death at the hands of the white eye soldiers. We must prepare ourselves."

———•———

The deerskin doorway of the wattle where Jesse was recovering flipped open. "Does dis be de house of de Yaller-haired hero named Yaller-hair?"

Jesse laughed for the first time since he was hurt. Just seeing Malaki's silliness and Leolla's smiling faces made him feel better. "Dis be de place!" Jesse mocked.

Ivy, who was putting a new dressing on Jesse's wounds, put her hand to her mouth and giggled.

"Y'all shorely do have a pretty nursemaid." Said Mal, holding Ivy's hand. "Tell me ma'am, iffen a bar ever bit me, would ye care fer me too?

Ivy, stroking Jesse's forehead, laughed. "If you are a friend of my yellow haired hero, I would, with pleasure."

"Who-o-o-e Darlin" Mocked Mal holding Leolla's hand, "Maybe we should leave and come back later,."

"Get in here, ye twa nuts. Ivy's been telling me all about her people, she has. Ye should hear. Like me, ye'll fall in love with her . . . her storys, tha is."

Leolla then knew that their happy trio had just become a happy quartet.

For the next month, they were inseparable. Every time Ivy's eyes turned in Jesse's direction and held too long, he felt a tug in his heart. They went everywhere and did everything together. They talked and laughed and did crazy things. It was more than Red Feather and Running Bear could watch without smiling. They had never seen their princess so happy.

Leolla told Ivy how she grew her "sweeter than sweet" potatoes and taught her how to fry them into pies in their rock oven without burning them and Ivy taught Leolla how to use bone tools to fashioned hickory wood and a piece of deer antler into a bow wrapped in sinew and strung with gut and searched for hours for just the right dewberry shoots to make into arrows which they tipped with red feathers, the trademark of their chief, to make them fly straight. They practiced at shooting paw-paws hanging in the trees until Leolla got quite good.

Malaki kept them all in stitches with his "Hog Breath Hanratty" stories, that is, when he wasn't out playing Indian stick ball with all the young bucks.

When Jesse got back on his feet, he and Ivy would take long walks through the forest and talk about their lives. Ivy explained that she was considered to be a princess because her father was chief of all Cherokee. She spoke of her love for her parents and how the Cherokee honor their forefathers as far back as their history permits. She also talked about Yellow Owl and his visions that someday the Cherokee will be driven from their land and how a white spirit horse with ears like the wing of Angels, would lead them to a new land where they could spend the rest of their lives.

Jesse, on the other hand had little to tell Ivy. He could only remember from the time he woke up in a hospital bed and was told that he was a British, or maybe Scottish, soldier who fought in the battle of New Orleans but could not remember anything before that.

He was especially interested in the white spirit horse mentioned in Yellow Owl's visions and wondered if it could be the same glowing, white mule who guided Malaki to the shell hole where he was laying unconscious. Ivy suggested that Jesse go see the medicine man about his loss of memory in hopes that he might know of a cure.

All in all, it was a magic and joyful time for them both. Ivy had made Jesse forget that only a month and a half ago, he was running from the Feds.

One morning, down by the river, Jesse was looking at himself in the water and trimming his, now picturesque, moustache while Mal finished the last of a sweetater pie, and without looking up, said, "Did ye ever think we don't even know what them federal boys look like. They probably ain't still in uniform and for all we know, they could be sneaking up on us right now?"

"Aye, I hear what ye say" Said Jesse. "We should tell the Indian lookouts to watch for them, but tis nae fair to get the Cherokees mixed up in our problems. What do ye think we should do. What be our next move?"

"I been thinking about that." Said Mal, "What did you think about Ernest P. Holman and his family?"

"I liked them. Why do ye ask?"

"Well, he lives close to that town of Sideways and he's probably in and out of there a couple times a month gettin' supplies 'n all and I figure he probably hears all the talk going around and sees all the people coming in 'n out."

"Aye?"

"What if we were to let him in on who we really are, and why the Feds are chasing us and how we are in a dire need for somebody who could keep his eyes and ears open in town and if he sees them boys, he could maybe get in close like and listen and if they are up to something, he could let us know.

"'Tis a bonny good idea," Said Jesse "But why would he do that?"

"Oh, I don't know," Said Mal, "Maybe because good friends are hard to find out here in the woods and the fact that we're buddy-buddy with all them Cherokee, he just might like to have a friend or two around their council fire."

Jesse thought . . . "Let's go see. First thing in the morning."

———•———

The trip down the mountain was a snap for Jesse, but Mal hit every low hanging branch, tripped over every log stepped in every hole and slid down every slope head first. He just couldn't stand upright and take ten steps before something else happened. Mal, on the other hand, couldn't get over what a good mountaineer Jesse had become.

"It's like ye wuz born in to it, laddy" He said about half way down.

They arrived at the Holman house that evening. Ernest was more than happy to see them and they all had supper together and when they were finished, all the men went out to "test ride" the new porch Sam had just built onto the front of their cabin where rocking chairs, a jug of moon and three corn cob pipes were waiting.

When they were settled and Melba was doing the dishes, Jesse lit up his pipe and started all the way back at the beginning from the time he was wounded in the battle of New Orleans and how Malaki saved his life and how they reckoned he was British because all that was left of his uniform was a piece of red cloth.

Then Malaki took over and told the part about how the federal government decided he was a spy and they sailed to the islands to get away from 'em. Then when they got word that they were right behind them and closing fast, they ran again and have been running ever since.

Ernest listened quietly, and when they finished, slapped his leg, "I figured it was something like that!" Shaking his head back and forth. "I sez to Melba the minute ye left that them people ain't no more spies than I am. I mean, what would a spy be doing away out here anyhow? I mean, What would a spy . . . . spy on?"

Jesse took over again and told why they had come there and that they needed a friend with good eyes 'n ears to keep them abreast of what's happening.

Ernest understood immediately and said that he was in town at least once a week and agreed to keep his eyes and ears open.

"Now, what do I do if I hears somethin' juicy?" He asked, "I'm gonna need a way to let ye know." He rubbed his chin and thought.

"I know, if I have anything to report, I'll go up to Eagle Rock, you boys know where that is, don't ye. It's half way up the mountain, and I'll fire my gun three times, and iff'n' ye hear me, you fire three shots back. Then I'll know you're on your way."

"That sounds like a good plan." Said Mal, "It shouldn't take us more than an hour to get down to Eagle Rock."

"Good!" Says Ernest, thoughtfully. "Maybe, when ye come down, ye could bring one of them Cherokee Indians with ye and I could let Melba and the kid come up and say hidy."

They all agreed and Jesse and Mal started home.

Mal was giggling.

"What?" Said Jesse.

"Oh, nothing," Said Mal, "I was just thinking about Ernest's great plan."

"What about it?"

"Well, it ain't exactly the kind of battle plan Capn' LaFitte might have come up with . . . but it should get the job done."

Little did they, or Ernest, realize that a discovery is about to happen that will change the lives of everyone.

Chapter 14

"Melba!" Ernest yelled as loud as he could, running across the yard, taking the porch in one single jump, crashing through the screen door and stepping on the dog's tail . . . "Melba! Where you at?"

"Ernest P. Holman, what in Sam Hill are you yelling about? Hush! What you doing with our Grandmas's savings jar out. You gone plum crazy?"

"Melba, you gotta hear this . . . As you know, I was up an out fore daylight this morning to get over to Sideways and see if I could hear anything about them soldier boys that' looking for Jesse and his folks."

"Yes, so what about it? Is this why . . . ."

"I'm trying to tell ye iffen you'd jes let me! When I was turning off the main road on to that deer path that leads down into Sideways, you know, by that old painted rock . . . ? I could hear the commotion from clean up there!"

"What commotion? Would ye say what you're trying to say?"

"GOLD! Melba. GOLD!"

"Gold?"

"Yes! They discovered it on our little Yahoola Crick out there.?"

"Gold in our crick?" Said Melba, whose eyes were now staring out the window.

"Yeah, well, not right out there, a feller named Leroy Withespoon and his two boys wuz making a cross in' spot down at the other end of the crick in Lumpkin County and they kicked over a rock doing it and found a three ounce nugget of gold under there! Now, they's people with pans and sluice boxes all over down there."

Melba sat staring with a frown on her face. "Lumpkin County? That the low end of Cherokee land, ain't it?"

Yeah, the boys wuz talkin' bout that. They sez that this feller Withespoon sent a letter to the Governor to see if it was agin the law to start a mine up there, but they ain't heard yet. I guess there's already been some trouble."

"Like what?" Asked Melba, looking up.

"They was talkin' about six of them fellers that went in together and decided not to wait for an answer from the Governor and took things in their own hands and fenced off a half mile section up the crick a mile or so from the county line and while they was panning and sluicing the area and making a mess, three Cherokee come up and asked what they were a doing on their land and one of them boys said that it weren't none of his business what they wuz a doin' and pulled him off his pony and threw him down the hill!

"Pon my soul!" Said Melba. "Did it . . . kill him?"

"I don't rightly know," Said Ernest, "But one of them other Indians went for his knife and them boys shot him dead . . . and the other one too! They would have gotten the third one, except he got one of em through the shoulder with an arrow and got away. Them things is bound to happen, I guess" Said Ernest, throwing up his hands.

"Come on honey. Bring the jar and lets get to town. We gotta buy some supplies and I want to talk to them fellers over to the land office about our homestead agreement. Where's all them papers I told ye to keep?"

"Our papers? They're folded up in the bible, why?"

"Who knows" Said Ernest, stopping in his tracks and gazing off in the distance. "We just might want to take them up on that option of another hundred acres. Think about it honey, that would give us pert nigh a mile and a quarter of creek front.

Chapter 15

President Andrew Jackson, now three years into his first term, was especially interested in the news.

"A gold strike in Georgia?" He screamed, "Mrs. Taylor, get the Secretary of State in here, now!

Secretary of State Van Buren came in. "I see you've already heard the news, Andy. What's this gold strike going to do to us?"

"What do you think, Martin" I'll tell you what it's going to do. It will bring every white settler and speculator on the frontier to Georgia expecting the government to make land available in what is now Cherokee territory." He said slamming his hand down on the desk "*What* . . . or *who* is standing in the way of getting those blasted Indians out of those hills and shipped west?"

He was referring to the Indian Removal Act, which was not working as successfully and he had expected. The Choctaw and the Chickasaw tribes, having been the first to accept the country's offer to exchange Native American land in the east for lands west of the mighty Quabalaka River, was a good start and opened up some territories for white settlers, but it bogged down and Jackson found himself with little information, no answers and was losing what little patience he had left and now . . . a gold strike to top it off.

"The *what*, Andy, is the Supreme Court. They ruled that the Cherokee Nation is not a sovereign and independent nation, and refused to hear the case and The *who* is Georgia who tried to extend their laws over the Cherokee lands and were blocked by our courts saying that they cannot do that, since only the national government had authority in Indian affairs. We're deadlocked, Andy."

"DEADLOCKED!" Screamed Jackson. "Enough! Contact Winfield Scott and be in this office with some answers first thing Monday morning!"

The Secretary of State and General Winfield Scott were waiting when the President arrived on Monday morning with a progress report on the gold strike along with news of trouble that was already brewing between the white settlers and the Cherokees when the President arrived. After coffee, they were escorted to a meeting room where a huge map hung with a vast shaded area indicating the territory belonging to the Cherokees.

"General Scott," Said President Jackson through squinty eyes, "We have just had the first gold rush in the history of the United States . . . That is good news! And, where did it happen? . . . On Cherokee controlled land! That is bad news! That gold belongs to the Union, not to the Indians! We must get . . . them . . . OUT of there . . . NOW!"

"How?" Said General Scott.

"With heat, My dear General," President Jackson said sarcastically, "You have a force of over 7000 militia, regular and volunteer soldiers at your command. Build a fire under those Indians. When it gets hot enough, they'll go."

Chapter 16

When Jesse first caught sight of the smoke curling up from the wattles of the village, his heart started beating faster. At first he blamed it on the climb but he had to admit it to himself, that wasn't it at all. It was Wings of Ivy. The day away from her made him realize how much he missed her. He had never felt this way before about a girl . . . any girl. He genuinely loved Leolla, but as a brother would love his sister. This was different. It was a feeling so strong, it hurt. He smiled to himself, "Could a yellow haired white eye who can't remember his own name, fall in love with a Cherokee princess? Nah-h"

When they crossed and were coming up from the river, they saw someone running toward them waving. At first they thought something had happened, but getting closer, Jesse saw that it was Ivy. She seemed excited. He waved back and started running toward her. They met in the lush, green pasture and she threw her arms around his neck and started kissing him uncontrollably. All Jesse could do was kiss back and silently thank God for this moment.

"When the sun was high in the sky and you weren't back yet" Said Ivy through her tears, "I thought the soldiers had captured you and had taken you away. The more I thought it, the more I realized that I could not live without you! I love you, Jesse Lafeyette McNabb, or whatever you're name is, tell me you feel the same."

"Love," Said Jesse with his eyes closed, "Is only a word, and no word is big enough to tell you how I feel."

They were still in an motionless embrace when Malaki caught up and passed them. "You better hurry that up, kiddies. I hear they's goinna be a big stomp dance around the fire tonight. We wouldn't want to miss that, now . . . . would we?"

From that time on, they were together constantly. One day, Jesse asked Ivy if Cherokees ever married out of their tribe. She suggested he go and talk to Red Feather. "He would know," She said, "And, I don't know why, but he already thinks of you as his son." Then she giggled.

The next day, he did. Red Feather explained that it was not allowed for any Cherokee maiden to marry outside our people. "However," He went on, "Once, long ago, there was another outsider that fell in love with one of our young maidens and asked permission to marry. The council met and agreed that if the tribe adopted him, he would no longer be an outsider and they were allowed to marry. They now live in the valley of the eagles on the far side of the mountain. There they live and raise horses. Is there anything you would have me ask the Council, my son?" He said smiling.

"Not yet, Chief," Said Jesse, as he felt his face turning red. "But, soon, maybe."

Chapter 17

※

Ernest was sitting at the corner table at the
Tip-Of-The-Top-Tavern on his second pint waiting for
Melba and *Miss goldilocks* to make up their mind on what
kind of dress would be best for the five year old daughter
of a big gold Ty-coon to wear on her first day of school.
He didn't mind, however, he actually enjoyed the time
alone to think. Mr. Hobson, over at the land office
had good news. He told Ernest that if they continue to
improve their homestead and keep up the taxes on the
hundred acres they were working, that come next October
he would be eligible for another hundred acres and all the
mineral rights that go along with it. He closed his eyes
and said to himself, *"It ain't never too late to get where you're
going,* Ernest P. Holman. Come next fall, you could be
king of two hundred acres of prime land and a creek full
of gold . . . to boot . . . Not bad . . ."
   While he had his eyes closed, he heard a familiar voice.
When he opened one of them, he saw that it was a bunch
of blue coats sitting over at the next table. He scanned
their faces and realized that The Lieutenant and the two
privates were the same soldiers that stayed overnight with
them back a month or so ago.
   The fourth sent a chill up Ernest's spine. He had seen
him before and recognized him as an ugly, animal-like
Indian who lived just outside the fort in an old abandoned
sod hut who goes by the name of Jimmy Big Dog. He
frowned as he remembered the first time he laid eyes on
him.
   It was late one night, several years ago and he was
having a pint in the very same tavern with Jeremiah
Blogget, who was sheriff at the time, and this dark form of

a man come charging through the swinging doors so hard, they crashed back against the wall. He remembered that his face was not painted, it was just dirty, but not so dirty that a body couldn't see that his skin was red and he had a long scar coming down out of his eyebrow and across his cheek that made his left eye look like it was half closed all the time. He wore a dirty buck skin shirt, a black, misshapen felt hat with a hawk feather in the band and long, matted, smelly dreadlocks down to his shoulders.

Jeremiah noticed him first and told Ernest that his name was Jimmy BigDog, a full blooded Cherokee who was once favored to be a sub Chief under Red Feather, but one night he got drunk and killed Lawson Baker, an eighty five year old homesteader while stealing his cow and thought, that he had also killed Orah Baker, Lawson's crippled wife, but she managed to crawl out to the road with an arrow in her back, where a passerby found her and brought her in to the Doc. When she came to, Doc called Jeremiah who came over to get her story. She was very weak but could talk and said that they were attacked by a crazy Indian who kept yelling "Big Dog kill! Big Dog kill!"

The next morning, early, Jeremiah and his deputy went out to see Red Feather, chief of all the Cherokee. Red Feather heard his story and summoned Big Dog. When Big Dog saw Jeremiah standing there holding Orah Baker's bonnet, he drew his knife and lunged for Jeremiah yelling 'Big Dog kill!"

Fortunately, Red Feather caught him mid air with a tomahawk blow across his head and he fell to the ground. When he rolled over, Red Feather stood over him pointing at the horizon and banished him from the tribe forever.

Jeremiah took him back to jail that same day and asked Doc to patch him up, but when he came over, he told Jeremiah that Orah Baker had died the night before without signing any kind of complaint. With no eye witness and no proof, the Judge had no alternative but to let Big Dog off with a fine and a lecture.

Looking out from under the bandage on his head, Big Dog hissed at the Judge and swore vengeance against Red Feather. He announced that, from now on, he will take the name of Jimmy and Jimmy Big Dog will live among the white eyes. He will eat and talk and drink like the white eyes, but when the time comes, Jimmy Big Dog will be the name of the brave who kills the Cherokee Chief, Red Feather.

Now, as Ernest listened to the group at the next table, Jimmy Big Dog was standing and talking much louder that the others and he could hear most every word.

"Red Feather die! All Cherokee go! Jimmy Big Dog show you how to find Yellow Owl!"

The soldiers pulled him back down to his chair and the lieutenant held his fingers to his mouth to shush him.

They hadn't noticed Ernest sitting there, and probably wouldn't remember him anyhow, so he decided to just listen a while longer. He heard the Lieutenant saying that he was glad to have new orders and that maybe now, they'll see some action. The one sitting next to him agreed and said that it ain't no fittin' job, chasing' around these mountain-tops for the ghost of a British spy who ain't never there where you expect him to be.

"Who cares, anyhow?" Said another. "That spy, if there ever was one, is more 'n likely back in London, sitting in a pub, having a pint and laughing out loud at us. That battle at New Orleans was fought over three years ago.

Ernest got up and started for the door and as he passed their table, he play-acted surprise and stopped. "Say, ain't you them army boys that spent the night out on the creek with the misses 'n me, bout a year ago?"

One of the soldiers looked around. "Yeah, Mr . . . er . . . Holesum, ain't it"

"Holman," Said Ernest. "Ernest Holman."

"Yeah, that's it, Ernest P. Holman. How you doing? How's that pretty wife and little girl of yours. Growing up, I bet."

"She shorley is," Said Ernest, with a big smile and a stuck-out chest. "We in town to get her all dressed up for her first day of school, come Monday. How you guys been. You still chasin' them spies? Did ye catch 'em yet?"

"Nah, We 'bout come to the decision that there ain't no spies up here. Probably never were. Come tomorrow morning, though, we all have to get back to work again."

"Work? Ain't ye working now?" Asked Ernest.

"Not so's you'd notice," Said the soldier. "But, tomorrow we're gettin' us a General up here to get us all organized and going again.

"A General? You need a General to organize what . . ." Sam looked around the table. "The four of ye?" and laughed.

"What makes what we say, any of your business funny man with face of a horse?" Growled Jimmy, wiping the rum off his chin with the back of his dirty hand.

"It's OK Jimmy." Said the Lieutenant. "He's a friend."

"Huh! . . . He looks like a horse face, hill-billy friend to me!

Ernest started to say something when the Lieutenant interrupted.

"There'll be considerable more come sunrise. General Winfield Scott will be arriving with a complement of over a thousand soldiers."

"A thousand soldiers?" Said Ernest, wide-eyed. "Is we at war up here?"

"No, nothing like that. They are here to *escort* the Cherokees down out of these hills to new land out west somewhere."

"Oh," Said Ernest." Did they agree to move?"

"AGREE? Hah!" Sneered Jimmy Big Dog. "White eye General Chief not come here with blue coats that stretch as far as an eagle can see, to talk to Cherokee and *ask* if they *agreed* to go or not. They go! Jimmy Big Dog will see to that. If they don't go . . . they die.

"Glory be!" Said Ernest, trying to ignore Jimmy altogether. "When's all this *escortin'* gonna happen?"

"Soon," Said the Lieutenant. "We've been building a tent camp down off the deer path road. We expect to start seeing a squad or two arriving tomorrow. They should all be here in a week and we'll start our Cherokee round-up then. I hear that there's over twenty thousand of them up here and the army just built a, what they call, concentration camps down at the foot of the mountain to put 'em in before they start out west."

"Who-e-e-e!" Said Ernest. "Looks like you boys got ye work cut out for ye. "I wish ye luck. It was mighty fine seeing all ye again." Then Ernest looked over at Jimmy and sneered. "Most of ye, anyhow."

The group said goodbye and Jimmy Big Dog spat out something in Cherokee that no one could understand . . . but understood.

Ernest nodded, "Same to ye, Jimmy Big Dog." And ambled through the door, walking slow at first, then he started running as fast as he could up the street to find Melba. He stopped and looked at the sky. They had to hurry if they were going to make a stop at the house, pick up his gun and make it to Eagle Rock and back before nighttime.

Chapter 18

✤

News of the discovery of yellow rock along Yahoola
Creek spread fast among the tribes and the killing of two
braves, as witnessed by Tall Trees, the third Cherokee,
at the gold miners site, had angered the tribes to the
point that they wanted to start attacking and killing all
whites found on Cherokee land. Yellow Owl called for
another council. Jesse and Malaki were both invited to
attend. They liked Jesse and trusted him and were on
the verge of adopting him into the tribe. Strong Eagle
considered them a valuable connection between the white
and Cherokee people and gave him the name of *Man Who
Hunts Himself*.

Yellow Owl arrived at sundown accompanied by Tall
Trees, the youngest council member and three other
chiefs from the Wakona Knob tribe. After the traditional
smoking of the pipe and a moment of silence, Red Feather
invited Tall Trees to talk.

"We were hunting small game up near the headwaters
of Yahoola." He said, "We heard loud talk and laughter
coming from down stream and went to investigate. We
saw a group of white eyes drinking fire water and dipping
metal pans into the water and dumping the water into
strange boxes that shake. Other than our bows, we had no
weapons and approached them in a friendly manner and
asked what they were doing on Cherokee land. The one
closest to me said something I did not understand and
pulled me off my horse and shoved me down the bank into
the creek. Just as I felt the water, I heard two shots from
a fire stick and saw Neeko and Bear Claw fall from their
horses. I readied an arrow and let fly just as the shooter

turned to me. It struck him in the shoulder and while the others saw to him, I found Neeko's horse and fled.

After another period of silence, Red Feather looked at Yellow Owl. How say you, prophet? What do your visions tell you?"

Yellow Owl had his eyes closed throughout all of Tall Trees' story. He slowly opened them and stared straight ahead and then rolled them up to Heaven. "There is anger! Much anger! Too much anger to be contained in the hearts of our people. It will overflow and there will be war. The White eyes have asked us to trade our land for land far beyond the great river like the Choctaw and Chippewa tribes have done and we said no. Now they are taking our land away from us. It may be true that their Great White Father and his generals do not know what is in the heart of the Cherokee. One of us must go and tell them. Everyone looked at Jesse and Malaki.

"Er . . . Great chiefs," Said Jesse, "We would be happy to go to Washington and talk to the Great White Father and his generals on your behalf, but we are being sought for breaking the white mans laws and until that is settled, they will not listen."

"Not only that," Said Mal. "They might even put us in their prison".

"Then Yellow Owl and I must go." Said Red Feather. "Who can make arrangements for us to . . ."

"Blam! Blam! Blam!" Three shots sounded from the direction of Eagle Rock down the mountain.

"Hear that, Jesse"

"Surely did!" Said Jesse. "Tha jes might be the answer to ye question, Red Feather. Mal, ye run and fetch ye musket and A'll explain to the council wha it means, A will."

"Got ye, Jess!" Said Mal, running out.

———•———

When they got to Eagle Rock, Ernest, Melba and little Tricia were waiting. Tricia looked at them and then looked up at her daddy.

"Dag-nabit fellers! I told Tricia ye would have a Cherokee with you fer her to see!"

"Sorry," Said Jesse, sliding down the last embankment. "A dinna think now wad be the time to talk to the Cherokees. They be up in arms n' mad. Maybe the next time . . . Wha have ye heard?"

"Plenty!" Says Ernest. There's trouble a-brewing." He then told him about his chance meeting with the soldiers and Jimmy Big Dog and the appointment of General Winfield Scott and his orders from President Jackson to bring in his troops and force the Cherokees, tribe by tribe, down out of the mountains, collect them in the temporary prisons they are building until all the tribes are together. Then the forced march to the west will begin.

"That sounds bad," Said Malaki. We gotta warn Red Feather!"

"Aye" Said Jesse "And Red Feather wants to know if ye could speak to ye army pals and see if they could arrange a meeting with the new white eye general, Yellow Owl an himself."

Ernest thought. "Shor could," He said. "It would have to be somewhere in the middle. I wouldn't expect them Cherokees would want to come into town and I know that general ain't fix'n to go to no Indian teepee, or whatever."

"How about right here?" Said Malaki, looking around.

"Here, on Eagle Rock?"

"Aye?" Said Jesse. There be plenty room for ten or so people to talk. We could even have a council fire, we could."

"Don't see why not," Said Ernest. "I'll ask 'em tomorrow. When do you need to know?"

"As soon as possible," Said Jesse. "How will we know?"

Ernest thought. "I know. They either gonna say yes or no, right?"

Everyone nodded their heads.

"Well I should have an answer by tomorrow afternoon and if it's *yes*, I'll fire three shots and you and your Chiefs can meet the next morning' at sun-up. If it's *no*, I'll just fire one shot and . . . what will be . . . will be, I reckon. How's that sound?"

Malaki giggled. "Ernest, my friend, I don't think Captain Jean LaFitte himself could have come up with a better plan." And winked at Jesse.

On the way back, Jesse spotted Red Feather, Running Deer and Ivy enjoying a picnic of berry water and Leolla Messer's Sweetater Pies down by the river and started toward them. Ivy saw Jesse coming and, in turn ran to meet him. Running Deer shook her head and smiled.

Jesse told Red Feather what he had learned about the Great White Father appointing General Winfield Scott to bring in his troops and force the Cherokee out. He talked of the concentration camp being built at the foot of the mountain and last but not least, he spoke of Jimmy Big Dog, as he is known in the white world.

Red Feather's head snapped around at the mention of Big Dog. "That is bad," He frowned, "Big Dog knows the way of the Cherokee. There will be no place to hide. If this comes to pass, we must fight . . . unless . . ."

"Aye," Interrupted Jesse, "We are arranging for ye and Yellow Dog to meet with General Scott an his party atop Eagle Rock within the next two days."

"That is good," Said Red Feather, we will be ready. Tonight, I will speak at the campfire and the dance of war will begin. It will last for two moons. The future of our way of life is in the hands of The Great Spirit." He nods, "I have spoken."

The next day, with the sun directly overhead, three shots were heard. The meeting was set for the next sun-up. Red Feather and Yellow Owl spent the day in private talking of a compromise to leaving their native land. Their wish was for the Cherokees and Whites to live together. As the braves from the other tribes filtered in, the dancing began and it lasted all day and into the night. When it finally stopped, Running Deer and Ivy embraced Red Feather and wished him well. He, Yellow Owl and five braves disappeared into the dark. Their plan was to camp along the way and be fresh by sun-up the next morning. The whole village was quiet that night.

———•———

Just before sun-up, Tall Trees sat straight up in his blanket and listened. It wasn't something he heard, it was what he did not hear that concerned him. The tree frogs were silent. The occasional grunt of a wart hog burrowing in the leaves was not there. No owl hoots, no beaver splashing in the water or wolves howling, nothing. He got up and armed himself with a tomahawk, his knife and bow and went out where he met Jesse, Malaki and Leolla standing by the fire, scanning the dark forest.

"What is it?" He said. "Why is there such a stillness.

"I noticed it too," Said Mal, throwing wood on the fire for more light and peering out into the darkness. "Something ain't right about . . ."

Then they heard it. A steady military drum beat from far out in the woods. It was mixed with rustling of leaves and the snap of twigs accented with an occasional rattle and clank of equipment being moved.

Tall Trees cupped his hands and let out a screeching war cry that echoed off the bluffs and dozens of braves suddenly came running, some armed and others just curious, all talking at one time. The drum beat was getting louder and louder. With it, they could hear the sound of marching feet. Everyone was squinting and searching for any sign or movement. Running Deer and Ivy joined the group and just as quickly as the sound started . . . it stopped.

The entire village went quiet . . . Deathly quiet. There was no breeze, the trees were motionless. No dogs barked . . . No babies cried. It seemed like the entire world had suddenly stopped what it was doing.

After what seemed like an eternity, a single voice called out.

"Attention in the camp! Major General Winfield Scott is coming in. Do not move or go for weapons. We only want to talk."

More silence. Then the sound of people breaking through the underbrush as three soldiers in blue suddenly appeared. Two with muskets flanking the third, who was carrying the flag of the United States. The two with muskets stopped and faced center as the flag bearer continued to within ten feet of the fire. Then, like the Gods had just given birth to him, an elegantly dressed officer appeared through the smoke. He was impressively tall, with great bushy eyebrows and a stern, steely expression on his face. The buttons and gold epaulets glistened in the firelight as he walked proudly, with his right hand inserted into the front of his dark blue tunic and his left hand on his saber. He wore a dress-blue hat with gold stars and a white plume trailing behind. He spotted Jesse's blond hair standing beside Tall Trees and approached him.

"I am General Winfield Scott of the United States Army. To whom am I addressing?" He asked.

"Oh," Said Jesse. "I'm Jesse McNabb and this here is Malaki Messer. I guess you could say that we're friends of the Cherokee and advisors to Tall Trees here, who is acting chief until Red Feather gets back. You see Sir, we are the . . ."

"Your Chief, Red Feather is not coming back!" He interrupted, looking at Tall Trees. "He and . . . and . . ." He looked at the sergeant standing beside him.

"Yellow Owl, Sir."

"Yes that's it, your prophet, Yellow Owl have both been arrested on charges of attacking and assaulting an officer of the United States Army and are both being held in the concentration camp below."

A murmur went through the camp.

"You should know that this entire area is surrounded by over one thousand soldiers whose orders are to escort the entire Cherokee Nation living in these mountains to their new home and hunting grounds west of the mighty Quabalaka River in the land of Oklahoma. I would strongly advise you and all your people to pack only what they can carry on the trail and prepare to move out within one hour's time. There will be no . . ."

"Er, excuse me General," Said Malaki, "Tall Trees here, ain't, how you say, authorized to order no move out like ye describe and Chief Red Feather and Yellow Owl left him with strict orders to not do nothin' until . . ."

General Scott snapped his eyes to Malaki. He pitched his head forward so he could slowly scan Mal from foot to forehead and looked back at Tall Trees.

"As unaccustomed as I am to addressing an Indian . . ." He said glancing back at Malaki, "I am even more unaccustomed to addressing his slave. Does he speak for you?"

Before Tall Trees could speak, a blood curdling scream came from the forest and Jimmy Big Dog leaped into the fire light.

"You talk too much talk, General! I, Jimmy Big Dog, who gave you Red Feather and Yellow Owl will now give you the scalps of all the rest!" With that, he let fly a tomahawk that caught Tall Trees between the eyes. He fell dead at Malaki's feet.

Something snapped in Malaki's head. His pirate instinct took over and he grabbed the tomahawk, ran into, and leaped over, the blazing fire, running straight at Big Dog. Not being able to see him, coming out of the light, Big Dog was caught off guard and Malaki smashed him against a nearby tree. Seeing the tomahawk, Big Dog drew his knife but Mal caught his wrist with his left hand and raised the tomahawk. Just as he was about to strike Leolla screamed.

"Malaki! Don't! Remember your promise to God!"

Malaki hesitated, just for a second, and when he did, Jimmy Big Dog buried his knife into Malaki's stomach up to the hilt. He fell at the foot of the tree.

Big Dog got to his knees, retrieved his knife and grabbed Malaki's great mass of hair and jerked his bloody head up off the ground. With eyes flashing, he snarled, "I, Big Dog will wear your scalp on my belt of wampum for all to see, Slave!" He started to cut . . . but stopped suddenly and stood up straight while his surprised eyes rolled back into his head and blood gushed from his nose and mouth. An arrow had just penetrated the left side of his neck and emerged from the right. It had red feathers. His body twitched and twisted and he fell on top of Malaki.

For the next minute, the entire camp stopped and stood in surprised silence as they watched the last signs of life leave Big Dog's body. Then, all heads turned slowly to see where the arrow came from.

There, with the fire still flashing in her eyes, Leolla stood motionless, staring straight ahead, with the bow still in her outreached hand.

"God forgive me." She murmured as tears started to roll down her cheek.

Jesse ran to her and pulled her to the ground just as another shot rang out and the bow flew out of her hand. She was shaking all over. Her anger had turned into hysteria. Jesse whispered in her ear as he held her tight. "It's ok, Leolla, you had to do it. You may have just saved Malaki's life.

A volley of shots then tore through the crowd as, what seemed like, hundreds and hundreds of blue uniforms rushed out of the dark, completely surrounding the whole camp, clubbing, shooting and bayoneting as they ran.

The women and children ran toward the darkness with soldiers close behind and braves ran for their weapons but the soldiers surrounded the ones they didn't kill, collected them into small group and merged with the others until they became like a great herd of cattle surrounded by a corral of soldiers, pushing and beating them as they stumbled down the mountain.

The firelight glistened off General Scott's saber as he ran from wattle to wattle, pulling out old women by their hair, whipping and herding the screaming children into the main group.

In the melee with all it's confusion, Jesse, Leolla, Ivy and Running Bear pulled Malaki back through the shrub grass and under an old hemlock and quickly covered themselves with leaves. Malaki was still alive but started to moan. Leolla held her fingers to his mouth as they all listened. Shots, screams, explosions and the sound of running feet were all around them but started getting fainter and fainter as the enormous horde stumbled farther and farther down the mountain.

Jesse waited until the screams became faint and crawled out through the shrub to get a look. The entire village had been torched and a thick blanket of smoke hung over the scene. There were bodies laying about and as he went from one to another, he found two women and three small babies still alive. He looked around for anything he could find to get them help. He didn't know just how badly Malaki was wounded, or even if he was still alive and knew he needed to get back and find out but these people needed help too. Running Bear startled him as she came up from behind. She picked up one of the babies and ran for what was left of their wattle house and returned with medical supplies and some food she found in the baskets inside. Ivy joined her and together they made pouches from blankets, and filled them with anything they could find that looked useful.

As they started back to their hiding place, Jesse heard a noise from the bushes and turned and drew his pistol. Slowly, he pulled back a low hanging pine branch and with as much authority he could muster, called, "Who be there?" There was another shuffle and Jesse stood straight and aimed. "Who be there?" The bushes shook and out came one of the most welcome sights he could have hoped for. It was Furball, the floppy-eared burro.

An hour later, with the invaders now out of sight, the group crawled from their hiding place, found a clearing at the edge of the village and built a small fire. Jesse moved Malaki closer to the light so Running Bear could look at him. His stab wound was deep but the knife seemed to have missed anything vital. The wound on his head was gushing blood, so she quickly took strips of tendon and a bone needle, and stitched it closed. She had Jesse hold the outer wound together with willow forceps while she took a red-hot knife out of the fire and cauterized it.

Jesse closed his eyes. "Do he be deid, Running Bear?"

"No, do you not see he is breathing ?" She said.

"Aye" Said Jesse, "But he didna cry out all the time ye was burnin' him. A just figured he . . ."

"He is still unconscious." She said as she smeared bear grease and moss ointment over his wound and covered it with a piece of seared rabbit skin. "If Big Dog had scalped him," She said, "He would be dead for sure but thanks to you, Leolla, he didn't. It is good now that he sleeps through all the pain."

"Is he going to come back to me?" Asked Leolla, with tears in her eyes

"We shall see," Said Running Deer, as she opened a small pouch and took out a pinch of fine powder and put it in a small gourd cup. "This medicine is made from the hawks's bill. It is powerful. It will tell you what you want to know. Bring some water, if you please."

Leolla did, and Running Deer slowly poured it over the fine powder. "If the powder floats on the top of the water, he will live. If it sinks to the bottom, he will die."

They watched as the powder swirled around and around. Finally, it stopped still and the powder stayed afloat. "He will live," Said Running Bear, "Now he must drink and be kept warm. Stay with him, when he awakens, your's should be the first face he sees."

Jesse went back for another blanket and while he was doing that, he saw something out in the darkness. Knowing that the soldiers would be coming back for stragglers, he motioned for everyone to be quiet. Ivy joined him and they climbed a big rock which got them higher than the treetops and gave them a good view of the far bank.

"It be right over yon," He pointed, "A canna see it now, but it was a wee light of some kind. A figured it be one of those carbide lamps tha soldiers use in the nicht time."

"A light." Ivy said out loud. "Do you remember Yellow Owl's visions?"

"Aye!" Said Jesse. "He, how ye say, hit it on the head, when he predicted the soldiers who would come and force the Cherokees out of the mountains, didna he?"

"That is true," Said Ivy, "But I am talking about his second vision. The one where a glowing horse spirit with ears like the wings of Angels would come and guide the

Cherokees who escaped the first attack to a place of new beginnings."

"Oh, that," Said Jesse. "A just figured that was just another of the many superstitions that make up your Indian lore. Why be ye thinking about that now?"

"Well, my love with golden hair," She pointed to a glow that was now on their side of the river. "Do you still think that is a . . . carbide soldier lamp?"

Jesse's eyes quickly went to where she was pointing. His body stiffened.

"Or . . . could it be the White Spirit Horse that Malaki calls *Glory*?" Asked Ivy,

Jesse didn't answer. He just stood motionless.

"Jesse?"

He didn't answer.

"Jesse, I asked you if it could be . . .

"Ivy!"

"Yes, Jesse . . ."

"She say there are many more Cherokees scattered around in different hiding places. We must find them an bring them here."

"There are? How do you kn . . ."

"Dinna ask, me Princess, A just know." Said Jesse. "Hurry, The White Spirit says that there is little time. We must find them and hide them. The soldiers are coming back."

They hurried back to the fire and Jesse told Running Deer what he knew. "How do we find them, Running Deer?" He asked. "After all that has happened, they trust no one. If we call out they will not answer."

"The chickadee." Said Running Deer.

"What?"

"We must make the sound of the Black Capped Chickadee. They know it as a sound that comes from a safe place and will come toward it."

Both Running Deer and Ivy went in different directions, making the sound of the chickadee. They listened . . . . Nothing. They went further into the forest and tried again, and listened. Ivy put her hand up in front of her lip and made a s-s-sh sound. Everyone listened. Finally, out of the darkness, they heard,

"Chic-a-d-e-e-e, Chic-a-d-e-e-e."

First to come into the light of their fire was Blue Turtle. He was an elder of the tribe and had a group of children who were holding each others hands and crouching behind the bushes with wide-eyed expressions of fear on their faces.

"Chic-a-d-e-e-e, Chic-a-d-e-e-e," More began to appear. Squaws with packs on their back, some leading livestock and armed, angry bucks, ready to fight. In an hour, one hundred or more were around the fire waiting to hear from Running Deer, wife of their Chief.

"My people!" Said Running Deer, "It is good to see that the Great Spirit has watched over you and kept you from harm and has hidden you from the white eyes. We have no news about Red Feather or Yellow Owl and hope that the The Great Spirit is watching over them as well. We hear from below that the blue coats will return soon in search of those of us they missed in their first attack. We must not be here when they arrive."

She took Ivy's hand as she and Jesse came to the front.

"You all heard Yellow Owl, our prophet, speak of his visions. It saddened and shocked me to have to stand and watch as his first vision came true, but we must go on and speak now of his second vision. Hear now, my daughter and *Man Who Hunts Himself,* our yellow hair brother. They have seen her light."

A sudden murmur, mixed with sobs and prayers arose, but quieted down as Ivy opened her arms to them.

"*Man Who Hunts Himself* and I have seen the glowing light of the horse spirit who will lead us to a place of a new beginnings. I ask you not to be afraid but happy instead, to know that she is here. She is close and speaks to *Man Who Hunts Himself* and has told him what we must do. Hear him now."

"The Spirit's name be *Glory*," Said Jesse, "She waits for us now doon on the river bank. From there, we are to follow her glowing light to a place of safety. A ask ye now to pick up what you have as quickly as possible and we will all join her there. A dinna ken where this . . . place of a new beginning is, we will see it together, but we must hurry. The soldiers will return soon."

It took about an hour, but the sight was inspiring. Well over a hundred Cherokees collected their belongings, made travois' for their injured and tied them to their horses and burros. Leolla walked beside Malaki, holding his hand, while Running Bear, holding two babies, helped Blue Turtle with all the other children. No one spoke.

When they broke through the underbrush and reached the riverside, there was no sign of Mercy or any other spirit light to be seen. The murmer returned among the confusion.

"What now, my golden haired hero?" Asked Ivy, "Where is your lady friend?".

Jesse had his mouth open to answer his smart aleck princess, but closed it before a sound came out, and listened. "She says that we are to keep her light in view and follow it at a distance. She will let us know when we are there.

"Look, there!" Cried Blue Turtle, pointing to a faint glow that appeared a hundred yards or so down an old deer path. "She is showing us all her light." Sounds of joy and amazement sounded from the tribe as they, one after another, saw the light and pointed.

As Ivy was telling them the plan, Jesse closed his eyes and sent three words to Glory in hopes that she could hear him. "We're ready, girl." When he opened his eyes, the light started moving down the path. The migration followed.

———•———

General Scott looked with pleasure at the thousands of Cherokees flowing out of the mountains and filling the concentration camps to the point of full and beyond. It had been a week now since he launched his first Indian Removal attack. His goal was the removal of fifteen thousand, or more Cherokees from the land and by his count, he was well on his way.

When word got around that the army had evacuated the Cherokees and that their land was going to be released for white settlement, a lawless rabble of scavengers couldn't wait for approval and moved in behind the army, burning, killing and claiming territory for themselves. The mood was one of celebration. A popular song at the time said it all.

All I ask in this creation,
Is a pretty little wife and big plantation
Way up yonder in the Cherokee Nation.

The winter was cold and the living conditions in the camp were inhuman. Many started dying from starvation and disease and stories of torture and killings were beginning to run rampant.

Among the first to arrive at the stockade concentration camp was Red Feather and Yellow Owl. Jimmy Big Dog had pointed them out to General Scott and he, without hesitation, arrested them and had Red Feather chained in a "public" place for effect and Yellow Owl, whom he considered the biggest threat of the two, was stood before a stone wall and six Cherokees were picked and, under threat of death, were forced to shoot him. General Scott could truly say that Yellow Owl was killed by his own people.

Fearing that some of these stories would get back to Washington, however, Scott ordered the commander of company A to march the first group of three thousand or so, to the rat infested stockades built on a pre-selected plateau below the town of Sideways, out of sight to the news media and hold them there.

His plan for Red Feather was to wait until every Cherokee was assembled, try him for murder and publicly hang him before they started the one thousand mile trek to Oklahoma, an inhuman fete that would claim the lives of over four thousand Cherokees, later to be known as "The Trail of Tears," A shocking embarrassment to our country.

In the meantime, however, General Scott, thinking just the opposite, saw his name and his mission as one that would go down in history and wanted the world to know that he was the one who finally ridded the country of an Indian problem that had eluded two presidents. "Who knows," He said to himself, "I just might be president myself, one of these days."

To make sure that no Indian was left behind to talk, he ordered Captain Charles Freeman, commander of company B to take his men back up to the top and comb the entire mountain range with bloodhounds. He was told not to return until every single Cherokee had been sniffed out of their hiding places and their villages destroyed.

The spirit light led the group to a deeper part of the forest where no paths existed and when Ivy and Jesse were sure they were not being followed, made camp. Leolla found and out-of-the-way corner and was making Malaki comfortable when his eyes opened. She squealed and Jesse came to see what the commotion was. Mal looked up at him and his mouth started to form words.

"Did . . . I . . . get him?" He said slowly.

"Well, not so's you'd notice, my friend," Said Jesse, "But I'm glad to see you've decided to come back to us. A laddie gets a wee bit tired taking care of all these women by himself, ye know."

"I wouldn't a missed it for nothin'." Said Mal as he looked up at Leolla. "And you, my Gullah girly, wait till ye hear what I been dreamin' about you." Tears welled up in Leolla's eyes as she giggled and kissed him all at the same time.

Jesse interrupted them and took Leolla's hand. "Speaking of ye waisted life," He said, putting Leolla's hand in his, "This is the lady that saved it for you. If she hadn't sent an arrow through the throat of that wild Jimmy Big Dog, you would nae be here with us tonight." Then he thought. "As a matter of fact," Said Jesse, "Ye most lost something else, too. Something that ye value even more than ye worthless life."

"What?"

"That great mass of hair o ye, that's what."

"You, honey? You did that?"

Leolla rubbed her hand through Mal's massive head of hair and kissed him.

"Whoo-ee" Said Mal, "Tell me more."

Jesse was right in the middle of describing how close Big Dog came to having his way with that bush that Mal called his hair and how Leolla got him with her first shot and . . . stopped, in mid sentence and looked at Ivy.

"Don't ask me how I know this, Ivy, but Glory has summoned us both."

Dawn was just starting to break as they walked the hundred yards or so down to a path that ran along a small creek and started up the next slope, when they both stopped in their tracks. Ivy gasped. Glory was still far away, but now close enough for them to barely see her outline for the very first time. She was standing heroically in front of a waterfall coming down out of the rocks. For Jesse, it wasn't just an inspiring sight for him to see, it was the *first* sight, close up anyway, of the stately animal that has been his guardian Angel and life-saving friend on, at least, two occasions. As he got closer and closer, a warmth started to fill his chest.

"What is it Jesse?" Said Ivy. "Are you ill?"

"A'm alright . . . A think. Just a bit woozy all of a sudden."

They walked closer and Ivy's eyes got big and her jaws dropped. "Look at her, Jess! She's beautiful!"

As they got even closer, Glory's eyes caught Jesse's eyes and they both stood very still. Jesse held his hand up to touch her nose and she moved forward to meet his hand. When they touched, the surge of warmth filled him completely and images started to form in his mind of herds of bleating sheep and castles and fishing villages and men with great mustaches wearing skirts of plaid and tams on their heads. Images that Jesse had never seen before. Or had he?

After a minute or so, Glory's great ears went back and she lowered herself to her knees. Jesse looked at Ivy, took her hand and they both climbed aboard as Glory rose and started walking up the creek toward the falling water. Ivy knew that falls as *Spirit Water* because it seemingly flowed out of an uninterrupted line of limestone cliffs that encircled the entire top of the mountain. The Indians believed they were put there by the Great Spirit to separate Mother Earth from Heaven. They drank from the water but considered the walls sacred and since they ran around the uppermost top of the forest like a frame and since there were no trees or bushes visible above them, Ivy was taught by the Prophets that the walls marked the end of the Cherokee's world and if any attempted to climb them, they would fall off the other side into a black eternity and never be heard of again. As far back as Cherokee history went, no one ever did.

Glory quickened her walk and soon started to trot. Ivy tightened her hold around Jesse's waist as her trot became faster and faster into a three-beat canter. Faster and even faster, they went and before Jesse and Ivy got a good grip on her mane, she was now at a full gallop heading directly toward the solid rock. Jesse knew that without reins, there was no way to slow her down. The trees and green underbrush whizzed by, the sheer rock face of the cliffs was getting closer and closer . . . the underbrush disappeared . . . the cliff was upon them . . . . Jesse closed his eyes . . . . Ivy screamed . . . . and Glory . . . stopped. All was quiet. A peace fell over the scene.

Jesse slowly opened his eyes and made sure Ivy was ok. "What just happened? Did she just run through solid rock?"

"I don't know," Said Ivy, still holding her fingers over her mouth, her eyes like a hoot owl. "Does Glory have the magic powers to do that?"

Jesse slid down and looked back. He saw what seemed like a rock tunnel coming up from the forest. He went back a few paces to get a better look and quickly realized that it was not a tunnel at all, but a "Z" shaped fault. A big crack in the stone that looked too narrow for anyone to get through, especially a mule. It ramped up to where they were and, when he looked up the other way, it went as far as he could see. Ivy was sitting on a stone and Glory was gone.

He hurried back to her and looked around. "Where is Glory?" He asked.

"I don't know." She said. "I got down to follow you and when I looked back, she was gone!"

Jesse squinted his eyes into the breaking dawn and looked up the path. Then, he turned and looked back at the way they had come in.

"We'll call it the *Glory Door*.

"I guess she is telling us that now that we are through it, we walk from here by ourselves. He took Ivy's hand and they started up.

For more than an hour, they went upward. Sometimes pulling each other over what looked like impassable stones and sometimes getting down on their knees or slipping through holes on their stomachs before they broke into the open and looked out. The sun had just come up and was now shining brightly and they found themselves looking at a happy, graceful waterfall pouring down into a rippling pond that was bluer than any pond either of them had ever seen before. They stood in complete silence staring at the unbelievable when an eagle, circling far out over the slopes, squawked a loud hello. In contrast to all the horror they had been through in the last three days, the complete, unfettered peacefulness of the little pond was overwhelming. A doe and her two fawns were drinking on the far side.

"Oh-h-h look," Said Ivy. "Aren't they sweet? They don't even seem to care that we're here."

"Probably not," Said Jesse. "Like as not, They hae nae see humans before."

They followed on down the animal trail they were on until it came to a rocky overlook. When they stepped out into the sun, they looked, rubbed their eyes, and looked again. They couldn't believe what they saw. It was a vast, beautiful valley that went as far as they could see, completely surrounded by mountain after mountain of dense forests and rock formations. They counted three more water falls, all cascading down from the high up rocks and running together into a white-water streams that finally settled down into a shimmering lake that looked as if it completely covered the floor of the valley.

"There it be," Said Jesse, "There be Yellow Owl's second vision. We must . . ."

He looked off toward where they had been. "Yes, Glory, A was just going to say that to Ivy. A was."

What?" She asked, looking off in the distance.

"She said ye must get back to your people before the soldiers come."

Chapter 19

❀

Oh'
I'm not so young
As I used to be . . .
When I was in my prime,
I'm turning now quite auld ye' see,
But I had a wee gud time.

To kiss the bonnie Lassie,
Show's I was never shy . . .
And the lad that doesn't
Do the same
Is not the man as I.

Scottish folk song

The year is 1836, Aberdeen, Scotland.

Mia McNabb looked down at the back wheel of her rented buggy submerged hub-deep in a muddy rut. Then she looked up at the grey sky as the rain started to fall again, brushed an unruly curl out of her face, tucked it back under her soggy bonnet that was new and stylish just two days ago and screamed.

She cursed the sleepy-eyed, all-night telegrapher who beat on her door in the middle of the night and woke her up in a panic with the message from her Grand Mama Bridgett She cursed the livery agent who charged her twenty pound sterling to rent an old falling top buggy with Emily, a tired old mare leftover from the Boer war to pull it for the weekend.

She cursed the hour she spent waiting for the swing-about bridge over the river Dee outside Aberdeen and, more than anything, she cursed the whole idea of driving, non-stop, to Inverness in the middle of the cold, foggy night.

She started to say a word that she learned from her Grand Papa, Fergus but caught herself, took two deep breaths and looked up into the grey clouds above. "I'm sorry, God." She said out loud "Please be with him and dinna let me be too late.

It was three in the morning when the message came in telling her that her Grand-PaPa, Fergus McNabb was on the brink of his last day of life on this earth due to a fall he took while riding the hounds. It seems that his hip was crushed, his collar bone broken and he was very weak due to the loss of a lot of blood from a cut on his head. The telegram, sent by Sinclair, their butler since time began, said the he was out of his head and making life miserable for anyone within earshot, screaming, "I Nae be going anywhere until I can see Mia McNabb! DO YOU HEAR ME? SEND FOR HER!"

Mia thought that strange. "Why me? Why not MaMa?" Then she thought. "I guess he knew that she was in London getting Ben situated at Cambridge. But still . . . why me?"

It was dawn and daylight was breaking through the clouds at last. With the river Dee behind her and with any luck at all, she should be at the foot of Loch Ness inside of two hours and from there it would be a straight shoot on in to Inverness. Then, it was an easy half hour on out to McNabb Manor, the country home in the hills overlooking the historic Old High Church. How many times she had made this trip. Usually, she was so excited she could hardly wait to get there. But today . . . it was different.

Finally, three hours after a "comfort" stop in town, a change of bonnet and some emergency oats for Emily, who was looking like she was going to turn herself out to pasture any time now, they turned up the long drive to the big home.

She was surprised to see the caretakers house still standing. It had to be as old as water but it's field-stone walls and thick, thatched roof just seemed to hold up forever. A lazy old cow with three-foot horns mooed a soft hello as she went by. The sun had broken through the rain clouds now and everything looked brighter and as she was pulling up in front of the arched, wrought iron gate, she noticed that the sun was reflecting off something out in the side yard. She pulled Emily up and got out to get a better look. It wasn't a reflection at all, it was a glow, an actual light coming from a beautiful whiter than white horse grazing out along Grand Ma Ma's prize garden. She had never seen such an animal. It looked like she was carved out of white marble with sharp, Gothic features and two, huge, graceful ears sitting dramatically atop her massive head, accenting her whole manner.

"Strange," She said out loud. "Ole Jim, the caretaker would never allow any live stock on the side lawn. She must have gotten loose."

She pulled on up in front, brushed herself off and stepped up on the massive front porch, raised the iron knocker and knocked three times. No answer. She tried again. No answer. In panic, she raised the knocker one more time . . . when the door opened.

"Oh, thank God, ye here!" Said Grand-MaMa Bridget holding Mia tight. "I didna think I could hold oot."

"Same old Grand Mama Bridget." Thought Mia. She still has the same big, blue eyes and the same freckles across her nose that she had as a young girl and like always, her life is in a panic. Like Henny-Penny, every time an acorn falls on her head, she screams to the world that the sky is falling."

"Hello, Grand Mama, Dae he still be . . . ?"

"Oh YES!" Said Bridget, "Bellowing like a bull, he be!" Gae up lass, we can talk on tha morn, we can."

Mia, topped the stairs and scurried down the hall, stopping to smooth her hair, and knocked . . . softly.

"COME IN, WOMAN. WHER BE ME GRAND DAUGHTER?"

Mia turned the handle, opened the door and stuck her head in carefully.

"DI YE HEAR ME, WOMAN WHERE BE . . . . Oh, Mia, that be ye?" Fergus said, looking with only one eye peeking out from under a huge bandage around his head. "Come oot o th shadow so me one eye can look at ye."

"Hello, Grand PaPa. How dae ye feel?" Mia, said meekly looking at his swollen face and the huge cast supported above him on a sling.

"Oh nae mind that," He bellowed. "Thay be trying to get rid o ye old Grand PaPa fer nigh on to ever, thay be, but as ye can see, a'm still here, A am. Come haud me hand. We have much ta talk aboot."

Mia pulled up the old wing-back chair, upholstered in the bright red and green McNabb tartan plaid and took his hand.

"A know ye mother is off wi ye brother and I hear that ye is off to the United States soon ta study medicine at tha Scottish Rite Hospital. Thon be right?"

"Aye, PaPa," Said Mia.

"Guid!" Said Fergus, trying to smile through a swollen jaw. "Have A ever told ye aboot the time ye Grand Uncle Duncan 'n A went to the States 'n fought in the Battle of New Orleans?"

Mia had heard the story about a thousand times in her growing up, but she could see clearly that she was going to hear it at least, one more time.

"That's whur Uncle Duncan be killed, was it nae, PaPa?"

"NAE!" That be what a want to talk ta ye aboot. He was NAE killed."

"But A always thought that . . ."

"That's whah everybody thought, even me!" But, while A was unconscious, "A didna ken whaur A wis!" He said humbly. "A didna ken if A wis in heaven or . . . ye know, doon, there, 'n A had a vision."

"A vision?" Repeated Mia.

"Aye, 'n in the vision, this big, white, glowing mule came in and . . ."

"Mule? Da ye mean tha big horse on ye side lawn?"

"Horse? On me side lawn? What did it look like?"

"Well, like ye say, she was big, she was! A dinna think A hae ever seen a horse so big n' beautiful. She had great big ears, she did and she was so white she glowed in the . . ."

"That be her, only she nae a horse! She be a MULE! On the side lawn, ye say?"

"Aye, Grand PaPa," Said Mia. "Here, A show ye." She walked to the giant arched window and pulled the drapes. "She's right doon th . . ."

"Wha?" Said Fergus.

"She be gone!"

"But ye saw her! Ye actually saw her!

"Aye, A did," Said Mia. "I thought that . . ."

"See? A told ye Grand MaMa, there's but one person on this earth that can, and will, believe me story, and that's ye! We are of the same blood, we be, 'n' ye feel all that A feel n' ye see what A see.

"In ye vision, Grand PaPa . . ." Said Mia, "Did tha . . . mule . . . talk, ?"

"Aye, but she didna move her mouth because she be holding this in it."

"What?"

"This." Said Fergus, pulling something from under the cover.

Mia looked down and he was flipping the latch on a rosewood box that looked very old. It was a weapon of some kind, like she had seen in pirate picture books. She reached down and took it out and ran her finger over the *McNabb* coat of arms carved in the handle.

"Our Da gave us each one a flintlock pistol like thon, he did, when wi became of age. Duncan hae one just like it and wi carried them into battle wi us." Said Fergus.

"And the white mule had it in her mouth?" Asked Mia.

"Aye," Said Fergus, "An when A took it from her mouth, A saw that it was identical to mine, except, when a looked close, A saw it had a chip in the handle like it was shot or something and it wa then that she talked, she did, Only she didnae talk, if ye get me meaning, n' she said, '*The one wha saved ye life, still lives.*' Canna ye believe? It was me brother, it was, that saved me life in that battle, 'n A just knew that God in His heaven above wud nae let him be killed fer doing it. He LIVES . . . or his children live . . . somewhere, an tha's whit A wanted to talk to ye aboot."

"Me! What can A . . ."

"Find him!"

"Find him? Why, after all these years, would ye want to . . ."

"Great Scott, woman, if love for me brither is nae enough, there be another, very important reason to find him before A die, there be"

"What be that, Grand PaPa?"

"When our Da passed, as ye probably know, he left the entire McNabb fortune n' all it's holdings to the twa o us to split right down the middle and be the responsible caretakers of the McNabb manor 'n clan and direct it's future."

"A knew that, Grand PaPa."

"But," He went on, "If it wer proven that Duncan dee'd in New Orleans, A am the sole beneficiary and, Heaven forbid, if this freaky hunting accident do me in, the whole shootin MacBang . . . goes to Bridget."

"Well . . . a'm sure that Grand MaMa will . . . ."

"Your Grand MaMa wi let Bruce McDuffy, her brother an no good brother-in-law of mine, wi all his high-powered lawyers and crooked judges, get control and sell it off, thae will, piece by piece fer shopping centers or vacation homes and such! The McNabbs wi die . . . while the McDuffys wi live!"

"But," Said Mia with her eyes closed and thinking, "If Uncle Duncan be still alive, it would . . ."

"Exactly!" Screamed Fergus, "It would all be his to see that the McNabb name lives forever and A pledged to myself 'n God above, A did, to find him before A die. That, my sweet, bonnie lass, be why A sent fer ye."

"But, Grand PaPa, Uncle Duncan has nae seen me since I be twa! How would he know . . ."

"Ye give him this."

"Ye gun?"

"Ay, "Find ye Grand Uncle Duncan and give it ta him. He owns tha only one like it and he will know who it be from. He will feel his brothers love once again, he will."

"But where . . .?"

"He lives somwhar in the States," Fergus interrupted. "A just know that and when ye gives this flintlock to him . . . or his family, it will say all that needs saying.

"But Grand Papa, the United States be a universe all in it's own, where

wud A . . ."

"On a mountain!"

"What?"

"On a mountain! That's wha ye start lookin'. If that battle left him with any life at all, he will take it up on a mountain to live out and A hear tell that they have mountains in America that reach neigh on to Heaven. That be wha ye'll find him. He be a Highlander . . . he be!"

"Well, A guess I could . . ." Started Mia.

"Atta girl! A knew A could count on ye. The Clan will pay all your expenses, nae matter how long it takes and A don know if God wi let me stay on this earth long enough for ye to get back, but tha be ok too, A can hear ye jus as well up in Heaven, A can. Find oot why he never returned . . . tell him we want him home and we love him and need him to save Tha McNabb Clan . . . wud ye now?"

Chapter 20

"Even though PaPa is still alive," Thought Mia as the packet ship, *Shenandoah,* approached the east coast of the United States, "Me promise to him amounts to the same as a death-bed promise." She, like any member of the McNabb clan, considers a death bed promise sacred above all mortal things and, as far as she was concerned, her

Grand PaPa was sitting, where he could get a good view, right on her shoulder.

She had already made up her mind to postpone her studies for a year or so and go directly to New Orleans, the scene of the battle to start her search. In preparation, she telegraphed The New Orleans Times-Picayune newspaper and outlined her mission. A return telegram arrived promptly from someone by the interesting name of *Bagwell Jackson,* who introduced himself as the Editor-in-Chief and Head Custodian of the Picayune Archives and last, but not least, the grandson of General Andrew Jackson himself, who had more than a passing interest in the battle. He went on to say that, in spite of the fact that The Times-Picayuen did not exist at the time of the battle itself, their reporters contacted and interviewed hundreds of participants who were actually there for it's thirtieth anniversary and after sorting and categorizing, had more than enough data to re-live the entire battle on paper and he was looking forward to meeting her. They made plans to meet upon her arrival.

She left New York City aboard The Seaboard Railroad and the big window of her compartment proved to be all the entertainment she could ever want as they clicked-clacked south through Virginia, along the foothills of the Quabalaka Mountain Range and on into the heart of Dixie. At Jacksonville, Florida, she switched to The Cannonball Express which took her across all the southern states she had read about in grade school. It all came to life as she crossed the mighty Quabalaka River into New Orleans. She knew that her brain alone would not be enough room to store all that she was seeing and all that she would be learning kept her diary close by and made notes all the way.

Dear Diary. I don't know why or how I find myself aboard a train, taking me back into time, yet forward toward my destiny all at once. I passed mountains that reminded me of the Highlands and bodies of water that took me back to Loch Ness. I wonder if they named Jacksonville after my Mr. Jackson's great grandfather. I find myself anxious to meet Mr. Jackson. For some reason, I feel we were meant to meet.

When they pulled into the Canal Street Station, she noticed how busy it was. People everywhere, street musicians, venders, red caps, wagon drivers swearing at other, lovers walking hand in hand, school children walking hand to hand, and about a million people who were obviously late getting to wherever they were going.

She took out Mr. Jackson's letter and re-read it. He said he would be meeting her at the station and would be wearing a white suit with a yellow flower in the lapel and a white straw hat. She looked out again. There must have been three hundred men wearing straw hats and even more wearing white suits. All she had to do now, was to find the one with a yellow flower in it's lapel. The Red-Cap took her bags up to the entrance and she followed until he put them down among a great crowd of people near the ticket counter. Panic was starting to set in when she felt a tap on her shoulder.

"Miss McNabb?" She turned and found herself face to face with a little yellow flower an without moving her head, rolled her big green eyes upward.

He removed his hat. "I didn't mean to startle you, My name is Jackson," he held out his hand, "Bagwell Jackson. I do hope you had a pleasant trip."

She turned and was nowhere prepared or anywhere near ready to deal with the rush that just went through her.

He was a head taller and when her eyes finally met his, they stayed there far too long. The sun coming through a large, colored glass arch above the main entrance backlit and haloed his head. He was tan and his features were sculptured, as in a *Monet* painting and his smile was as inviting as a puppy dog's nuzzle.

"It wa?" She said and caught herself, "A mean, it wa so nice of ye to meet me."

"I assumed that you would be tired from your trip, so I took the liberty of booking a suite at the Loadstone Arms, an old in-town plantation, made over into an elegant bed and breakfast not long after the war. It's on the edge of the French Quarter which is close to all that's going on in N'orlins, but without all the noise and hustle-bustle. I'm sure you'll like it. I have a carriage waiting by the Basin Street entrance."

Mia hardly heard a word he said. She was still looking into those eyes.

"What" . . . Oh A mean, aye . . . Thank ye ever so much . . . A carriage? . . . How romantic . . . er . . . I mean . . . How nice.

He took her luggage and led her through the crowd to the side entrance and a "two people" carriage with a black leather canopy, trimmed in bright red tassels and a handsome driver who was her image of a Venetian gondolier was standing elegantly in front holding the reins of the shiniest, black stallion she had ever seen.

The driver looked down at Mia. "Bonsoir Mademoiselle"

She was taken back and didn't know what to say an blurted out. "N a bonny g'day ta ye too, Laddie."

There was a moment of pure silence as they looked at each other, then, un- controlled laughter broke out.

Mia somehow knew that this moment was a magic start of something that was going to take her the rest of her life to play out.

Dear diary, I don't know what higher power is guiding me, but I feel like I have been cast to appear in a Shakespearean drama that made it's opening on Kingussie Way in Inverness and is soon to be

*playing here on Bourbon Street in New Orleans, Louisiana and
I don't even know my lines yet! Bagwell is wonderful. (I wonder
what his close friends call him . . . Bag? . . . nah-h-h.) More later.*

They had breakfast at Brennen's the next morning and
Mia had a chance to start at the beginning and fill Mr.
Jackson in on her mission that started with two brothers
in 1815 at the battle of New Orleans, the return of one and
the search for the other.
"I must tell you Miss McNabb . . ."
"Mia . . . ."
"I beg your pardon?"
"Please call me Mia." She cooed.
"OK, Mia. Then you must call me BJ,"

*(Oh . . . So that's what his close friends call him! Did you get
that, diary?)*

"Very well," Said Mia as she wrinkled her nose. B . . . J."
"As I was saying," BJ went on. "I am genuinely moved
by a family like the McNabbs who protect and support
each other generation after generation. It portrays a deep
belief in the hereafter that is shared by each and every
member, no matter where he or she is. All families should
have that strength.
After the last bite of her first crab meat omelette, Mia
left on the arm of her handsome host who guided her five
blocks through the historic French Quarter to 12 Royal
Street, which was the three story red brick and wrought
iron home of The New Orleans Times-Picayune.
BJ had everything ready in the archives conference
room with a giant map of the area south of New Orleans
showing the actual battlefield where Andrew Jackson
was dug in on the northern edge to stand off the main
attack and the southern edge where Jean LaFitte and his

privateers were dug in and handily repelled the secondary British attack coming out of the swamp.

He had a ledger with names, through actual documents and here-say of every British soldier, and their commanders who participated and the same for every American soldier and their commanding officers.

He had laid out every headline and article published about every skirmish as well as every unfounded story and superstition coming out of the ranks as well as when and how the British sailed away and what happened to our troops afterwards. There were statistics of how over 2000 British were killed, wounded or captured to only 333 Americans and post-battle articles of what happened to those who fought.

For three days, Mia poured over the data. She found the names of Fergus and Duncan McNabb among the British forces. She found the name of Fergus listed among the British wounded but she did not find the name of Duncan McNabb among the British dead or captured. He just disappeared.

She was sitting and staring out at the people going up and down Royal Street, at odds as to where to look next when BJ came in with a few secondary interviews conducted among the troops who made it back alive with their beliefs, charms, superstitions and stories of how and why they think they made it out.

There was a story about a rabbit's foot tied on the muzzle of a musket that guided every mini ball that came out of it. There were stories about voices and visions some heard talking to them in the heat of battle, guiding them. There was even talk about a big white horse that shined in the dark and the one about a gold watch his momma had given him with her picture in it that took a British mini ball right in her face and saved his life.

Mia, in her despair almost overlooked it. She had already laid the articles aside and was putting on her hat when the words, *a big white horse that shined in the dark* hit her like a sledge hammer.

"BJ . . . Come quick!"

"What?"

"Leuk at this! It say that one of the fighters saw *A big white horse that shined in the dark!*

"So?" Said BJ, "If I had been going through what they did, I probably would have seen big, white elephants!"

"You don't understand, it wasn't a white horse he saw, it was a white *mule*!"

"A white mu . . ."

"Aye, a white mule wi big ears! The biggest ears A've ever seen!"

"The biggest ears that *you've* ever seen?"

"Aye, me . . . oh . . . er . . . A guess A didn't tell ye aboot all that. Sit down."

Mia then told BJ about driving through the gates into the McNabb country home and being surprised by what looked like a big, white, horse on the side lawn. A horse so white, it appeared to shine in the early morning light and when she mentioned it to her Grand PaPa, he couldn't believe what he was hearing and got quite agitated and when he quieted down, he told her that he had a vision while he was in his coma that had the identical white horse.

"Only Grand PaPa said it was a mule."

"A white mule . . . with big ears . . . that shines in the dark?"

"Aye," Said Mia, "And when I went to the window ta show Grand PaPa, she be gone!"

"You're saying," Said BJ, holding his chin and looking off into space. "If we could find the soldier that saw the big white horse, it could possibly lead us to Duncan McNabb."

"Aye!" Mia said excitedly and moved her hand to his. "Don ye see, it's be our first real breakthrough!"

"That it is," Said BJ as he leaned over and kissed her forehead. "It is."

BJ took the article to Annette, his assistant, and asked her to trace it's origin and get back to them as soon as she hears. The next day Annette caught up with them at an outdoor table in front of a small Creole restaurant named *Aimee, Babet*. She had been able to trace the quote from the article to a wounded LaFitte privateer who was being tended in an emergency sick bay set up on the docks running alongside the old Customs House. A little more digging led her to the exact spot, but noted that it had since been dismantled. However, she did find out that the medical installation had been run by a Doctor DuPhol. Doctor Drey DuPhol, known to his shipmates as *The Fixer*.

The next day, BJ and Mia paid a visit to the commandant of the US Army headquarters only to find out that after the battle, LaFitte was awarded a pardon for his piracy by President Madison only to disappear back into his dark side and was never heard from again. Doctor DuPhol stayed on and started a practice on Galveston Island in Texas.

Dear Diary . . . Tomorrow, we are taking "The River Belle" down river to the coast. Can you believe it, BJ and I will be on one of those stern wheeler steam boats with jazz music and card playing and long dresses and waltzes and romantic star-lit nights and big yellow moons and . . . oh yes, there we will board the "Spanish Main", a sailing vessel to take us on to Galveston Island to talk to a Doctor DuPhol.

Chapter 21

Jesse held Ivy's hand as they excitedly ran back down the fault, past the waterfall and onto the deer path leading back to the small valley where the band of cold, tired and hungry Indians were hiding. Jesse stopped and took note of every landmark and memorized them. They had been on the back of a White Spirit Horse galloping at break-neck speed coming up and they hardly had time to take in the sights.

They walked for two hours or so when Jesse spotted smoke coming up from behind the next foothill.

"Would ye look at tha." Said Jesse. "If General Scott be wondering how to find the Cherokees he missed, all he needs ta do is look up."

Jesse thought it would be best if they approached quietly. The last thing he needed right now, was an arrow in his backside. They quietly climbed up the gentle slope, maneuvered an overhang that hid the area from prying eyes, broke through the tall grass and Ivy made the sound of the Black Capped Chickadee. When they heard a melodious answer, they crawled forward and were surprised to find eighty to a hundred more Cherokees milling about since they left. Running Deer and a young buck, known as Little Wolf greeted them with mixed feelings. Running Deer had been crying.

"I am happy to see you safe, Princess but the news we have heard from down below about your father and Yellow Owl is not good."

He then told her about Yellow Owl's fate and the fact that Red Feather was locked in a wooden cage and hoisted up above the heads of the milling Cherokees and was awaiting trial for the murder of Jimmy Big Dog. He also reported that a full company of soldiers had been ordered to come back up to look for any of us who are still here. He said that Cherokee scouts, at the risk of losing their children had been forced to show them where to look and that they had started at daybreak this morning and would be back on the mountaintop inside of three hours.

Ivy looked around at all the faces. Sadness hung over the group like a dark, unwelcome cloud. A mother stood nearby with a crying baby. She went to the mother and took the baby in her arms. It quit crying. Then she took Jesse's hand who, in turn, took Running Bear's hand and the three of them walked to the top of the overhang. Ivy held up her arm.

"Listen to me, my people. All is not sad. I know that there are unanswered questions. I know that many have lost loved ones. I realize that our way of life has been shattered, but we are Cherokees. We will go on as we always have through the ages. The White Horse Spirit has led us to the Glory door, the entrance to a safe land where we can start a new beginning. We must simply get to it. Tend your wounded and make ready to leave within the hour. I and The Man Who Hunts Himself will lead you to the Glory door. Kill the fires and scatter the ashes. Bind your horse's hoofs with deer skin and sweep the area with pine straw. Leave no sign that the Cherokees were ever here. Little Wolf will show you how and he and his tribe will follow behind and erase any signs of our travel." She gave the baby back to it's mother and raised her other arm. "Stand up, my people and let us go find our new life."

It took a little over an hour, but two hundred and twenty three Cherokees were packed and standing on the road ready to march and when Little Wolf and his cover-up crew finished, not one human sign remained. The soldiers would never know that they had been hiding there.

They traveled quietly. The babies did not cry. The dogs did not bark and the horses did not whinny. By sundown, the entire tribe was standing along the great rock wall looking up at the Glory door, confused. One by one, Jesse and Ivy escorted each one through and up the fault. It was so narrow, and most were so scared, it took another four hours to get them all through. When the last horse and travois passed, Little Wolf and his tribe stayed behind to sweep that area, replace the foliage and rolled a large stone out to the middle of the fault itself. The Glory door was gone to the human eyes. When the first of the band reached the peaceful pond and waterfall, smiles started to cover their faces. They waited there until all were assembled and started down the animal trail to the overlook together. When they saw the endless green valley surrounded by the mountains, their silence became cheers and laughter. Hope and happiness returned to their faces.

It took another five hours for everyone to get to the far end of the valley where families started breaking away from the "herd" to seek out their new homes. Little Wolf and tribe started to collect wood and logs to build their very first council fire near the lake but far enough back that no one could see the smoke from the other side. As the flames grew and the logs cracked, The Cherokee stood proud once again. They were safe at last and it was now time for them to talk of their future.

Jesse, Ivy, Leolla and Running Deer worked the entire day, with Little Wolf's help to fashion an elaborate *lean-to* for their new home and moved an impatient Malaki into a comfortable bed of pine straw covered by a soft bear skin. When all were settled, the ladies went out to gather berries and nuts and gave Jesse and Malaki their first opportunity to plan their next moves. Jesse told him that Little Wolf and three braves were starting out at daybreak to secretly flank the searching soldiers, canoe down the

River of Stone and find out just where and how they was holding Red Feather and report back.

"That's good!" Said a perky Malaki. "I don't know just how yet, but we'll get him back before they start that march. Now, since I ain't had nothin' to do but lay here while ya'all drug me clean out to the far side of nowhere and back again, I've had a lot of time to think."

"About what, A'm afraid to ask?" Said Jesse.

"Well," Said Mal, looking off over the peaceful valley, "Short of not having no front door, Glory shore showed good taste when she picked this place."

"I know," Said Jesse. "tis beautiful, is it nae?"

"Yep, n' jes as soon as Andy Jackson's boys and all them gold rushers see it, they gonna' think so too."

"I know, we canna keep it a secret forever, 'n Jackson wi nae be satisfied until all Cherokee land is in the hands of white settlers." Said Jesse.

"That's 'zakley whut I been thinking." Said Mal. "What we need is to have this whole valley, clean up 'n over the mountains, safe in some white-eyed settler's hands."

"Wi do? But . . ."

"Yep," Said Malaki smuggly, "A white-eyed settler that would then turn around and give it to the Cherokees. As long as he plays by the rules, that white-eyed settler can do anything he wants with that land and he is free to in-vite anybody he want, to visit him. It's his, ain't it?"

They both sat in silence, thinking. Then, simultaneously, they both shouted out the same name.

"Ernest P. Holman!"

"Tha be a great idea," Said Jesse. "This area be so hidden, it nae likely tha anyone, even the early pioneers, ever ventured beyond the great cliffs, but as sure as me name ain't Jesse, tha surveyors know it be there an it be described on the books as *land beyond the cliffs to the top of the mountain.*"

"That's right," Said Mal, "And Ernest already said that he was in good with that man Dobson at the land office who told him that he will soon be eligible for another claim."

"And the time be right, too," Said Jesse, "While everybody else be snapping up and fighting ore tha parcels o land down ta the *gold* end of Yahoola Creek and are so busy stealing fra the Cherokees, they nae going to notice wha's going on up here on the north end 'n when abody by ye name of Ernest P. Holman stakes out a claim on *the land beyond the cliffs to the top of the mountain,* tha army would be pleased as a pig eatin' slop to know tha it be safe in the hands of a white eye . . . and off tha books an Ernest could officially invite the Cherokees to move onto the land and the army could nae do a ting aboot it. There be no way in the world tha wud ever find the Glory door and to them, it wud look la naething but a wall of worthless rocks leading to nowhere, it wud. If tha happened to see smoke coming from up there 'n checked with the land office, they wud just find oot tha it was someone named Ernest P. Holman who has tha claim up tha somewhere."

"That's right!" Said Mal, smacking his sore knee, 'n if they ever did hear that the Cherokee wuz living up there, it would be too late. As long as Ernest improves it like the government says he must, he can do whatever he wants with his own land and once they move in, the whole tribe could all work together and build some settler-like cabins and wattles to live in and for Red Feather, when we get him back, they could build a larger structure and if anybody questioned it, Ernest could tell 'em that it was the General Store or something. Who knows," He went on, "Someday they might have a whole town up here and name it, what did you call that hidden entrance? *"Glory Door"* that's it, we could call the town *Glory Door!*"

Jesse laughed. "A town wud be guid," He said "But one wee thing keeps a bothern' me, it do."

"What's that?"

"They nae going to get all what they need to build a town through that wee crack in the wall, d'ye think?"

Chapter 22

❧

Mia and BJ arrived at Galveston Bay and disembarked from the *Spanish Main* at mid-day. The docks were busy with stevedores loading cotton bales on wagons, vendors selling tamales and seamen from every nation talking in every language. Mia was beside herself.

Even though their separate quarters on the *River Belle* and the *Spanish Main,* were proper in all respects, Mia's diary was getting a little warm with her adventures and secret thoughts. The entries were mostly about, or included, BJ and her infatuation with him was growing with every moonlit night.

Dear Diary . . . What do you think. Is he not the grandest, most handsome, exciting man you've ever seen? To think how close I came to saying yes to Bobby Neason McKay, back in Aberdeen, that night he asked me t' marry him. We got out of that jus in time, did we not?

They reserved a carriage and driver to take them to Galveston Island and a place called *Campeche.* It was the home port for Jean LaFitte after his participation in the Battle of New Orleans. Doctor Drey DuPhol was the attending physician for LaFitte and his crew during that time. When the US Navy strongly suggested that the privateer leave Galveston Island, Dr. DuPhol stayed behind and set up his practice.

B.J. was doubtful that they would get much information about the identity of a wounded pirate who remembered seeing a shining white mule spirit several years ago in a sick bay after the battle of New Orleans, but he really didn't care. His strong feelings for a certain bonny lass and her impossible mission had gotten the best of him. As far as he was concerned, this trip could last forever.

They got a good dose of Galveston history as they rode through the tropical neighborhoods of adobe and Spanish tile ranch houses contrasted with European homes with decorative brick and ironwork. Mia found it hard to contain herself.

Dear Diary . . . Do you think that a bonnie, Scottish lass and a handsome, intellectual historian in search of a white mule could find happiness living on an island in Texas riding on plain old horses? . . . Really, Diary, ye shud nae put thoughts like that in me head.

When Doctor DuPhol had been notified by wire that a representative of the New Orleans Picayune Newspaper would be arriving and requested an interview with him about the whereabouts of certain casualties treated by him and his staff during the battle of New Orleans, his defences went up.

The Feds had already confiscated all his files months ago. All, that is, except the Brit file that Glory returned and, no one knew about his visit to Little Majorca Island before Jesse and Malaki left for the mountains.

He looked out his office window which overlooked the front drive. Soon, he saw a carriage with a well dressed gentleman in a white Panama hat and a strikingly pretty lady get out.

("Hm-m-m, They look harmless enough but if they are coming here in search of Jesse, they'll get nothing from me. ")

"Doctor DuPhol?" Said B.j. "So happy to meet you! My name is Jackson, Bagwell Jackson from New Orleans . . ."

("Jackson . . . Probably related to Andrew Jackson".) Thought Doc.

"And this bonnie lassie is Miss Mia McNabb, from Inverness, Scottland."

("McNabb? . . . From Scotland? . . . Probably a made-up name. Still . . .")

"How do you do, Miss . . . er . . . McNabb. So nice to meet you both" Said Doc. "What can I do for you?"
"We are here in search of one Private Duncan McNabb, a British infantryman who fought in the Battle of New Orleans and was presumed killed in action. However, certain things that have happened recently has given us cause to think otherwise." Said B.j.

("I knew it! They're after Jesse")

He sat back in his chair, rubbed his chin and frowned. "McNabb . . . Duncan McNabb? I can't say I ever knew anyone by that name. It's the same name as yours, Miss McNabb. Are you related?"
"Aye," Said Mia, "He be, or wa, me Grand Uncle, and it be Mia." She cooed.
"Pardon me?"

148

"If ye please, call me Mia."

"Oh, yes . . . . er Mia," Said Doc, also falling completely under her spell. "What leads you to believe that he is still alive?"

"Well," Said Mia, glancing at BJ, "It be me Grand PaPa, Fergus McNabb who really believes it. Duncan be his younger brother wha saved his life in the Battle of New Orleans, he did, and was wounded, he wa, but Uncle Fergus beconvinced that he wa nae killed and be living somewhere in the United States, 'n he sent me to find him."

(Hm-m-m, Quiet a story. I suppose his name could have been Duncan . . . or not? Anyone can make up a story.")

"And how do you fit into this . . . er . . . manhunt, Mr. Jackson?" Asked Doc.

"Well, I suppose you could say that my knowledge of the Battle of New Orleans got me here." Said B.J. "You see, I'm director of the Archives Department for the New Orleans Pickyune and we have the most comprehensive collection of historic data, stories and articles ever assembled on the subject of The Battle of New Orleans and Mia . . . Miss McNabb . . . decided that I would be the logical start of her mission."

"You, personally?" Asked Doc.

"Well, yes, as a matter of fact." Said BJ. "You see, General Andrew Jackson was my grandfather and . . ."

("There it is! His Grandson, no less!")

as history professor at the University of Tennessee, I documented my Grandfather's actions hour-by-hour and day-by-day throughout the whole campaign and when the Pickyune heard of my efforts, they invited me to join their organization."

"That's quite an undertaking." Said Doc, "But what brought you all the way down here to talk to me?"

"It be a small, human interest article wi came across in the archives," Said Mia, "An article aboot the laddies ye tended in ye hospital tent and the things they saw and heard and thanked for coming through tha bloody war alive."

"Thanked?"

"Aye, one had a rabbit's foot tied to his gun sight. Another praised a gold watch, he did, wi his mother's picture, for taking a mini ball that was intended for his heart and another spoke of a spirit that protected him. It be his testimony wha brings us here."

"Oh? What was his story?

"Tell me Doctor," Said Mia, "Have ye ever seen or heard aboot a large white, glowing mule spirit tha saves lives in battle?"

(Uh-o-o-o!)

"What a strange question Miss MacN . . . Mia. Why would you ask that?"

"Because," Said Mia, "The day A went to see Grand PaPa on his near-death bed in Inverness, A saw a shining light oot in their garden. It was moving and when A pulled me buggy up closer 'n stopped, A saw an enormous horse-like figure wi grand, large ears and when I got oot, it looked up at me and a warm . . . , maybe . . . secure feeling went up me spine. When A asked Grand PaPa aboot it, he most fell out of his bed, he did.

He said the same spirit mule came to him in his dream while he be in a coma and told him that his brither, Duncan, be alive. A know it sounds a wee far fetched, but Grand PaPa wa convinced that if somehow, A could locate that spirit, A would find me Grand Uncle. So when A read the article aboot ye young lad who see it, A copied down

your name, A did, and showed it to BJ. He researched it 'n
we discovered that you wa here on Galvestion Island."

("This is incredible, she saw Glory! How could this be?")

"Miss McNabb, I . . ."
"You didna answer me question, Doctor." Challenged
Mia
"Your question?"
"Aye, ha ye ever seen or heard aboot such a spirit?"
"Miss McNabb, Many young men rant and rave about
things they see or hear in their pain. I am a man of science
and if I can't remove a mini ball from it, put a splint on
it or bandage it up, I can't afford to take their babble
seriously. I hate to say it, you are nice folks, but I'm afraid
you made the long trip down here for nothing."
"But Doctor . . . A"
"Come, Mia," Said BJ. "Let's not take up any more
of the good Doctor's Time." They got up and started to
leave and when Mia approached the door, she stopped in
her tracks.
"What is it?" Said BJ.
"BJ, I left a wee package in the buggy, I did, wud ye
please bring it in?"
Puzzled, he did and handed it to Mia. She took it and
she turned to DocDuphol.
"Doctor," Mia started. "A respect wha ye just said, 'n
apologize fer taking up so much of ye time, I do, but ye,
being a military Physician 'n all, wud you mind taking a
look at the contents o this package and give us your . . .
opinion?"
Doc untied the cord and pulled the oil-skin wrapper
back and his heart stopped. There, before him was an
identical match to the flintlock pistol with rosewood
handles and the same McNabb coat of arms that he pried
out of the hand of a young British soldier, fighting for

his life. Without moving his head, Doc's eyes rolled up to meet Mia's.

"Please sit down . . . Miss McNabb, I . . . have a story to tell both of you that is hard to believe, but it is true."

He poured them both a glass of wine and sat with his eyes closed for a few minutes and then started all the way back to the end of the Battle of New Orleans and a black pirate named Malaki Messer who brought in a half dead soldier with what was left of a red tunic hanging from his shoulders. He picked up the gun Mia had put on his desk.

"He had a gun that was an exact match to this one. Malaki was ranting about a strange white mule he met on the battleground and carried them in.

"He did?" Said Mia, wide eyed. "I mean, he was?"

Doc went on then and told them everything. He told them about the fact that the soldier had lost his memory completely and how they gave him the name Jesse Lafayette McNabb. He told of his recovery and his trip to Little Majorca Island on Jean LaFitte's ship to escape goverment agents trying to arrest him as a spy and his last sight of him when he said goodbye to him, his ex-pirate friend, Malaki Messer and his wife Leolla as they headed up into the mountains to hide out and find a new life for themselves.

Mia was very interested in that part. She couldn't forget Grand Pa Pa Fergus' words after she asked him where to start looking. "Look ye on a mountain, lass." He screamed. "He's be a Highlander 'n if he be alive, he be there."

Chapter 23

For the next two week, hardly a day went by without Little Wolf returning to the secret valley outside the rock cliffs with two or three or ten more Cherokee, from other tribes who had hidden from the soldiers and were now looking for shelter and answers.

During this time, Jesse had been letting his whiskers grow and when they were long and scraggy, he rubbed them down with lard and charcoal, giving special attention to his mustache and goatee to darken them and give him the grizzled look of a miner who's face had endured about six winters and as many barrels of rum too many. Then, he added and lit up the corn-cob pipe he got from Reverend Thornberry, pulled a shapeless, floppy old miners hat down over his blond hair, threw a little dust on Furball's head and lead her over to the water's edge to look at their reflection in the water. He had loaded the little burro with enough supplies to last a week and covered them with an old canvass tarp, tied on a shovel, a pick and some pans for effect and seasoned them all with more dirt and moss out of the creek. He looked, and he was satisfied. If by chance he were stopped by soldiers on his way down the mountain, he would be just another miner, looking to get rich quick, and dared anyone to question it.

Malaki, who was supervising the whole new look, said, "I need to be going with you! You will need me."

"Oh, gud!" Said Jesse, "A dinnae need a stove up ex-pirate wit nuthin save his sea legs ta slip dun the mountain at night wit wee notice to da Blue Coats!" Said Jesse sarcastically. "Nae a gud idea!"

"Is that right?" Quipped Mal, "Listen to you. You don't even speak American and that yeller hair of yours will shine like the moon if ye lose your hat! How ye spect to get away with it?"

"Ahv been practicin' ma hill-billy talk." Said Jesse in fairly good southern. "Sides, ah ain't spectin to stop n'talk to nobody, nohow, leastwise, not much.

"OK, Ok," Said Mal, giggling at his accent. "Ye sound great. Now, let's sit down and go over the plan again."

Once again, they discussed how Jesse would slip out the Glory door just after nightfall and make his way past the River of Rocks and head straight down the mountainside until he reached the same deer path they had followed on their way up and to the fork in the road where he will turn right until he comes to Yahoola Creek. There, he will go straight upstream to the log home of Ernest P. Holman, come daybreak and fill him in on all that has happened. He hadn't had a chance to talk to Ernest since the meeting with General Scott, or the killing of Jimmy Big Dog and the army's attack and how they escaped. Not to mention the whole, not to be believed, story of how a shining, white mule named Glory led them all through The Glory Door, a secret entrance in the rock cliffs to a vast, hidden valley where over two hundred Cherokees were now hiding out.

"That's right," Said Malaki, "You tell him all that and it should at least get his attention and after he's had time to soak it in, you can tell him about our idea of his registering a claim on all that land to build himself a farm and later on when the heat's off, legally inviting the Cherokees to come there and make it their home."

"Ye got it" Said Jesse, smoothing his grubby mustache. "Wish me luck. It be getting dusk soon and A haven't even said goodbye to Ivy yet. A better get oot of here soon, before ye start trying to get oot of tha bed again."

He gave Leolla a hug and crossed over the compound to where Running Deer and Ivy were having supper in their lean-to.

Ivy saw the old miner and his burro and started to take her mother and run, when Furball made a *ee-e haw* noise that only Furball can make, and she stopped.

"Jesse, is that you?"

"It shorly is!" He said in his fake Southern. I figure that If A can fool ye, me lassie, I can fool anyone. How do A look?"

"Awful!" Teased Ivy, "Is this what you plan to look like when you're old and worn out?"

"Maybe, but ye, my princess, must remain, furever, as sweet and beautiful as ye be right now. What have ye heard frum Little Wolf?"

"He reports that thousands of Cherokees have been bunched up together in a camp that is far too small for them, with conditions that are inhuman. He said that there was little food and no blankets to keep them warm. Red Feather has been caged and hung on display in the middle of it all and they expect to start the march west just as soon as all the soldiers have finished their sweep of the mountains.

"Tha be a humiliating, painful confinement" Said Jesse, rubbing his grubby chin, "But at least Red Feather be alive. I'll be talking to Ernest in the morning and hear wha he thinks."

"After you speak to Mr Holman, what do you plan to do?" Asked Ivy.

"I be hangin around for a day or so while he talks to the land office. I nae see how they could refuse him. He be the perfect homesteader, he be white, with wife 'n wee one and A would think that the army would jump at the chance to unload some more Cherokee land into white hands and get it off their books. Maybe A can meet up with Little Wolf during that time.

"Are you going to see if you can get close to father?"

"As close as I can get with oot getting caught meself."

"Can I come with you?

"Come with me? Of course not! A pretty Indian princess like ye couldn't be seen running around tha mountains wi an old geezer like me!" Said Jesse, "First off, it wad nae do ye reputation any good and second, it's be dangerous and if anything ever happened to ye A would just . . ."

"You would what?" Asked Ivy quietly.

"A'd just die, I reckon." Said Jesse, moving closer to her. "There is so much A need to say to ye and now an A dinna have time."

Ivy came close and took his dirty old face in her hands, looked into his eyes and parted her lips. Jesse put his arms around her and drew her close. When their lips touched, his heart skipped a beat and his skin tingled from top to bottom. They held each other's lips for ever.

Finally they parted. "That, in case you don't know," Ivy said, "was not a goodbye kiss. You must watch out for yourself."

Jesse was about two feet off the ground. "Nae cud happen ta me now, me love. Just knowing that I'm coming back to ye for anither kiss la that . . . will keep me safe forever."

"The Great Spirit be with you, my yellow haired old man."

"Goodbye ma'am," Jesse said in Southern, "Y'all take care, now, ye hear?" He straightened his old hat and as he took a step toward Furball, he stopped and turned. "There is just one other thing I need to say to you, ma'am afore ah go."

"What's that, my love?"

"Ye got charcoal on ye chin."

━━━•━━━

Jesse cleared the secret entrance just after dark, went around the huge stone and started down the mountain at a brisk pace. He lit his carbide lantern, as any self-respecting miner would do after dark, and even hummed a few bars of *Yankee Doodle* as he walked. He came within sight of two different groups of soldiers escorting more Indians down the steep trail. He waved at one and they went on but he was actually stopped by the other.

"Howdy, mister," Said a burly blue coated Sergeant just before he spit. "These hills ain't the safest place in the world for man your age to be wandering about. Where you headed fer?"

"Well, sonny," Said Jesse, taking a piece of paper out of his pocket and unfolding it, "I tell ye in jes . . . a minute. "Oh yeh, here tis. A's headed fer a place called Yahoola Crick, ever heered uf it?"

"Who ain't," Said the sergeant. They discovered gold down there a couple months ago."

"Thas whut I heered. I aim to go down and re-leav that crick uv some uv it's nuggets, if I ain't too late."

"If I was you," Said the Sergeant, "I'd find a place to sleep and go on in the morning. It ain't safe to walk around up here at night. There's Cherokee Indians running around everywhere."

"That sound like good advice, sonny" Said Jesse as he pulled his pipe out of his mouth and spit. "Good luck to ye now."

The night was clear and the moon was as bright as he'd ever seen it and he was making good time. About a mile further, he broke into familiar territory. When he looked around he recognized the flat, open area as Eagle Rock, the same place Yellow Owl and Red Feather met with General Scott and were arrested. Since he was tired and the open flat area inviting, he looked at the moon, realized he was way ahead of schedule, he built a small fire, spread out his blanket and made camp.

Soon, the moon disappeared behind some low-hanging clouds, the fire burned out and Jesse went to sleep, only to be awakened two hours later by a rock tumbling down the mountain and coming to rest about six inches from Furballs's left, rear hoof. Jesse stayed motionless except for his right hand moving slowly up his leg to his flintlock that was tucked into his belt. There was a scuffling sound and more gravel poured into the open. Cocking the pistol, he rolled over and aimed it at the noise.

"If ye is animal, skedaddle outta here!" He yelled. The light of dawn was starting to break through the forest.

"If ye is human, come out where I can see ye . . . real slow."

Amid more scuffling, a dark figure started to appear from behind some bushes. It appeared to be a seaman of sorts, dressed in dark pants, a black P-coat with it's collar high and a sailor's watch cap pulled down to frame a red feather sticking out between two very familiar big, green eyes.

"Ivy? Is that you?"

The two brown eyes blinked and rolled up, trying to work their way around the red feather and reflected the first light of day. "Of course it is . . ." She said, indignantly, "How many other Cherokee Princesses do you know?

Jesse rushed toward her and took her in his arms. "A should be mad, but A hae nae figured oot how to be mad at ye and in love with ye at the same time. What be ye doing here."

"Well," She said. "When we kissed and I watched you walk away without giving me an answer about my father, I knew you were going to try and free him."

"That may be," Jesse grunted, holding her out where he could see her eyes, "But ye must go back. This be too dangerous fer a woman."

"I am not a *woman*," She said with fire in her eyes. "I am Wings of Ivy, Princess of the Cherokee and the daughter of Red Feather, who is the Chief of the

Cherokee, and, if you try to rescue him, won't come with you . . . without me."

"What?"

"He won't come with you. I know him and, if they don't kill him, he will feel a responsibility to march West with his people. With Running Deer in hiding, I am the only one he will listen to. I must be the one to tell him about the hidden land beyond the Rock Cliffs. I must be the one to remind him of Yellow Owl's vision. I must be the one to point out his responsibility to the ones who stay behind to start a new beginning. Then he will see the wisdom of it all and come with us. Do you understand?" A tear rolled down her cheek.

Jesse listened in silence, tilted her face up to his, brushed the tear from her cheek. "Aye, A do understand, but the thought of something happening to y . . ."

"And another thing! . . ." Ivy interrupted.

"What?"

"As I watched you walk away, it occurred to me that I just might . . ."

"What"

"That I just might be seeing *you* for the last time and I . . . well, I decided that I would rather die with you than try to live the rest of my life without you."

Jesse tilted her face up to his. She pulled off her watch cap and her eyes batted twice and then closed. There, in the middle of nowhere, with no one watching, a grizzled old gold miner and a beautiful Cherokee princess, kissed.

(*Thank Heaven no one was watching . . .*)

———

They arrived at the clearing outside Ernest P. Holman's cabin mid morning and saw that he was out front talking to a Blue Coat. Jesse told Ivy to wait while he found out what was going on.

Ernest saw him immediately and waved for him to come on in.

"Jesse boy!" Said Ernest, looking him up and down. "I thought that was you, but I waren't sure. Why the get-up?"

Jesse shook his hand and looked at the soldier. "Can we talk?"

"OH," Said Ernest. "Excuse me bad manners. "Jesse McNabb, I'd like you to meet Corporal J.C. Potts. I knowed his daddy back in Ohio and he sent me a letter saying that J.C. was part of the Blue Coat regulars sent down here to help with the Indian situation and asked me to keep an eye on him and . . . well, here he be."

Jesse started to shake his hand and pulled back when he noticed that he was holding a muddy old gold-miners pan.

"Er, excuse me, sir" Said the Corporal, humbly "When I heard, over to the Fort that they discovered gold in that crick over yonder I come out to see for myself and Uncle Ernest invited me to try my luck. It's a pleasure to meet you, sir."

"Gud fer ye, laddy." Said Jesse. "Have ye turned into some kind of a rich gold ty-coon yet?"

"I can't say that I've had much luck, sir," Said J.C. "But just getting out here and away from that Indian concentration camp was worth the trip out."

"It be bad?" Asked Jesse.

"Bad ain't the word for it." Said J.C. "When I enlisted, I thought I was going to be part of an army that was bound to protect these people but as it turns out, I seem to be part of an army of human vultures who are not only bound to wipe the Cherokees off the face of the earth, but draw the last drop of blood from their veins while they're doing it. I've seen soldiers force one Indian to shoot another Indian to save his own life. I've seen whippings and beatings and hangings that would put slavery to shame. I never knew people could be so cruel to other people and if that ain't enough, there's this lawless rabble that follows us around in case we overlooks something. They are even worse than the soldiers because they don't have no rules and regulation to stop them. They want' em all dead so's they can steal their land and mine their gold. They considered them poor Indians lower than animals. I'm sorry to say that I have been part of it"

"It's special good your here to meet J.C." Said Ernest. "You see, he works back in the mess tent and has pulled the duty, every morning, of giving them Indians the only meal they going to get all day long and he was just telling me that one of them Cherokees is a Chief, named Red Feather. Ain't that the same Chief they tricked down to Eagle Rock fer that meeting with that General Scott who arrested him?"

Jesse held up his hand. "It is, but hang on, young man. I've got somebody with me who needs to hear this." He turned toward the forest and whistled.

A dark-coated figure came out of the woods toward them.

"That ain't one of them pirates ye was talking about, is it?" Asked Ernest.

"No" Said Jesse. "This somebody more important than that. You must meet her?"

"Her"

"Yes, her," Said Jesse as Ivy approached, taking off her watch cap and letting her black, flaxen hair tumble down to her waist and waving. "Ernest P. Holman and J.C. Potts, I would like you to meet Wings Of Ivy, a Cherokee princess, the daughter of Red Feather and the love of my life."

"Well I be knocked down n' hog tied if she ain't the purtiest princess I ever seed." Said Ernest, as he stepped forward to take her hand and help her get the rest of the way out of the bulky P-coat.

"It is my pleasure," Cooed Ivy. "Jesse didn't tell me you were so good looking." At that moment, Ernest became her slave.

"This is Corporal Potts, honey and he has something you need to hear."

"Howdy, Miss . . . er, Ivy. I was just telling them that one of the Cherokees I feed every morning is Red Fe . . . ." He paused. "Did he just say you are the daughter of Red Feather."

"He did," Said Ivy.

"Well, you'll be happy to know that, as far as I can tell, he's alive and well. The camp, on the other hand, is jam-packed with thousands of Indians who are hungry and cold and sick and, to keep 'em in line, the General decided that their Chief needed to be put somewhere where they could see him all the time and show them that he ain't going to be any help to 'em atall. So, he ordered us to build this cage-like box to put him in it and ordered us to hoist it up above their heads so all could see. He is left there, night and day with no blanket to keep him warm and only one meal a day, but that Chief don't let on for nothing. He just keeps standing proud, like he knows something that we don't."

"You say that you give him his meal every morning," Asked Jesse. "How do you do that?"

"Well, the mess cook cooks up this mess of . . . well, food and puts it in a bucket and gives it to me and I take it to Sergeant Splinter.

"Splinter?"

"Yesser," Sergeant Burt Splinter. He's drunk most of the time, The men say he's *some piece of hardwood* "Said J.C. "Get it? *Splinter? Piece of hardwood?*"

"I got it, said Jess, taking his corn cob out of his mouth and smiling. Now, tell me what does he do with the food?

"Well, he looks inside the bucket to make sure that there ain't nothing in that bucket but . . . . food. Then he takes the key that is on a string around his neck and gives it to me. It fits the padlock that holds the cage door shut, and I take it to the two armed guards stationed by the cage. They lower it, unlock it, put the bucket in, lock it back up, give the old bucket and key back to me and I take it back to the Sergeant. That's all there is to it."

"Da the padlock be special in any way?" Asked Jesse.

"No, it's just an army-issued padlock with a brass key."

"Da all the keys look alike?"

"Yes, they look the same, but they's all different, of course." Said JC.

Jesse stopped the conversation and looked at Ivy. "Ivy, could ye and J.C. go on in and see if Melba could scare ye up a fried egg or tae? A need to talk to Ernest.

After they were out of earshot, Ernest looked at Jesse. "Are you thinking the same thing I am?

"A think so," Said Jesse. "If we put the same kind of key on the same kind of string that the Sergeant Splinter wears around his neck an give it ta JC, he could feed Red Feather the way he always did, only the key that he gives back to the Sergeant would be the . . . ."

"Fake one!" Ernest said suddenly.

"Aye, and JC would give us the real one, we give it to Ivy, we do, an if we could make a noise, or something, to get those guards away from the cage, while they are making sure no Cherokees gets out, we'll smuggle a Cherokee in to get her daddy oot."

"Ivy!"

"I'm afraid it be," Said Jesse. "Unfortunately, she be the only one tht could convince Red Feather that there be no way to stop the white eyes from marching the whole of the Cherokee nation west and that he be needed to stay behind and lead the Cherokee who are hiding in a new land, just as Yellow Owl predicted."

"That sounds like a good plan," Said Ernest, "And I'm sure that JC will play along. He's really upset to see how the Indians have been mistreated, but what is this new land you speak of?"

"I'm glad you asked that, my friend." Said Jesse, putting his arm around Ernest's shoulder. "Shall we go to breakfast and talk?"

Chapter 24

✲

Jesse spent the next two days filling Ernest in on all that has happened, starting all the way back to Yellow Owl and his two visions and how they were now coming true.

He told how General Scott, under the guise of the meeting Ernest, had arrested Yellow Owl and Red Feather. He described the army's attack, the killing of Tall Trees by Jimmy Big Dog, the killing of Jimmy Big Dog by Leolla, the wounding of Malaki, the round up of all the Cherokees and their forced march down the mountainside.

Then he talked about the hundreds of survivors who hid out that the army didn't find and the appearance of Glory, the white spirit horse that Yellow Owl saw in his vision who led them all through The Great Rock Cliff to a hidden valley big enough for the remaining Cherokees to inhabit and start all over again.

"That's great!" Said Ernest. "Wait till I tell JC. He will be tickled pink that at least some of them Cherokee are going to make it."

"Yes, well, there be a catch." Said Jesse.

"What's that?"

"Well, since they won't own the land, the army will eventually find them and kill or run them off again unless . . . ."

"Unless what?" Asked Ernest, suspiciously.

Then he told him about their idea of Ernest registering a claim on the land, moving onto it and after a time, inviting the Cherokees to live there. "It would be legal and above board," Said Jesse, "because a land owner can do anything he wants with his own land."

"Haw!" Exploded Ernest. "That's a great plan! Ole Stanley Hobson, over to the Land and Assay Office and I have gotten pretty close and he's expecting me to show up any time now to register a new claim. Now he don't know it's going to be *All the land beyond the cliffs to the top of the mountain.* Ain't that a hoot?" Said Ernest, "Ole Stanley Hobson is busy trying to keep everybody happy down at the bottom of the mountain and he ain't even going to think twice about a piece of land that he, or nobody else neither, even knows is up there."

"I thought you would spark to the plan," Said Jesse. "What kind of a man is Mr. Hobson?"

"Hobson? I don't know. Why do you ask?"

"Would he be the kind of man that would accept a bit of . . . well, financial encouragement to move your claim to the top of his list?"

"A bribe?" Said Ernest, thinking and rubbing his chin. "I suppose he might be, he don't make much in that office and he's been there for forty years, but Melba and I ain't . . . ."

Jesse held out his hand. "Here, look at these . . . ."

"Wow! Where did ye get them?"

"They're the two gold nuggets that Little Wolf found at the site where the miners killed that Indian. He said he was up there and got hungry and was pulling up some wild onions at edge of the creek and there they were, looking at him, big as ever. He gave them to me to give to you in case you needed them. They're probably worth two or three hundred dollars."

"Whoo-e!" Said Ernest. "That's gonna blow ole Stanley's whistle. He spends all his time watching people bring gold nuggets in to him, getting them assayed and then taking 'em right back out again when they leave. Now, I'm gonna bring some in, get 'em assayed and leave em for hisself, just for doing what he would do anyhow, only quicker!"

"Done!" Said Jesse, "Now all we needs to dae is tak a wee bit o'time and plot oot how we can pluck a Red Feather outta' the General's tail so's he can float up to see it all, we do"

A week later, they met again.

"This here key," Said JC, holding it up for Jesse, Ivy, Ernest and Little Wolf to see, "Is identical to the one that fits the padlock on Red Feather's cage, when we get ready to make the switch. It ain't going to be no trick for me to give it to the sergeant in place of the real one. They look just the same. The real trick is how to get Miss Ivy inside, the night before I do it, so's she can mix with all the rest of them Indians and tell them the plan to free Red Feather, and get the two of 'em out the next night without them guards seeing it."

"A pretty good trick," Said Jesse, "How ye gonna do it."

"Well, me and Little Wolf have been thinking about that, I'll let him tell you what we came up with."

Little Wolf took a stick and drew a square box in the dirt. "This," He said, "Is the white eye camp . . ." Then he broke the line on one side with his moccasin. "And this is the front gate where the Sergeant Of The Guard's quarters are." Then he drew a small box at the extreme back corner of the compound. "This is a locked-up shed where White Eyes store food and keep it away from bears and raccoons and such. It is built onto the outer log wall and has only one door and no window."

"It ain't guarded," Interrupted JC, "And since I work in the kitchen, I carry the only key to it.

"One of the logs on the outer wall has been loosened," Said Little Wolf and can be pulled back far enough for Wings of Ivy and me to enter the shed and wait until it is time."

"Yes," Said JC, "And when I unlock the door to get some fat-back for cookin', Miss Ivy and Little Wolf slips out and loses themselves in among all them other Indians.

"We can easily blend in with the rest of our people." Said Little Wolf," And we will go to those we know well and tell them about our plans.

"Now, like I said before," JC interrupted again, "The sergeant is drunk most every night but he always hangs his Army Colt in it's holster on the bed post before he goes to sleep . . . and he *does* sleep! He don't wake up 'til I bang on his door and then he always does the same thing. He gets up, takes the bucket over to the window for light, opens it up and looks in it for a while to make sure nobody put no gun or . . . no decent food in there, I reckon."

"Then he gives you the real key, right?" Asked Jesse.

"Yes," Said JC, "And I go on my way, meet the guards, give them the key, they lower the cage, puts the new bucket in, take the old one out and gives it me with the key to take back to the Sergeant, which I do. Only this time, JC goes on with squinty eyes, "I stop at the well and get a drink of water and leave the real key under the bucket for Miss Ivy, who's out there milling around and I go on and give the fake key to the Sarge.

"Pretty slick," Said Jesse . . . but,"

"I'm not through," JC goes on. "Now comes the good part. You see, Sergeant Splinter comes from up north somewhere and is always talking about how scared he is of all the snakes we have down here, especially rattlesnakes!"

"Rattlesnakes?"

"Yep, and on this pertickler morning, Little Wolf is going to be hiding under that window with one of them buggers in a gunnysack!"

""He is?" Said Jesse.

"Yes, and when the Sarge sends me out the front door, Little Wolf gives me a little time to get back toward the mess tent and lets that snake loose through the window and runs, knowing that when it rattles, Sarge is gonna be scared out of his skin, and will most likely grab his Army Colt and start firing away and the two guards at the cage are the closest and are going to hear the gunshots and come running to see what it's all about."

"Oh-h-h," Said Jesse, "That's when . . . ."

"Yep," Said JC, "That's when Miss Ivy picks up the real key and she and Little Wolf run over to the cage, lower it, let the Chief out, throw in a couple bags of corn meal for weight, raise the cage back up and while hundreds of Indians are running around crazy-like and screaming, Miss Ivy, Little Wolf and Chief Red Feather will make their way back to the food shed, hide behind all the boxes and wait for nightfall to cover their escape.

"The whole thing will be over in five minutes," Said JC and that's when I re-lock the food shed, run back to see if poor ole Sarge is OK and help restore order. By the time they's blowed the head off that rattler and settled down, they ain't even going to think about the Chief 'till sun-up the next day when I have the real key back in my pocket, and we feed him again."

Chapter 25

✿

Two days later, General Winfield Scott sat behind
his huge desk at the U.S. Indian Agency reading for the
second time, a letter that had just been hand delivered to
him from Andrew Jackson, President of the United States.
It read:

*Dear General Scott. I assume, by now, you duly note the
importance of "The Indian Removal Act" to our country and why
it must be carried out to the letter, as soon as possible, in order
for our newly established country to move forward and realize it's
vision.*

*The removal of 13,000 Cherokees from the mountains of Georgia
and marching them over two thousand miles to selected lands in
Oklahoma will not be easy and calls for the most stalwart effort on
your part. You must not waver.*

*The whole of the Cherokee Nation must realize by now, that
they are a defeated nation and it has been done so by the United
States of America, not the British or the French, but by the
Americans. That realization alone will make the march go easier.
If, however, some of them still stand off and need more convincing,
look for the opportunities to publicly demonstrate our strength and
commitment. Their spirit must be broken. When I told you to build
a fire under them and they will move, you did and it got things
moving but don't hesitate to make the fire even hotter under some
to make them move faster. I understand that the concentration
stage is near completed and I wait to hear when the march will
actually begin.*

Scott called for his orderly. "Is Captain Freeman of Company B back in camp yet?

"Yes sir," Said the orderly. He arrived night before last with over 800 more Indians who were admitted into the stockade."

"Good! Contact him and tell him that I plan to start the march westward within a weeks time and have him in my office, first thing in the morning."

"Yes Sir." Said the orderly

———•———

"Captain Freeman Sir. Reporting as ordered."

"Yes, good morning, Captain." Said Scott. "I understand your mission was successful.

"Yes Sir, we admitted 836 additional Indians to the camp last night and all their villages and belongings have been dealt with."

"Good, as you know, we plan to start the march within days."

"Yes Sir, the column is now being formed and the supply wagons are standing ready. Will we have wagons for the sick and elderly, Sir?"

"No!" Said the General emphatically. "This country has leaned over backward to provide land for them red skins to live on. All they have to do now, is get there." The United States Army has been provided to, he smiled, *oversee* their immigration until they reach the forced destination. There will be no exceptions. All will walk! Do you understand?

"Yes Sir! Will that be all, Sir?

"One other thing, Captain."

"Yes Sir."

"What is the status of that *Chief Red Hat*, or *Little Feather* or something like that? The one we captured up on Eagle Rock. You know, you were there.

"Chief *Red Feather*, Sir," Said the Captain. "He is still in his suspended cell hanging in the middle of the camp, Sir. I talked to the Sergeant Splinter, who is Sergeant of the Guard this morning Sir, and other than the fact that he found a rattlesnake in his bed, all is well. Why do you ask, Sir?"

"Red Feather must be brought to trial."

"Trial, Sir? On what charge?"

"Murder!" Said General Scott.

"Murder?"

"Yes, Captain. You remember the night we were in their camp er . . . negotiating with their chiefs and a man on our side by the name of Jimmy something . . . Jimmy . . . Big Dog, I think, yes that was his name, *Jimmy Big Dog*, an Indian turned white I believe, found it necessary to . . . er . . . negotiate on his own and was killed, by one of his own kind, as I understand."

"Yes Sir, I remember. He received an arrow through the neck." Said the Captain. We never determined who shot it."

"Who?" Said Scott, "Well, I didn't exactly see it happen either, but I would venture to say that it was shot by this Chief Red Feather himself. Everyone knows that he's a hot head and there was a bad blood between him and this Big Dog fellow. In my book, he let fly that arrow, wouldn't you say?"

Well," Said the Captain I don't know . . ."

"Let me put it this way, Captain," Said Scott sternly, "If I made that accusation in a court martial, you would back me up, would you not? You were there."

"Yes, Sir," Said the Captain, ". . . All the way, Sir!"

"Good," Said Scott. We must make an example out of him."

"How, Sir?"

"Tomorrow, morning, I would like you and a small detachment to join me at his cell when I officially charge him with murder and we will then escort him to the solitary confinement cell at the Agency to await trial. He must be tried and publicly hung before the march begins."

———

His only goal was to stay alive. Red Feather knew and believed this. He can't give up. A Chiefs sole responsibility in time of battle is to stay alive but he knew he was weak, very weak. His weight was now about half what it was when he was arrested and put in the cage hanging in the center of the compound.

His ribs protruded like a skeleton . . . and his arms and legs were like the branches of a tree in the dead of winter. The small bucket of food they gave him every morning was all that was keeping him alive . . . barely. He had taken his one and only blanket and ripped it into smaller pieces to fashioned a crude coat to cover his arms and legs. The pieces were held together by sharp pieces of wire he was able to pry loose from inside his wooden cage.

The screams and noises coming from all his people in the camp was all he had to remind him that he was still alive. He used to be able to call out to the guard and ask for water, but now when he tried to part his lips, they were so parched and chapped they bled and the blood trickled down and clotted on the end of his chin, so he stopped trying. Frostbite had already gotten one fingertip and two toes and his cage was not big enough him to move around and he was forced to sit in one position without end. His muscles had been taxed to the point that there was nothing left and all he could do was let the weight of his whole body rest on raw nerves. The pain was unbearable.

He thought about his Christian teaching and wondered if this might have been what Jesus felt on the cross.

At times, when the pain was more than he could bear and he wanted to cry out loud, he didn't. He was a Chief and there was suffering all around him. He knew that his cries would just blend in and be heard by no one except himself, so, somehow, he endured his pain.

Sometimes, when the night was as black as the raven's wing, he would have visions that persons or spirits would come and help him escape, but help never came, so his hope disappeared. But the visions? They kept coming.

Like now. At this very moment, he was having a vision that someone was lowering his cage. "Food, maybe there's food." He thought to himself. "Maybe it's morning. No, this is different. I hear a voice up close. A familiar voice!" He thought but didn't respond. It was too painful to part his lips.

"This vision is different," He thought, "Why is it not going away like all the others. He put his hand over his mouth, took a deep breath and gathered enough strength to partially open one eye. There she was. He was looking straight into the face of a beautiful lady.

"Maybe it's an Angel. No, she has tears in her eyes. What was that?" He listened. The vision was talking.

"Father?"

"Father! Did I hear right? I never thought I would ever hear that word again. Maybe it is the Heavenly Father that is talking and He has finally come to take me to His bosom. There it is again! I'm coming, Oh Great Spirit . . . I'm coming . . . but wait! The voice I hear is . . . it sounds like . . . it is! That's Wings Of Ivy's voice!" He held his hands on either side of his head to block the onrush of daylight that was sure to come when he opened his eyes and with great effort, he slowly lifted his lids to see.

"It is *her* face I see! It is *her* eyes that are full of tears. She is calling to me from far away, from out of a fog."

In a crackled voice that was hardly audible, he put his tongue to the back of his lower teeth and muttered, "Yes.s.s, daughter."

The voice responded with a surprised "OH!" And spoke again, in an excited whisper. "You're alive! You're alive! Oh, thank you Great Spirit for keeping him alive."

"How can this be?" He thought as the vision spoke again.

"Father, listen closely. We haven't much time. Little Wolf and I are here to take you out and away from here."

When she took hold of his leg to straighten it out, it surprised him and he screamed out.

"Shush-s-s-s-" She said, putting her fingers to his lips and looking around for any sign of the guards coming back. "Make no sound. Can you move?"

Red Feather shook his head from side to side.

Ivy looked around. "What can we do Little Wolf. He can't move?

Little Wolf stood and moved as much of his body as he could into the cage with Red Feather, knelt down and whispered into his ear.

"My name is Little Wolf, Great Chief. It is a time for complete silence, I know you are in pain, but it is very important that you do not cry out as we pull you out of the cage."

He looked away to take the soft scarf from Ivy's neck to rolled up for Red Feather to bite on and when he looked back, a bright beam of white light came down upon the chief's face and he started smiling. When Little Wolf looked around to see it's source, it went out . . . and Red Feather was at peace. Together, they hurriedly drug the chief with all their strength until he cleared the cage. He made no sound. When Little Wolf took the scarf from his mouth, he discovered that Red Feather had passed out.

"It was a blessing," Said Little Wolf, "He felt no pain."

They then quickly put two forty pound bags of corn meal into the cage, re-locked it and hoisted it back up in the air, pausing just long enough to see that the cage had no marks or other evidence that it had been tampered with.

Satisfied, Little Wolf looked at Ivy. "I pray, my Princess that the Great Spirit is still here to give you the strength it will take to help me lift him up. Ivy stepped forward and sat him up while Little Wolf knelt and put his left arm around Red Feathers back and his right arm under his legs, took a step back and with all their mite, using every bit of strength they both had, stood up. The Great Chief made no sound.

"I will have to carry him all the way, my Princess, you lead the way."

Ivy could hear a commotion coming from the direction of the front gate and shots were being fired, but she could see nothing. The surrounding Cherokees had formed themselves into a solid wall of people and on her signal, they parted and let the strong young brave carry their Chief through their numbers and then closed their ranks behind them. Wings of Ivy, Little Wolf and Chief Red Feather disappeared . . . like magic.

Chapter 26

The dream, we dreamed

There was a time when corn grew strong
And the harvest time was nearing.
A time when life was seldom wrong

And the bluebird's song endearing.

We dreamed a dream of peace and love
Though different in our ways.
And we prayed as one to God above
Who made our nights and days.

Our braves were young and unafraid,
But their dreams were turned to fears
When white men came with sword and blade
And cut their trail of Tears

A long, long Trail of Tears
A FOLK SONG/1838

The next morning, Corporal JC Potts, holding a bucket of food, banged on the Sergeant's door. It opened quicker that usual and surprised him. When he stepped inside, he came to attention and saluted the General himself and his detachment.

The Sergeant stepped forward and took the bucket from JC, looked in it and gave him the key from his neck.

"At Ease, Corporal!" Said the Sergeant Splinter. "Looks like this might just be the last meal your Chief-y Boy is going to get. You know General Scott and Captain Freeman?"

"Yes, Sir-s," Said JC, coming back to attention and saluting again.

"They are here to re-arrest The Chief on charges of murder. Unless they feed him again before they hang him, I reckon this will be the last breakfast our big Chiefy will be needing.

"Breakfast!" Said General Scott. "How apropos! Why don't we all accompany the Corporal this morning, Sergeant. We can all serve Chief Red Feather his

176

breakfast. I venture to say that it will be a great wake-up experience."

"Very good, Sir!" Said the Sergeant, handing the bucket back to JC. "A very good idea, Sir."

It was an overcast morning and daylight had not quite arrived yet. JC swallowed hard, as they started for the compound. The two guards came to attention when they saw the General's party coming out of the darkness.

"How is your prisoner this morning, soldier?" Asked General Scott.

"All's quiet, sir. I suspect he must still be asleep."

"Lower him down, then, soldier." Said General Scott. He'll wake up when he hears about the breakfast we have for him this morning."

The two guards faded into the semi-darkness and the squeak of the ancient, wooden pulleys could be heard as the cage was lowered. Then, all was silent. The General waited . . . and waited and then stepped forward and spoke.

"Well, what is it guard? Is he awake or not?"

"Yes, Sir . . . I mean No Sir . . . I mean . . . ."

"What do you mean!" Said Captain Freeman. "Speak up soldier!"

"I mean . . . Sir . . . He ain't here!"

General Scott looked at Captain Freeman, who went quickly to investigate. "He's right, Sir, Chief Red Feather is gone!"

"Captain Freeman, arrest these guards and put Sergeant Splinter under house arrest! We will deal with them as soon as we find out who allowed this to happen. In the meantime, turn out the guards! By sun-up tomorrow, I want every one of these heathens ready to go!"

Throughout the night, all gates were swung wide open and Cherokees spilled out into the clearing. Guards with sticks and some with whips lined them up into endless lines. Whatever belongings they had left were tied into packs and worn on their backs. Some had shoes . . . some didn't. The long awaited march would begin at daybreak.

———•———

Jesse, who had been waiting with Furball outside the rear of the concentration camp peered into the darkness for any movement at all. The plan was to wait until midnight when Ivy and Little Wolf could safely slip Red Feather out through the corner of the food pantry where they had loosened the log and get him back up the mountain to where Running Deer and the rest of the Cherokee were waiting, before daylight.

It was now twelve forty five and he had heard nothing, so he tied Furball to the nearest branch and decided to crawl up to stockade and see if there were any sign of them. He had gone about thirty feet when he heard the call of the Black Capped Chickadee come out of the darkness.

As much as he had practiced making a noise that sounded like a Black Capped Chickadee, when no on was around, his efforts still sounded more like sick frog than anything else, so he decided to answer with his imitation of a coyote, which he thought was pretty good, and kept crawling toward the chickadee. About twenty feet further, he pulled a low hanging limb aside and found himself staring directly into Ivy's eyes. She immediately put her fingers to his lips for silence and whispered into his ear that Little Wolf was waiting behind and needed help with Red Feather who was unable to walk. Jesse nodded and followed Ivy back to Little Wolf. Together, they were able to get Red Feather to his feet and silently half drug him to where Furball was waiting and helped him up onto his back. While Little Wolf followed behind to hide any tell-tale signs, Jesse and Ivy went on as far as Yaholla

Creek before they stopped for Little Wolf to catch up and they could talk.

"Little Wolf," Said Jesse. "Am A glad to see ye. Did ye have any problems getting out?"

"No," Little Wolf said under his breath as he took Jesse's chin and turned his face toward his so he could speak low without anyone hearing him. "I must tell you, my friend, that the cow does not moo in the dark."

Jesse's squinted his eyes. "The what . . . disna what?"

"The cow does not moo in the dark. If anyone who knew that, heard you moo, they might have sounded the alarm."

"That wa nae a moo!" Whispered Jesse, "Ye, of all people, should know that. It be a coyote call."

"Oh," Said Little Wolf, going on to another subject. "Our Chief, Red Feather must have a place to rest and regain his strength before he can proceed back up to his people. He cannot make the journey tonight."

"Hm-m-m," Jesse thought and then looked up. "Little Wolf, if ye could leave a not-so-hidden trail downstream leading to the tracks going west, that will be left by the marchers on the Trail of Tears, an merge ye trail into theirs, General Scott an the searchers, who will show up by daylight for sure, will ken that Red Feather has gone tae join his people, he will, an they will fall in behind at a fast clip an since thair wee band can march faster, thay should catch up wi the head of the column in a matter of hours. Then . . . when he see that Chief Red Feather nae thar, he be mad as a bear wi oot his wallies, he will, an we wil have da time ta git on our way. A be sure tha by now, General Wifield Scott ha issued orders to shoot the likes o us on sight. He wants us deid, he dae. He wants us deid!"

"That is so," Said Little Wolf.

"Now, while ye are doing that, Ivy and A will take the Chief and wade upstream, so's not to leave tracks, to

Ernest Holman's place. Red Feather should be safe thar til he can walk on his own.

Then, when ye get a chance, you could double back, hiding ye tracks, and go upstream to wha the creek crosses the deer path up near the fork and, if ye see no one, head straight up until ye're back to the cliffs. Then find Running Deer and tell her all that has happened and assure her tha her precious Red Feather be safe, he is, and will be home soon."

"That is good," Said Little Wolf. "Go with God." He turned, said goodbye to Ivy, checked Red Feather once again and turned back to Jesse. "I do not know where we all will end, but Little Wolf will not let the Cherokee people forget what *Man Who Hunts Himself* has done for all of us. I pray to the Great Spirit that you will be safe and that we will all be together again soon." He turned and left.

Chapter 27
❊

For President Andrew Jackson, the escape of chief Red Feather was the final straw. He had gotten excited when they discovered gold but he wasn't anywhere near ready for a *Gold Rush*. His excitement turned to sheer anger when he got reports that hoards of gold miners were trespassing on what is still Cherokee land, claiming it as their own and killing any Indians who objected, and more reports that some 200-300 Cherokees had slipped through General Scott's net and were hiding out in the Quabalaka Mountains somewhere, and were probably being led by weak, but still walking Chief Red Feather made him furious. With Red Feather running free, he knew he was out of time.

The first thing he did was order the immediate dishonorable discharge of a Sergeant Burt Splinter for drunkenness and dereliction of duty.

Then, armed by the passage of the *Indian Removal Act,* which was passed in 1830, *(by one vote, mind you,)* and in spite of the fact that it was the coldest winter in history for that part of the country, he quickly and officially signed the order that would allow an armed force, some 7000 strong, made up of militia, regular army and volunteers, under the command of General Winfield Scott, to take the 13,000 Cherokees collected in concentration camps and began a one thousand-mile march through nine states, west to the designated Indian territory, now known as Oklahoma . . . "NOW!"

For the Cherokees, there was nothing left for them. Their homes had been burned and their horses, cattle, hogs and sheep were all taken or slaughtered by the lawless rabble that followed on the heels of the soldiers. Their land and large farms were taken by the government to be raffled off to white settlers in a lottery later on.

The Cherokees themselves, even though it was one of the coldest winters in history, carried only scant clothing and most were on foot without shoes or moccasins. For warmth, they were given blankets from a hospital in Tennessee where an epidemic of small pox had broken out and because of that, townspeople would not allow them into their towns and villages along the way and forced them to go around, adding many torturous, freezing miles to their journey.

Horizontal snow blizzards blew across the plains almost daily and streams and rivers froze over 8 or 12 inches thick which they had to break through just to get water to drink. The larger, fast moving rivers that did not freeze over were impossible to cross due to raging ice floes and many died huddled together waiting for unwilling ferry men to take them across. Those who did agree to ferry them, charged $1.00 per head, *(locals who crossed daily, paid 12 cents)* and even then, it was sometimes hours or even days before paid up Cherokees finally made it across.

Many were robbed and murdered by locals who later charged the US Government $35.00 a head for burying them. Before the *"death march"* was over, 4000 of the 13000 Cherokees died. The trek, was to be dubbed by survivors and future generations of an ashamed nation as, *"The Trail of Tears."*

A private John C. Burnett, a soldier in the regular army wrote: "Future generations will read and condemn this act but I do hope posterity will remember that private soldiers, like myself, and Indians, like the four Cherokees who were forced by General Scott to shoot their Indian chief and his children, had no choice in the matter. We had to execute the orders of our superiors.

Another was quoted: "The Government was bound to protect these poor people, yet alas, with shame, I confess to aiding and abetting the vultures in human form who drew the last drop of blood from the veins of those unfortunate people. "

Yet another soldier who participated in the removal said years later: "I fought through the war between the states and have seen many men shot, but the Cherokee removal was the cruelest of all.

Overall, all tribes together, 48,000 Native Americans were removed to Oklahoma, leaving over twenty five million acres open for future white settlers. Newspapers all over the country were up-in-arms at the cruelty of the United States Army and how the now President, Millard Fillmore, ex president Andrew Jackson and General Windfield Scott could perputrate such horror on anyone., even if they were indians.

Slave states as well as abolitionist, North and South were appalled and angry social and political groups all over, were rushing their Senators and Representatives and demanding an immediate and public apology. Media sources in countries all over the world had heard and published commentaries about the cruel Americans.

Chapter 28

✵

The Year is 1838, Aberdeen, Scotland.

"Bridgett!" Fergus McNabb yelled, sitting in his wheel chair and peering out the giant leaded windows overlooking the East pasture and flower gardens. "Bridgett McNabb! Is ye' deef, lass? Bridgett! I need ye'! Don ye' hear me? BRIDGETT!"

He listened. Finally, there was the sound of wooden heels hitting wood coming from the far end of the long hall leading from the kitchen to his room. It was mixed with female grumbling and inward chatter and got louder and louder and then stopped, just outside his door. It slowly swung open.

"Bridgett! There ye' be, lass! Ye' took ye' wee gud time gettin' here. A kud a ben deid an ye' nae know it. Where ye' been?"

"In the kitchen, cookin' ye' breakfast, Ye' Majesty. It may dawn on ye' one of these mornings that A got other things to do than jus take care of ye' all the time wi out stop. What dae ye' want now?"

Fergus peered over his right shoulder. He could see that she was not to be trifled with on this dull, overcast morning. He smiled. "I wonder, Me lady if I might please borrow the use of ye' gud eyes fer just a moment?"

She came in suspiciously. "Whit now?"

"Come look out to the east, whit de ye' see?"

She looked, took off her wire frame specs, wiped them off with her apron and looked again. "I don't see nothing that nae been there since God made Scotland, wha do ye ask?"

"Look again, what is that shining light down at the end of the drive?"

Bridgett looked again. "All A see is the kerosine welcome light that's been there fer forty years. Ye man Flannagan lights it ever nicht and blows it out every morning, he does. There, see?" The light went out. "What did ye think it be?"

"I jes thought," Said Fergus, "That it might be the white mule angel come back."

"The White Mule Angel? There better not be no white mule in me garden. Ye' be like Johnny-One-Note, Fergus McNabb, that's all ye' talk about. Thay's nae been no one who's ever seen her but ye'"

"That' nae true!" Said Fergus. "Mia did!?

"So she said." Mumbled Bridgett under her breath. "Why are ye off on that subject again this morning, anyway?"

"The shining, white mule appeared in my dream again last night."

"She did, did she? Well, why don't ye jes talk to her in ye dream instead of screaming ye head off for me"

"I couldn't."

"And why nae?"

"She couldn't talk."

"And why nae?"

"She had a letter in her mouth."

"A letter?"

"Aye, she was bringing a letter to me, but A woke afore she gave it to me. What do ye think?"

"Fergus! Ye soft-boiled eggs is hard boiled by now and the ham that goes with it will be tough as shoe leather if

184

A don' get me back to the kitchen. The only letter a know anything about, anyway, is the one that came last night for ye. It be from Mia."

"WHAT? A letter from Mia? That's it! What did ye . . . ? Where be it now?"

"Right here," Said Bridget, pulling the letter out of her apron pocket.

"Bridgett, how cud ye . . . !" He stopped. "Wud ye kindly close the door on ye way back to the kitchen. I'll jes set 'n read me letter."

Dear Grand Pa Pa,

I apologize for not writing sooner, but this search for Grand Uncle Duncan has been like nothing I have ever done before. There is no mission you could have ever sent me on that could be so frustrating yet so rewarding. So far, it's been like an exciting high sea adventure that has wrapped itself around an unsolvable mystery and landed me smack in the middle of a love story. I'll tell you more about that later.

As you know, I postponed my studies and headed straight to New Orleans in Louisiana to talk to a newspaper archivist and student of the Battle of New Orleans named Bagwell Jackson who has been my guide, and for three days, we immersed ourselves in every article ever written on the battle and those who fought it.

There were personnel lists of soldiers, both British and American, and The Scottish Grenadiers were listed and it didn't take long to locate yours and Grand Uncle Duncan's names. Unfortunately, no personnel list were made after the battle and Grand Uncle Duncan was not listed among the casualties. He was just gone. We found a Jamie McNab, a Grantly Mankenabb, a Carbide McNuttly, but no Duncan McNabb.

We kept searching and were about to run out of hard data. All we had left was few human interest articles about strange or unusual happenings reported among the wounded. You know, PaPa, good luck charms, visions, superstitions and stuff like that and I ran across a report about a large, glowing, white horse with big ears that hauled in a boy off the battlefield in time to save his life and then disappeared. It didn't say if he was American or British, so I thought nothing about it and was putting on my hat to leave when I remembered that mule that I am convinced I saw, in your side yard and the one you said you saw in your dream and an overwhelming feeling came over me that the mysterious mule is who I'm really looking for. Don't laugh at me, Grand PaPa, but I believe that if we can find the white mule, we will find my Grand Uncle Duncan. So, I went back to read the article again.

It was attributed to one of Jean LaFitts's pirate bunch who fought with General Jackson and he was being treated in a temporary hospital run by a pirate Doctor named DuPhol. BJ (that's what we call Bagwell) and I went to the wharf where the temporary hospital had been erected but it was gone and Captain LaFitte had sailed to parts unknown. We checked with Army headquarters and their records showed that he had sailed for the Sea Islands off the coast of the Quabalaka Mountain range with a full crew and two passengers. They didn't know about the two passengers, but LaFitte and his crew sailed back around the cape to Galveston Island in Texas. We are on our way there now, as I write. Love you, . . . Your favorite Granddaughter . . . Mia.

"I knew it!" Said Fergus, slapping his sore knee, "She be me, in lassie form! Bridget! Bring me a quill and some paper. Did ye hear, Bridget? BRIDGET!"

Fergus scheduled a meeting with the Clan's legal adviser and secretary, Otis McNabb, who is the oldest son of the clan's only banker, Charles McNabb and arranged for an account to be set up in Mia's name at the Bank of Scotland which has affiliations in both New Orleans and New York.

When Otis brought the papers out for him to sign, Fergus asked him to quietly close the door so they could conduct their business in private and then rolled his wheelchair over to a draped area behind his huge mahogany desk and pulled the cord to expose a large map of America, showing a call-out of it's Atlantic coast and the Gulf of Mexico and invited Otis to take the large chair facing the display.

"Otis," Fergus asked seriously, "Can ye keep a secret?"

"Well, I . . . Can I keep . . . Well, Aye sir. The legal profession is built on secrets and many be entrusted to me. I venture to say, that I would not be a successful lawyer if I couldn't."

"Good! I talk to ye now as me friend but far more important than that, I talk to ye now as a McNabb."

"Aye, Sir," Affirmed Otis.

"Some say I don't have many, if any, years left as head of our Clan. If I die before me beloved Bridgett, as ye know, She will inherit me complete estate and the future of the Clan."

"Aye, I know ye will, Sir." Said Otis.

"I must personally assure that the McNabb Clan does not die and be taken over by the McDuffys!

"Aye, but since the demise of Duncan, ye are the only one that . . ."

"That is so . . . IF . . . there were a demise of Duncan."

"IF, Sir?"

"Aye! I realize that the battle of New Orleans was fought over thirty years ago and no one has heard a word about Duncan since, but I have reason to believe that Duncan is still alive and ye cousin Mia is in the States now, following his trail. I'm thinking that I should go there and help her look."

"Go there? But Sir, ye body nae be up to it and ye wife . . ."

"My wife must not know we are going! This is the secret ye must keep."

"We, Sir?"

"Yes, Otis. I need ye to go wi me, being as how me leg is a bit under the weather."

"But, Sir . . . I . . ." Stuttered Otis. "What evidence do ye have that . . . ?"

"Never mind that!" Said Fergus, "Tis a feeling, it is that I have, more than hard evidence and some mysterious characters have emerged in the cast of characters and it's plain to see that it is going to take more than one person to track them down. Mia needs our help."

"I don't know what to say, sir. I canna jes up and . . ."

"Just say YES, Otis." Said Fergus. "For the future of the clan, say yes!"

"I . . . Aye, Sir."

"Good! It should be, if I have to say so meself, quite an adventure."

"Aye Sir . . ." Said Otis, staring off in space and realizing what his Great Uncle had just asked him to do and smiling. "Quite."

"Now, we canna miss a step, there is a stage leaving Aberdeen for Liverpool in two weeks. That should give me enough time to get more on me feet and trump up some cock-n-bull story to tell Bridget, and enough time for you to draw up whatever passports and papers we will need along the way and, this is the important part, arrange passage on the *SS Baltic,* under some trumped up alias. The *Baltic* is that new fangled transatlantic steamer with side-wheels, that has been breaking all speed records between England and the United States. We must be on that stage, me boy, because it connects to the departure of that ship. Canna ye do that for me Otis?"

"Aye . . . Sir."

"Good. Now be off wi ye, lad, afore Brigett gets home.

Chapter 29

Ernest had just gotten back from his meeting with Mr. Hobson at the Land and Assay Office and was now hopping around behind Melba like a jackrabbit, trying to tell her about it.

"Melba! Would you stop canning them 'maters and sweeping out that dog hair long enough to hear about your future?"

"We already got us a future, right here on the crick! A crick, I might add, that might just have a little gold in it too. I don't see why you would throw all this away just to go up on top of that mountain and live with the Indians!"

"I ain't throwing nothin' away, Melba. We's going to keep both. Didn't I just finish that new bedroom on the back so's we could have the *master* bedroom all to ourselves?" Asked Ernest, with a smirk on his face. "I ain't doubtin' that we got a nice little farm here, but we could put a hundred nice little farms like this 'un up there on the mountain top and still have to go on horseback just to borrow a cup of sugar from the next door neighbor. It's BIG, honey, bigger than you could imagine."

"But we've just gotten to know all the people around here and I just don't like the idea of having to start all over again." Said Melba.

Ernest listened to what Melba was saying and thought for a minute, then he looked up. "Well-l-l, now," He started, "According to what Mr. Hobson is saying, I don't think we know all these people around here jes as dang much as you think we do."

"What do you mean by that?"

"Mr Hobson says that since the army pulled out, taking them Indians west, that more and more of that white rabble is pouring in from all over. He says that there ain't a day goes by that a hundred or two hundred more settlers don't show up with their gold panning pans looking for a spot along the crick to start dippin', and you know what, there jes ain't too many spots left along that crick to handle em. He says that things is heating up and he's afraid they jes might boil over.

"Has there been trouble?" Asked Melba, quieting down a lot.

"Not yet, but with the Army gone, there ain't no law, to speak of, and there's been different groups forming up and turning into mobs. Right now, they're fighting amongst themselves, but Mr. Hobson thinks that it's jes a matter of time afore they take the law into their own hands and try to take over more and more of Yahoola Creek going north. The headwaters of that crick starts up there behind them bluffs, you know."

"You mean the land on top of the mountain? The land you are talking about that might soon be ours?"

"Yep, and Mr Hobson said that because the land all sits back behind that wall of cliffs up there with no good way to get in, the surveyors just left it in one piece. He's guessin' that it's more that two or three hundred square miles of beautiful valleys with a 300 acre spring fed lake smack dab in the center, just waiting for someone to come build on it and when the news gets out that the whole dang parcel was given to one person, all heck jes might break loose."

"One person? You?

"Yep." Said Ernest, "But up there, we could have a farm twice as big as the one we have now and Tricha could make friends with the Cherokee children and we could grow corn, raise cattle and roam and explore forever. We might pan for a little gold ourselves and who knows, we might even find some."

Then, as time goes on, we could maybe start a mercantile store for supplies, since the Cherokees would need a white man to do the ordering and shipping and such. It would be like a partnership between the Indians and us and the beauty of it all is the fact that we own it fair and square. It ain't out of the question, you know, a body could probably build another whole town up there. Maybe one day we will."

"Did you sign the papers already? Asked Melba.

"Yep, but Mr Hobson said that he needs your signature too, and he said that a parcel of land this big must have the signature of the Governor of Georgia or the Lieutenant Governor acting for the Governor.

He has to go to Augusta anyhow, to file some other claims that have been given out and thought he might be able to kill two birds with one stone by getting our claim signed and filed on the same trip."

"Is he going soon?"

"Just as soon as you sign this." Said Ernest, fishing in his pocket. "You remember these two gold nuggets Jesse got from the Indians, don't you?"

"Yes."

"Well, I showed them to Mr. Hobson and told him that it would be worth these gold nuggets to be able to put a plow to the ground and get some seeding done up there before the rainy season and thought maybe they would help defray some of his cost of making a special trip to the capitol and all."

"What did he say?"

"Nothing . . . He just got tears in his eyes. Come on, honey sit down and let's sign these papers before something else happens.

Before she could, however, they heard the sound of the chickadee and gravel hitting against the window.

"What was that, Ernest?"

"I don't know," Said Ernest, and as he goes for his gun, it happened again, the call of the chickadee and gravel against the window.

"Hello! . . . Anybody home in the house?" Someone called softly.

Ernest looked out the front window. "It's Jesse, honey. Looks like he's got a couple Indians with him. One's hurt, looks like.

Melba looked out. "Why that's . . . Ernest, ain't that the Chief we met up atop Eagle Rock?"

"It shorely is!" Said Ernest. "It's Red Feather, hisself. Go get some covers out of the trunk and make up the bed in the new bedroom. It looks like we gonna need em."

While Ivy and Melba were tending Red Feather, Jesse told Ernest all that had happened, including the fact that Little Wolf had laid down a false trail to draw anybody hunting them, off to the west.

"Who-e-e!" Said Ernest. "I bet that general is madder than a wet hen."

"Aye, ye have to know he is. Said Jesse, "But we fixed it so's he won't know if the chief decided to go on the march with his people, or if he opted to go back up and be with the Cherokees that were overlooked and are still on the mountain. In either case," Jesse went on, "He dinnae know how weak the Chief be and we needed a place for him to recuperate and, at the same time, give the General juist a wee time to search. A dinna think the good General wud peer inta people's homes, especially nae homes in town. If it is gud for ye and Melba, a will stay here wa Ivy while Little Wolf goes to Running Deer and tell her about her brave Chief."

"Well, Jesse lad," Said Ernest, "You come to the right place. The ladies will take good care of the Chief, and I got lots to tell about Mr Hobson and the land."

A week went by and Red Feather got stronger by the day. Ernest had heard about the famous chief and was very proud to meet him and made it a point to visit and talk to him anytime he could. It was obvious, the more time they spent together, the more they trusted each other. They laughed a lot and when Ernest could get his hands on a copy of the Sweetgum Gazette and read him the news articles about the Trail Of Tears, he would sit very quiet with his eyes closed and listen intently as the articles and headlines described the deadly, torturous plight of the Cherokee and how the country, as a whole, was in an uproar at the cruelty of the United States Army and the disbelief that the now President Millard Fillmore, ex president Andrew Jackson and General Windfield Scott could perpetrate such horror on anyone, even if they were Indians.

Wings of Ivy and little Tricha spoiled him rotten. Red Feather took an immediate liking to Tricha and gave her the Indian name of *Hair of Sunshine.*

When he was strong enough, Ernest and Jesse brought a survey of the land north of the rock cliffs. That is, if you want to call it a survey. Since no one had actually been beyond those cliffs, it told them very little. What was most notable to Ernest, was the fact that there was no visible entrance. However, that was not thier mission. Right now, they wanted to let Red Feather know what their plans were.

When they told him the plans for Ernest to get the property, all legal like, and invite the Cherokees remaining in the mountains to live there Red Feather just sat there quietly. It was a lot for him to accept. That land had been sacred and forbidden to the Indian for generations, but after looking at the survey and knowing that the White Horse Spirit led them there just as it was predicted in Yellow Owl's visions, he not only understood but got quite excited about the new beginning.

Ernest figured from the survey that the land ran close to 300 square miles and they sat for hours looking at the area and calculating how much of it could be cleared and devoted to planting corn and beans and potatoes and how much should be left for hunting and fishing and trapping.

Ernest had about eight hundred dollars in yellow rock nuggets and he and Melba had their grandma's savings, which was more than enough for seed and plows, etc.

It was becoming clear, and very exciting to them all, just what he, Jesse, Malaki and Red Feather, could accomplish if they can find a way to live and work together.

On the down side, getting in and out of the property was still a problem. The sheer, unassailable cliffs that literally fenced in the whole top of the mountain offered no ready answer for getting people in and out, especially oxen or horse-drawn wagons.

Ernest got a piece of Tricha's notebook paper and started to draw a map showing the deer path trail they came up and how it abruptly ended at the cliffs. Then he marked the crack in the wall where Glory led them through the fault and together, they agreed that there was no way to widen it at that point.

They looked at another area where the cliffs jutted out suddenly toward the closest mountainside and wondered, if it would be possible to build up the deer path to where it was close or even with the rocks and cut down some of the giant, tall pines growing there and bridge across at the top of the cliffs. It was far fetched, but it was the only thought they had for now. What they did agree on, due to what they were hearing from below, was to keep the secret entrance a secret.

Skipping over the fact that they didn't know how they were going to get in and out yet, they still talked about opening a general store where together, they could sell produce and the Indians could sell baskets and bead work and furs and pelts to other settlers. Ernest talked about transforming his house, barn and corrals outside the town of Sideways into another general store and J.C. Potts could run it.

"Who is this J.C. Potts you speak of?" Asked Strong Eagle.

"He's the one who brought you your one meal every day that you were in your cage, Father," Said Ivy. "And he was key to helping us get you out of there."

"Aye," Said Jesse, "In more ways that one."

"Since his enlistment is running out," Said Ernest, "He's decided, after the Trail Of Tears, the army ain't the place he wants to spend the rest of his life and he didn't want to go back to Ohio, so after the excitement of Chief Red Feathere's escape and all the friends he's met along the way, he wants to stay in the mountains, and it didn't take me long to figured out that he would be the perfect one to put him in charge of it all. He really does admire the Cherokee people and he would be proud to offer Cherokee products to all the folks going in and out of Sideway. Maybe, later on, we could even open another store in Sweetgum. It's getting to be a big place, I hear."

Ivy waited until they had finished and then put some marks of her own on the map showing where wattles could be built alongside the log cabins that the whites will live in and how Ernest and Red Feather could build their quarters together to form the governmental center of the village.

Great tears swelled up in Running Deer's eyes. She was painting a mural story on a giant deerskin. It was to be the history of the capture of Red Feather and Yellow Owl and the attack on the village by the blue coats, showing the Great Horse Spirit leading her people through the great stone cliffs.

She had been too busy working with all the children to think of herself up until now but as she put the finishing touches to the bone white Spirit figure leading a line of Indians toward a rising sunset, and as the story came back to her mind, she couldn't hold back. She laid her face against the big mule's image and with a tear rolling down her cheek . . . she prayed.

"Please, Great Spirit, tell me if you can, where is my Strong Eagle. Tell me he is alive. Can you talk, Great Spirit?"

She heard the sound of the Black capped chickadee come out of the darkness and spun around and returned the call. The sound occurred again and as she stared, a face came slowly into the light. It was Little Wolf.

"Forgive me, Mother Chief, for not getting back before now. I know how anxious you have been to hear of the great chief, but I had to hide until the dark of night in order to escape a band of soldiers. But I am here now, Mother Chief . . . with good news.

5:30 *P,M*
46 hours
before Inauguration:

"So, as you can see, young lady," Said President Elect Ernest H. McNabb, "It seems that a horse spirit with ears like the wings of an angel, named *Glory* has seemingly played a large part in the history of my ancestors and consequently a large part in my election to . . ."

"Well, was she . . . ?"

"Was she what?"

"Was she an Angel? . . . I know I promised to ask only one question, but . . ."

Ernest smiled, pursed his lips and rubbed his chin. "Can my answer be . . . off the record?"

"Absolutely, Sir . . . I promise."

"Then I will answer. As the world already knows, I am a Christian . . . a devout Christian and being such, I truly do believe that God watches over and guides us all, and at those times when He cannot directly protect us, I believe He sends his Emissaries of Divine Light, or Angels to guide us through what ever ordeal we may be involved in."

"Emmissaries . . . you mean like the white horse spirit?"

"Yes, but one cannot actually be sure until Jesus comes again. Then we'll all know. Not everyone sees them and more often than not, they disappear just as soon as their work is done."

Pepper opened her canvas brief case with a big red *PJ* printed on it and spread out some old clippings on the desk. "I brought these along for reference, Sir. Their out of our archives and they talk about you and a white mule named *Lucy* that was your constant companion when you were young and there are pictures of you campaigning with her in the *Lucymobile*. Was she an Angel too?"

Ernest got a far-away look in his eyes and thought for a minute. "Ah yes, Lucy, I loved that mule. Maybe someday in Heaven we'll find out if she was an Angel or not, but If you ask that question to anyone on the streets of Sweetgum, they will give you an emphatic *YES*. However, I don't know just how many votes I would have gotten if I had gone around telling folks that my red, white and blue wagon was actually a chariot being pulled by an Angel. If you check back with your archives, you will note that *Lucy* and the *Lucymobile* were never seen again after I was elected Governor."

"You've never, ever seen her again?"

"Never."

"Have you, yourself, ever seen *Glory?*"

"Ah-ha! Another question!"

"Well . . ." P.J. said sheepishly, "It's kinda like the same question, only a smidge different, don't you think?"

Ernest laughed. "I suppose, and somehow, I knew it was coming. This answer must also be off the record?"

"Yes" Said Pepper.

"Then my answer is yes, I think I've seen her."

"Think" When?"

"It was back in the fifties and I was a young Marine Leutenant in North Korea. The Red Chinese were a sneaky bunch, in that they hid in underground tunnels during the day and came out to raid us during the night and the only way we could get to them was to find their tunnels and go in after them."

"Did you ever do that?"

"Well, yes, as luck would have it, I was leading a squad of fifteen, or so, men when we stumbled onto one of their entrances. It was pitch black in there but we went in anyway. We were getting our eyes accustomed to the dark when a bunch of Reds jumped us and forced us back into a blind tunnel with no way out except through them."

"What did you do?"

"There were so many of them, there wasn't much we could do, except get captured or killed or worse. We couldn't see them, but we could hear them screaming at each other and rattling their equipment as they got ready to rush us. I saw their commanding officer draw his saber and yell, *'HAP SHE DAH!'* I think that means *Charge'* and they came at us, as my daddy used to say, like a herd of turtles."

"Did you get killed?" Asked Pepper, with an impish grin.

"Well, no, but I *figured* we were goners. Then, all of a sudden, above all that commotion, I heard a loud 'EE-E-HAA' sound and every one of those Reds stopped in their tracks and turned to look. It was coming from a brilliant white light that appeared behind them. The Koreans were dumbfounded and falling all over themselves. The light got brighter and brighter and their commanding officer kept backing up right toward me and when he got close enough, I managed to grab him in a head lock as pretty as you please and when all his men looked around and saw what was happening, she led me and all fifteen of my boys right through the middle of those gooks and out another entrance.

When we got back to our lines and I turned the Red officer over to the MPs, everybody was patting me on the back and shaking my hand and calling me a hero. I even got a medal, can you believe that? I didn't do anything but run."

"Was it Glory?"

"I don't know, but if I ever do get up close to that lady, I'm going to pin my medal smack on her .... tail or somewhere."

Pepper giggled. "So . . . ?"

"So what, young lady?"

"Did Fergus ever find his brother?"

"Young lady, when I granted this interview, you said . . . . oh, what's the use . . . , would you like a sandwich?"

Chapter 30

After the departure of the army, escorting the Cherokees west, there was very little law and order left in the high country. Word had gotten out that several hundred Cherokees along with Chief Red Feather had escaped the army's round-up and were living beyond the cliffs at the top of High Mountain. No one in Sideways thought much about it, one way or another, however, because it was a good half day's climb and, none of their business. Besides, they had problems of their own.

The gold was petering out at the bottom end of Yahoola Creek leaving a lot of miners dead broke and hungry, but more important than that, they had nobody to blame for their troubles. When their claims ran out, they kept moving north, up the creek with their pans and sluice boxes whether they owned the upper claims or not and fights were breaking out. So far, six people had been killed and still, not a day went by that more and more *gold rushers* didn't flood in looking to get their share.

The tavern in Sideways became the center of the festering problem. Hardly a night went by without a fight or a killing. It was getting bad, and sitting smack in the middle of it all, was ex-Sergeant of the Guard Burt Splinter.

After his Court Martial, he had but one friend left, his bottle. He had officially become the town drunk. But, as disgusting as his slobbering and staggering presence was, he not onlyl had all the drunken miners around him, he had a bitter hate, beyond all hate, for the army and a hate beyond even that for the famous Cherokee Chief Red Feather. His escape had not only gotten him cashiered out of the army, it had also made him a laughing stock of the whole mountain.

One night, he was sitting at the bar while a miner, who had his claim jumped, swore vengeance against another miner and drew out a pistol to kill him. Splinter took an empty bourbon bottle and crashed it over the miner's head. The entire tavern went quiet as Splinter stood over the unconscious body and spoke.

"I am tired of sitting here night after night listening to all you lilly-livered babies sit around," He made pretend quote marks with his fingers, "Feeling sorry for yourselves. Poor little miners, belly aching 'cause you done run out of gold. Well, why don't you do something about it?"

"Ah, sit down!" Said a miner. "Your're drunk. You don't know what your're talking about!"

"Yeah," Said another drunk, "Siddown!"

"I may be drunk, but I ain't stupid!" Belched the Sergeant.

"Yeah? What do you know about it?"

"I know why ye run out of gold!" Said Splinter proudly.

"Yeah, why?" Said another drunk who was trying to get out of a chair and didn't make it.

"The Cheroke-e-e-s!" Splinter sounded out with vengeance. The tavern got quiet again while they considered what the Sarge had just said.

Finally, the same miner who had given up trying to get out of his chair said, "The Cherokees?" They ain't stealing gold. They don't even know what it's used fer. They call it yeller rock."

"They may call it that," Sneered Splinter, "But thanks to them white injuns they got living up there with 'em, they know what it's used for now and they done dammed up that crick at the headwaters, taking all that gold for themselves. That's why you all ain't got none!"

"Yeah? Well, let's just say what ye say is true, what can we do about it?"

"We can blast them out of there, that's what."

"Big Talk!" Said yet another miner. "I just come down from up there and not only did I not see no injuns, there ain't even no way fer a body to get behind them cliffs. If ye can't get back of them cliffs, ain't no way you could could live there. It's as simple as that.

"Yeah?" Said Splinter, "Well, this morning I went over to the Claims Office and asked ole Stanly Hobson about it and he told me that the whole top of the mountain up there has done been claimed by a white man named Holder . . . or Holdup . . . or Hang Over or some such name."

"I heer'd about them white injuns," Said a miner, "And how they was adopted by the tribes and I heard that they took a bunch of slaves up there with 'em, too! probably run-aways."

"I heard that too,!" Said another, "And I also heard tell some of them fellers up in Illinois is talking about making it agin the law to own slaves. He said there might even be a war fought over it. Can you believe that? A war between the states over slaves? Maybe we ought to blast em out of there!"

"A body could get hung for that!" Said yet another.

"Whose gonna stop us? The army's gone!"

"Yeah, but how we going to do that?" Said the same miner. "I mean, we ain't got no dynamite or nothing."

"Don't need none." Said Splinter, downing another shot and swinging his leg over a chair. "Some of you boys know me, and you know that I was in the army, before I . . . er . . . voluntarily changed professions. I was Sergeant of the guard and part of my job was guarding the munitions compound, over to Fort Sideways, where they keep all them field cannons they used back in the Battle of New Orleans and I still got the keys to all them locks. With an eight horse team and your help, we could help ourselves to one of those twelve pounders, the one we called *Napoleon*, and three or four of them explosive shells. That cannon is deadly accurate and there ain't no cliffs or no injuns that can stand up again a twelve pound *Napoleon*." Silence fell over the entire tavern.

No one noticed a lone figure who had been sitting back in a dark corner behind the coal stove as he got up silently and slipped out through the swinging doors. Ernest P. Holman needed to get this news to Jesse and Chief Red Feather as soon as possible.

Chapter 31

The year is 1825, *Aberdeen, Scotland.*

Even before they boarded the stage for Aberdeen, Furgus and Otis read the headlines in the Aberdeen Citizen about the cruelty dealt to the thousands of Cherokees Indians in America, who were being forced to endure hardship beyond human endurance during their march from the Quabalaka Mountain Range to the Oklahoma Indian Territory and how the people in towns along the way were calling it *The Trail Of Tears*.

"I say, Otis, look ye here. Is that not the same Mountain Range that Mia mentioned in her letters?"

"Aye, Sir." He said scanning the article. "Are ye sure that is where we should be going?"

"We canna be of help to Mia if we don't get into the thick of things, my boy, now can we?"

"Nae, Sir." Said an unsure Otis.

Fergus laid the paper down and picked up Mia's letter to read again for the fifteenth time.

Dear Grand PaPa.

Big News! I can't believe it. As you know, B. J. and I, (He's still wonderful. Tell me, PaPa, how would you feel about having the grandson of Andrew Jackson in the family, some day?) are on Galveston Island talking to Dr DuPhol about Grand Uncle Duncan, if there is an Uncle Duncan, and he wasn't very talkative at first, until I showed him the flintlock pistol. Then, his eyes got big and he sat us down.

He recognized it immediately as a perfect twin to the one he took from a wounded soldier (probably British) who had lost his memory. He was brought in by a black pirate who was ranting about a "big white mule with big ears" and since he didn't know the soldier's name, they gave him the first name of Jesse Lafayette and gave him McNabb for a last name, because they read it on the gun handle.

Doc said he treated him until he could get around and then helped him escape to an island named Little Majorca with the same black pirate whose name is Malaki Messer and a woman called Leolla, (I don't know who she is.) because the US Goverment was looking to try the soldier as a spy. Can you believe that? Grand Uncle Duncan, a spy?

Doc has arranged for us to sail there. He said, when he went there to warn him about the Government, was the last time he saw them and they were headed into the Quabalaka mountains. (You sure called that one, Grand PaPa.) We should arrive there next week. I understand that the Quabalaka Mountain Range is still pretty primitive with only a few settlers and a lot of Indians.

We will keep you up on our progress just as soon as we can.

Lots of love . . . Mia

Fergus folded the letter and put it into a folder entitled "Duncan", zipped up his briefcase and sat down in the waiting room to think of anything he might have forgotten.

"Otis, did ye . . ."

"Aye sir," He said, "I left the letter you wrote Ms Bridget on the dining room table where she canna miss it. I must say, sir, a stroke a luck, it was, that her mother called her over to help wi the cannin."

"That it was, that it was." Said Fergus, "It saved me from having to invent some cock-n-bull story that she would catch me on anyhow, it did. I just told her I had been called away, unexpectedly, on business and would be in touch. I told her nae to worry because ye be with me. At least, she trusts ye. Ye's her favorite, ye are." He closed one eye and rubbed his chin. "Now, me boy, did ye . . ."

Aye, sir. The stage will arrive in Liverpool two hours afore we board the *SSBalti,* sir. All arrangements have been made and our quarters are ready."

"An when we gets to New York, did ye . . ."

"Aye, sir. Arrangements have been made to board the two masted schooner, *SS Carolina* which wi drop us on Little Mijorca Island, where we wi be met by a Mr Moses Thornberry who be, among other things, a mon o de cloth and the Da of the mysterious *Leolla,* he be. A must say, sir this whole trip is going to be quite . . ."

"Expensive?" Said Fergus. "Of course it be expensive! A say *drat that!* Life denna be cheap! And if a discover that one o da lives belongs ta me brother, Duncan, it be worth it . . . at any price!"

He didn't say anything about the stabbing pain that was going down his left leg and never stopped until he sat down. He also didn't mention the fact that, even with his cane, he could only get a hundred yards or so before he had to rest. The thought of riding a stage and two ships for six days just to get him to the place where he could trek up a mountain, was not a good thought atall.

He thought of the great white mule and took a deep breath, closed his eyes and prayed. "A dinnae ken who ye be, white spirit. Is ye an angel? If ye be, I hope ye can keep me going, 'til I kin hug me brither, I do."

Chapter 32

❧

There was much happiness and never ending stomp dances when Red Feather made his way through the *Glory Door,* The main and only entrance to the New Cherokee Valley. and once again joined his people. Running Deer and Ivy watched proudly as Red feather donned his red ceremonial headdress.

Red Feather looked over and smiled. "It may be the new beginning for our tribe," He said, "But it is not the beginning for squaw and little squaw to watch while their great Chief . . . gets dressed. Ivy giggled and they left their makeshift lean-to wattle and stepped out into the sun.

Oh, I almost forgot. Said Ivy, Mr. Holman gave me this letter to deliver to Leolla. He said it was from her father on Little Majorica Island. Have you seen her?"

"They have a fire over by the lake." Running Deer said, pointing. "They talk with *Man Who Hunts Himself.*

Ivy found them by a big rock close to the entrance. Jesse and Malaki were in heavy discussion with much finger pointing and sweeping of arms like imaginary explosions, while Leolla was sitting alone and looking bored. She sneaked up behind Leolla and gave her a quick hug. Leolla squealed and jumped."I didn't hear you coming."

"You must never hear an Indian coming, my sister," Said Ivy, "We learn how to sneak up on people and deer from the day we are born, didn't you know?" They giggled.

"I didn't want to disturb the generals in their war room over there, but I have a letter for the general's wife from her father."

Oh good, Said Leolla I could use a little daddy sweet talk in amongst all this danger and threats of war." She opened the letter, scanned it and looked up with a puzzled frown on her face.

"Is it bad news, Leolla?" Asked Ivy, looking at her big frown.

"Well, no, not really. It's mostly for Malaki. Some of Daddy's flock are in trouble. He wants him to help.

Malaki came up behind Ivy and slipped his arms around her waist. "And how is the prettiest little Princess in all the Cherokee Nation doing today.

"She's doing fine," Said Leolla sternly. "And I would appreciate you getting your hands off her! Here," She giggled, "Here, it's a letter from Daddy and it's mostly for you.

Mal read the letter, rubbed his chin and made a hm-m-m sound.

What is it, Mal?" Called Jesse, walking up.

"It's from Papa Thornberry. It seems that three of his flock are missing and he needs my help."

"Oh?"

"Yeah, old Millard Posy, remember him, over at the lumber yard in Sideways? He just passed away and his will stated that the three Gullah slaves he owned, were to get their freedom when he went. He loved them slaves. He even named them after himself. There was Pat Posy, Paul Posy and Philbert Posy, that is until they changed his to Longfeller. I remember them well, we used to play together."

"Longfeller Posy?" Asked Jesse. How did that come about?"

"Well, for two reasons." Leolla went on, "One, was the fact that he was over six and half feet tall. Pat and Paul stopped growing somewhere around six feet, but Philbert just kept growing and growing and when he topped six foot six, folks just started calling him . . ."

"Longfeller." Said Mal, rolling his eyes.

"Yes, but not yet. That's not the whole of it," Said Leolla, anxious to go on. "I told you how much the Posys loved those boys, well, when they were about four years old, Mrs Posy decided to teach them how to read and write and she got out all her old learning books and commenced to teach them the alphabet and how to form them letters into words. Just little words at first, like *boy* and *dog* and *tree* and such and they learned fast and it was no time atall, that they were writing and reading words just like the white kids over in the school house. Then, one day, Philbert wrote the word *boy*, and then he wrote the word *toy*, and started giggling. When Mrs Posy asked him what he was laughing at, he pointed at the words and said "Dat *boy*, sounds jes like dat *toy*!" and laughed again and clapped his hands and from that time on, he started searching out words that sounded alike and put them together into sentences. Then, soon after, he even started talking in what they call *rhyme*. You know, little storys that has words that sound like each other."

"That's interesting," Said Mal, yawning. "What does that have to do with Longf…"

"I'm coming to that. Mrs Posy remembered a little book she had stuffed in an old trunk somewhere that was written by a writer named Henry Wadsworth Longfellow. He's a famous poet who lives up north somewhere, and when she gave it to Philbert to keep, she looked down at the name and said, "Philbert, since you like poetry so much, and since you stand as tall as a Lodgepole Pine, I 'spect we ought to change your name to *Longfellow*… And, they did. The only thing was though, when it was first spoke by a slave, it came out *Longfeller* and that's what stuck with him all his life."

"That's some story!" Said Mal. "I'm sorry I asked."

"It has always saddened me when someone passes and I'm sure the Posy boys will miss Mr Posy, but I'm also sure that when they get their freedom, they'll be happy again."

"I don't know," Said Malaki, "It says here in this letter that they disappeared!"

"Disappeared?" Asked Jesse, "How did they disappear? A slave don't run off from his freedom. Where did they go?"

"Well, Pastor Moses goes on to say that a miner come up from below and said that three slaves were chained to a tree, smack in the middle of the miner's camp down on Yahoola Crick.

Pastor Thornberry says that he contacted the sheriff over in Sideways and asked him to go down and check on it and the sheriff took a copy of Mr. Posy's will and showed it to a man named Splinter, Burt Splinter and he told him that the will is not worth the paper it's printed on. He said that mountain law is the only law they practice and mountain law says that if a slave's master dies, they are still slaves for who ever gets to 'em first and evidently, the miners took them the very same night that Posy died.

"What did the sheriff say?"

"Nothing, evidently. It says here that the sheriff has not been heard from since".

"Did they kill the sheriff?"

"It don't say," Said Mal "But they say they would kill the slaves too, if anybody interferes.

Malaki folded the letter and gave it back to Leolla, and put both hands to his mouth like he was praying.

"Splinter . . . ? That name is familiar. You know him Jesse?"

Before Jesse could answer, Little Wolf walked up.

"Splinter was Sergeant in white eye army who guarded Red Feather. Him bad man."

"Aye," Said Jesse. "I remember now. He was stripped of his stripes and kicked oot of the army after Red Feather escaped. He be the same drunk Ernest overheard in the tavern stirring up all the miners again the Cherokees. I hear it's gotten bad. There must be eight, maybe nine hundred of them now and since the gold petered oot and the army left, they've gotten mean, they have, They are most all drunks and killers and evidently are writing their own laws." Said Jesse. "He be the one that wants to blast us off our mountain top. We bloody well better watch him.

"Well, Yes," Said Leolla, "But what about the slaves?"

"The slaves," Pondered Mal. "Jesse, you still got them miner's clothes?"

"Ae."

"Good, I have a thought. Do you think you could get in touch with Ernest and have him see if Mr Dobson, over at the assay office, has cashed in them three gold nuggets we gave him. If he ain't, let's you, me and Little Wolf get together down on Eagle Rock. Them slaves ain't goners yet."

Ernest Holman, holding the three gold nuggets, Jesse, in his miner clothes, smoking his corn cob pipe and Malaki and Little Wolf met atop Eagle Rock three days later.

"I don't know why I needed to make the borrow of Mr Dobson's gold nuggets," Said Ernest. "He weren't just all that willing to give 'em up. What you up to Malaki?"

Mal smiled and put his arm around Ermest's shoulder. "Ernest, do you know them rocks with that old bear cave back under 'em that overlooks Yahoola Crick down south of your place? You know, near where the crick makes that big hairpin turn?

"The cave that . . . yes, I know it, why?"

"Anyone ever find gold in it?"

"Oh, no! They've gone over that area seven ways from Sunday. Ain't nobody ever found no gold atall back in there."

"What would you say them drunken miners crave even more than the licker that they keep trying to drink the world out of?"

"That's easy," Said Ernest, "More gold!"

"Right," Smiled Mal. And if a miner, say one that nobody knows, came whoopin' and hollerin' and flashing a handful of nuggets that he said he just found back in that cave, what do you think would happen?"

"They'd be panic, that's what. They'd be another gold rush bigger that the first one."

"Right, and they would probably rush off and leave those slaves unguarded, would ye say?

"Oh-h-h, Yea-a-a-h," Said Ernest, starting to understand.

"Now, Little Wolf, if there wern't nobody watching, how long would it take you and me to sneak in and snip that chain and get those slaves out of there and up the hill?"

"I would say about three minutes, Big Hair." Said Little Wolf, smiling."

"Well," Said Malaki, What would you boys say to dropping in on those miners tomorrow, say when the sun is high and will shine good on those gold nuggets, and do us a little slave saving?"

Chapter 33

✿

The *USS Mailsailer* was just pulling away from the dock and Pastor Moses Thornberry heard the *toot-toot* goodbye from his friend Lester Whiteside, and waved. Lester, a tall, red-headed offshoot of an Irish mother and a Jamaican daddy has been the barefooted skipper of the little mail steamer since they first started making deliveries from the mainland fifteen years ago.

He looked down at the little canvas pouch Lester had given him. "And looky here," He said out loud, "This looks like another week's worth of good news and bad news and happy news and exciting news and any other kind of news that keeps all us island folks talkin' to the rest of the world."

Every Tuesday, as long as Moses cared to think back, he has taken the walk down the path from The Gullah Church and Social Center to meet Lester, pick up the mail, bring it back up to the Center and put it in little cubby holes. Then, the best part, he would dust off the cane-bottom rocker, put his feet up on the porch railing and set back to wait for them who come to fetch it. He loved his life. His was truly the arm that reaches out every week to join the people of Little Majorca Island with their loved ones across the water, and more like than not, Moses is more excited than anyone, to see what he brought

Today, however, it was so pretty he decided to sit in the shade of a palmetto tree, light up a corn cob, and read his first. There were three. One was from someone named *Mia McNabb*. It was postmarked Galveston Island, Texas. "Hm-m-m" He thought, "McNabb? That's the same name as young Jesse but I don't know any McNabbs in Texas."

The second one was from someone named Otis McNabb and it came all the way from Aberdeen, Scotland. "Hm-m-m," He said again. "Another McNabb." That's also the same name as young Jesse, but I don't know any McNabbs in Scotland."

The third was a more familiar, long awaited, letter from Leolla and Malaki.

Moses hefted and weighed them all in his mind and decided that the one from Texas and the one from Scotland was probably going to boggle down his mind and require some heavy thinking and he just couldn't imagine, after waiting so long for any news from Leolla, how he could read and enjoy her letter with a boggled down and heavy mind, so he opened her's first.

Dear Daddy,

First off, I would like to apologize for not writing for so long, but if you got the newspaper from the mainland, you will get some idea of what has been going on here on the mountain. In my last letter, I told you about getting attacked by a bear

and being saved by the same Spirit Horse, or mule or whatever it was that Malaki swears he saw after the Battle of New Orleans, and how Jesse was hurt and taken to the Cherokee Village, where they nursed him back to health. Well, we have been living with them ever since, but there is more to it than that.

If you get the papers from the mainland, you've probably read the headlines about the terrible treatment of the Cherokees here in the Quabalaka Mountain Range by the United States Army. They attacked the village and forced over twenty thousand Cherokee people, in the dead of winter, with no blankets or warm clothing atall, to "walk", mind you, over two thousand miles to the Oklahoma, Indian Territory. A great many of them died along the way. They, and the country are calling this shameful and agonizing trip . . . The Trail Of Tears.

However, as predicted by their Holy man, the army didn't get them all. Jesse, Mal and I, along with about three hundred Indians hid and are now living in a secret, secluded valley that the army can't find. It is so-o-o beautiful, Daddy, you will love it. The Cherokee have adopted us into their tribe and have given us Indian names. Jesse has become "Man Who Hunts Himself" and Malaki is now "Big Hair". Don't you love it?

Don't worry about us, with any luck at all, this will be a new beginning for us all. There are lots of plans being made and after we get settled we want you to come here and meet these wonderful people. Please say you will. I know they will love you and all your stories.

Now, Malaki wanted me to give you a progress report on the Posy slaves. As you know, they were being held in the miner's camp and, so far, nobody knows what happened to the sheriff, but my two heroes and a young Cherokee named Little Fox went after them.

Jesse dressed up like a miner an plans to go into the miners camp and distract them while Mal and Little Fox cut the three posy boys loose and bring them back here to safety. They will be a welcome addition to our group, in that they worked at the lumber yard when they were owned by Mr. Posy, and we are hoping that they can set up a new saw mill and help us build our town.

The miners are really mad and I'm sure our troubles are not over, but I'll let you know when it is safe and perhaps you could come and see us.

I haven't told Malaki yet, but I'm pregnant and I miss my Daddy.

All our love
Leolla.

"She's WHAT??" Moses let out a whoop and threw his letters in the air. One flew back into the water. "How about that, Ole Man Moses Thornberry? After all this time, you is going to be a Granddaddy!" He yelled, as he fished the letter out of the water and put it on a rock to dry out.

"I just knew, when I woke up this morning and looked out at God's pretty earth, that this was going to be a good day!" He looked up at the sun. "And looky there, it ain't even noon yet. Then he looked down, at the other two letters. "Hm-m-m-m, Hope I didn't speak to quick. I best see who else wants to talk to me afore I do any more high-steppin'" He opened the one from Mia.

Dear Pastor Thornberry,

You don't know me, but my name is Mia McNabb, I am the Great Granddaughter of the honorable Fergus McNabb who lives in Inverness Scotland, which is a town in the Scottish Highlands.

Over a year ago, he sent me to the United States to search for his younger brother Duncan, who fought with him in The Battle of New Orleans back in 1812. During that battle, Duncan was feared killed after having saved the life of his older brother, and for over twenty years, Fergus has lived with that reality.

However, recently, due to a vision he had while in a coma, of a great white mule who told him, in words, that "He who saved your life, lives," he is convinced that the vision was referring to his brother and his lost hope has been restored. That was when he sent for me.

I sailed to the United States and for two and a half years, my colleague and I have been searching for Duncan McNabb. My colleague's name is Mr. Barnwell Jackson, of the New Orleans Pickyune newspaper where my search began and even though we quickly confirmed the existence of a Duncan McNabb, there was no clue that would tell us if her was dead or alive. His name did not show up on any of the rosters posted after the battle. He just disappeared.

Then, going through the archives, we came across an article of a wounded soldier who saw a glowing, white mule on the battle field and I was reminded of the one in my Great Grandfather's vision. It wasn't much, but it was a clue.

So far, that clue has led us to military bases, hospitals, pirate ships and ultimately here to Galveston Island, Texas where we interviewed a Dr. Drey DuPhol, the attending physician to the pirate Jean LaFitte and knew of the existence of a young British soldier who lost his memory and had a gun with "McNabb" written on it. They gave him the surname of Jesse Lafayette and with the gun, our elusive wounded soldier became Jesse Lafayette McNabb . . . who is traveling with a Malaki and Leolla Messer, (formally Leolla Thornberry) which brings my search to you.

We will be arriving on Little Majorca Island one week from today in hopes that you will be able to help us.

I remain yours, sincerely, Mia McNabb

"Well, I'll be dogged," Moses mumbled to himself. "I think I'm the only one in this whole family that *ain't* seen that big white Mule. Wouldn't it be something, though, if my boy Jesse, or, what was it . . . oh yes, *Man Who Hunts Himself,* turned out to be the Honorable Duncan McNabb, a rich clansman from the Scottish Highlands? Nah-h-h, things like that don't happen in real life . . . . but, still . . ."

He took off his old, felt hat and bowed his head. "Lord, with all the fighting and wars and trouble going on, I want to thank you for watching over all my loved ones. Maybe, someday, we can learn how to live in peace and love for each other and we could haul out that old golden rule of yours and dust it off and, maybe, do a better job of living by it than we have been.

Thank you for saving the Posy slaves, Lord. They're good people and after living half a lifetime as slaves, they surely have earned the right to know what it feels like to be free.

Now that I'm thinking about that, Lord and since I'm praying anyhow, I'd like to put in a good word for that feller up in Illinois. Lincoln, I think it is. Be with him, Lord. Lead him, and maybe someday soon we could have a world without slavery. I just hope, beyond hope, that we don't have to kill each other to get it.

Oh! One other thing, Lord, if that big white mule named Glory is one of your angels . . . I would ask your to give her a big hug for me. She surely is doing a good job of watching over a lot of people I love.

Thank you Lord. I guess that's all for now and I better get back to my letters. It appears that I haven't met the whole family yet.

In thy name I pray, Amen."

Moses looked at the return address on the envelope. "Mia McNabb introduced me to Fergus McNabb, brother to Duncan McNabb . . . who could be Jesse Lafayette McNabb. I guess, Otis, you're about to tell me where you fit in to all this . . . . ain't you.

To: Reverend Moses Thornberry
P.O. Little Majorca Island
United States of America

My good Sir,
My name is Otis McNabb. I am banker, adviser and personal companion to The Honorable Fergus McNabb, head of the McNabb Clan, here in Inverness Scotland. It is our understanding that you have already met my cousin and his Great Granddaughter, Mia McNabb, who is searching for his brother, Duncan, who was reported killed in the Battle of New Orleans but may still be alive.
According to Mia's letters to her Great Grandfather, it appears that her search is coming to a head in the Quabalaka Mountain Range just north of Little Majorca Island on the mainland. She also informed us that your daughter and her husband are with

Master Duncan. That is, if it is indeed Master Duncan, and she intends to form a party to go into those mountains and culminate the hunt.

With headlines on the front pages of most newspapers around the world reporting the trouble with the US government and the Cherokee Nation living in those mountains, Fergus feels it is not plausible to ask Mia, no matter how eager she is, to face this alone. I also feel that you have the same concern for your daughter.

You have our sincere promise that any costs or expenses occurred by her while she is searching in your area, will be met by us, without question. An account has been set up in her name at the Bank of Scotland in New York City and funds will be made available.

So, even though Fergus McNabb is not of the best of health, he has asked me to arrange passage to the US and on to Little Majorca Island as soon as possible. I have done so and we will be arriving in about a week to ten days. We seek your advice on the best form of transportation up into those mountains, what supplies and arms we should take and advice on who we should include in the party to assure our safety.

Since we will be en route, it will be impossible to reply to this letter, but hope this request is doable.

Our sincere thanks,
Otis and Fergus McNabb.

"Uh-u-u-huh!" Moses grunted as he checked the date on this one. "I would say, Mr. Otis McNabb, that you couldn't be more than a day behind your Grand Niece. "I surely do hope we have enough beds for everybody," He mumbled as he headed over to Silas Jones' blacksmith barn to see if he still had that herd of donkeys in his back corral.

Chapter 34

❧

"I don't know, Sarge. Nobody said nothing about requisitioning a twelve pounder *Napoleon* for training purposes. I know ye got the paper signed by Captain Freeman 'n the keys to the compound, 'n all, but . . . well, I heard you got yourself in some kind of trouble down there and I . . ."

"Look here, Private!" Yelled Sergeant Splinter, what I do in my own life ain't none of your business. All you need to know is that I am a sergeant and you is a private and I got six men and an eight horse team waiting out yonder and we have orders to have one twelve pound *Napoleon* and three of them explosive shells in front of General Winfield Scott's office before dark. Now hop to it!"

"Maybe I ought to check this out with the Lieutenant first, Sarge, cause . . ."

"We are already two hours behind schedule, Private! If I have to go back and tell Captain Freeman that he has to go tell General Scott that we are delayed because a private . . . what is your name anyhow, private?"

"Lobinski, Sergeant . . ."

". . . because a Private Lobinski wouldn't release the cannon until he found Lieutenant . . . and what's his name?

'Leu . . . Lieutenant Jasper," Stuttered Private Lobinski.

". . . until he found Lieutenant Jasper, just who do you think General Scott and Captain Freeman and Lieutenant Jasper are going to point their fingers at?"

"I . . . I see what you mean, Sarge. I guess it's OK if you will just sign this here release form, I'll open the gates."

"Good, Private. I will be sure to let the General know how cooperative you have been."

"Geese, Sarge, thanks a lot. I appreciate that."

"Think nothing about it, Private. You're a good man."

———•———

By sundown that night, the twelve pounder was hidden in it's covered wagon under a blanket of pine needles back behind the miners camp. Ex-Sergenat Burt Splinter was sitting with a group of drunken miners by the fire, passing the jug and congratulating themselves. With a chaw in one cheek and laughing his head off, Splinter was telling the boys about his trip.

". . . And this stupid Private Lobinski was so scared by the time I got through with him, he 'bout peed his pants!"

A roar of laughter rose around the fire and Splinter turned his head and spit into the night and it landed on cheek of one of the three slaves chained to a sycamore tree at the edge of the camp.

"Oh, did ye see that?" Said the Sergeant, "Good shot, huh?"

The miners laughed and then they all started spitting to see if they could do as well. Pat, Paul and Oglethorp Posy turned their heads and closed their eyes, protecting themselves as best they could, but to no avail. When they looked up, the light of the fire sparkled off the tobacco juice running down their faces. Splinter and the miners rolled all over themselves laughing.

"Better clean 'em up 'fore morning, boys." Said Splinter, "We going to need to help push and pull that cannon up the hill, that is, if they ain't too sticky. They were laughing so hard they hardly heard the yelling and screeching coming from up the hill. Splinter grabbed his rifle and stood up.

"Wait boys! Listen!"

They all stood and squinted out into the darkness. Splinter cocked his rifle.

There was more and more yelling and the sound of feet snapping twigs and the rustle of trees until, finally, an obviously happy miner rolled out of the trees into the light of the fire.

"Stay where ye are!" Said Splinter in a low, guttural voice. "Make a move, and 'I'll shoot ye."

"Whoa, Hoss! Said the miner. "Don't get ye back up. I just saw ye fire and decided to drop in . . . and . . ."

"Who are you and what's you doing down here yelling your blessed head off? What you so happy about?"

"Oh, excuse me, boys, me name is Millhouse, Jacob Millhouse. I heard about all that gold you boys are scraping out of this here crick, and thought I'd come and try my luck. That's where I been, upstream doing a bit of panning."

"Where are you going now."

"Where am I going . . . Oh, nowhere in particular. I jes thought I would amble into town and talk to the land feller and see if I might get me one of them claim papers.

"Oh, you *did*, did ye" Said Splinter, "I don't see that as something to be so happy about. We ain't done more than ten ounces in the last two weeks. Just where you going to make this claim?"

"Well, you know the area up around that ole bear cave up . . ."

"You mean up where the crick makes a hairpin?"

"Yep, you see . . ." The miners looked at each other and then burst out laughing."

"Good luck to ye, greenhorn." Said Splinter, wiping the tears out of his eyes, "Ain't no miner that's ever come around that ain't panned that cave. There ain't nothing, I mean nothing within a hundred yards o'that ole hole. As a matter of fact, that's what we call it, *The Hole of No Gold.*"

"Oh," Said the miner, standing up and brushing himself off. "I guess I'm lucky to have run into ye gents." His hand instinctively moved down to the big pocket of his old buckskin jacket and clutched something. "I'll be taking me leave now. Nice meetin' up with ye." He started off into the woods.

"Wait!" Yelled Splinter. "You're just *too* ready to go. There's something you ain't telling us. You never did tell us why ye is so happy."

With that, he spun the old miner around and crossed his big arm around his neck. "You tell us what you're up to, or so help me Hannah, I'll break your dirty neck!"

"OK! OK!" Said the old miner. "Let me be and I'll tell you, but you got to know that just as soon as I get me one of them claim papers, that cave, 'specially the back end of it, is mine!" Splinter released him and stepped back. The old miner waited until they all had stepped back and slowly reached into the left pocket of his weather-beaten old coat and pulled out a small pouch of deer skin tied at the top. He untied it, pulled back the corners one by one and when he did, the fire lit up the three nuggets inside like fireflies in love. A gasp spread through the group.

One of the miners started to lunge toward the old man, but stopped suddenly and looked around at the faces of the men around him, and then darted into the night and up the hill. The others, including Splinter, stood there for a total of one second, and then . . . all ran into the dark after him. The old man stood scratching his chin and peered off into the woods. Finally, in a loud voice, he said,

"What ye think, Mal? Should we be getting back?"

"I'll be right with ye, old man," Said Malaki, coming out of the darkness with Little Wolf one step behind, holding the big wire cutters he borrowed from the blacksmith, "Just as soon as we have a word with the Posy boys, here. Who knows, they just might want to come with us."

The three slaves, who had been confused by the old miner, looked up as Little Wolf started his snipping and when they realized what was actually happening, all three broke out in white, pearly smiles.

It took just three minutes to cut them free and all disappeared into the night, except Little Wolf who stopped and looked at the evacuated camp. Satisfied, he reached up and took a bright red feather from his headband and placed it on the empty chains hanging from the tree.

"Are you coming, Little Wolf? We don't have all night, you know.

"Yes, Big Hair, I was just leaving a thank-you note from our chief."

When Splinter and the miners reached the old cave, there was a bit of pushing and shoving at the entrance but Splinter bullied his way in first and lit a torch. There was water seeping down the rocks in the back, which kept the ground soft, if not muddy, all the time. Splinter held the torch close. There were no tracks or signs anywhere that anyone, much less, a miner named Millhouse, had been in the cave for at least three months. When they went back toward the entrance, the only tracks were those that they, themselves had made.

"I think that old Millhouse feller wuz joshing' us Sarge." Said the miner they call *Sludge.*

Splinter was standing silent, looking back toward their camp. "Joshing us ain't the why of it, Sludge. They's more to it than that . . ."

"The slaves, ye think?" Asked Sludge.

"The slaves! That's it! Come on, boys! Back to the camp!"

The fire had died down by the time they arrived and Sludge jumped over it and went directly to where the slaves were chained, and stopped suddenly and looked back. "They's gone, Sarge!"

Splinter walked over. His face was beet-red. Sludge was standing there staring at the chains he held in one hand and the red Feather he was holding in the other.

"What's this Sarge?"

"Red Feather!" Screamed Sarge, whose face had turned from red to the color of the coals in the fire. "That's a message from Red Feather!"

"What are we going to do, Sarge?"

Splinter stood looking out into the darkness. Then he snapped around and grabbed Sludge's sleeve. "I'll tell you what we are going to do, we're going to answer this message. Grab some men, turn that cannon around and lash it down!"

"But Sarge, it's black as pitch out there. How we gonna see what we're shooting at?"

"We don't have to see 'em! Just one of them shell will blow a hole in that mountain forty feet across and will kill anything around it for another forty feet." Said Sarge, "They're obviously headed back to their cliffs by the way of Eagle Rock. Give *Napoleon* 'bout fifteen degree elevation, aim it just to the left of that tree yonder, load it up like I showed ye and wait for my order!"

"OK, Sarge," mumbled Sludge but . . ."

"GO!" Screamed Sarge. "Before they get too far!"

Little Fox couldn't see where he was going, but he had the forest sense of a Cherokee and the night eyes of a wildcat. He scampered ahead of the others and was approaching the base of Eagle Rock. Jesse and Mal were not too far behind him and the Posy slaves were bringing up the rear.

A great thunder sounded from below. Little Fox stopped, his eyes widened and he screamed. "TAKE COVER!"

Malaki and Jesse jumped behind a fallen log just as a great explosion happened about twenty yards ahead of them. When the smoke cleared, Jesse yelled. "Is everybody alright!" He heard a "Yes" from Little Fox and mixed noises from the slaves.

"Come,! Hurry!" Yelled Little Fox. They could hear sounds of trees cracking and underbrush being crushed by the huge boulders tumbling down the mountain side that had been torn loose all around by the shell.

"I do not think they will shoot another of their precious shells in the dark," Said Malaki, "But we better not take the chance. HURRY! It will be light soon and we must be through the Glory door before then!"

Little Fox reached the fault in the cliffs first and helped Jesse and Mal through. He looked at the sky. Dawn was starting to break. He went back down the hill about twenty feet when Pat and Paul Posy appeared around a gooseberry bush, huffing and puffing. There was no sign of Longfeller. By the time light arrived, all were out of sight.

Just before dusk, that night, Cherokee lookout guards scoured the mountainsides for any movement. Their job, above anything else, was to make sure that no one gets, even a little, close to the Glory door. When they gave the "all clear," Jesse, Malaki and Little Fox quietly slipped out again and back-tracked down the mountain to find Longfeller.

Unfortunately, the Cherokee guards were looking for a cannon and watched primarly what was going on at ground level. What they didn't know was that two days ago, Sergeant Splinter had posted a miner in the top of a giant sycamore tree on an adjacent mountainside, armed with a high-powered army telescope. His job, night and day, was to watch for any movement, man or beast, along the base of the cliffs, that might pinpoint the secret entrance. He spotted Little Fox who was the third coming and going in that general area he had seen in the last three days. He guessed the the secret entrance had to be somewhere around there. At least, he thought, within cannon shot. As he watched Little Fox, Malaki and Jesse dissappear down the mountain, he took comfort in knowing that Seargent Splinter and the miners were now on their way up the mountain with *Napoleon*, to be placed on a flat rock shelf half way op his adjacient mountain. Once they were sure of the exact target, it woud be impossible to miss it from there. He waited fifteen minutes and was now on his way to report his new findings to the sergeant.

Chapter 35
✿

Stanley Hobson leaned back in his chair and unbuttoned the bottom three buttons on his vest and looked up to Melba Holman who had just cleared his dinner plate and was serving him a small after dinner rum cake. "Mrs. Holman . . . I"

"You can call me Melba, if you like, Mr. Hobson."

"Then you can call me Stanley if you like, Melba. Ernest does. What I started to say . . . Melba, that was the tastiest, most satisfying dinner I'v ever et. What was it you call it, again."

"Around here, it's called *Iron Pot Wapiti Stew,* with roastin' ears and Irish potatoes right out of our garden."

"*Wapiti?*" Puzzled Stanley, what exactly is *Wapiti?*"

"Oh, that's the Cherokee word for elk . . . or deer. In our language it's venison, but since I got the recipe from Running Deer up on the mountain, Ernest and I decided to call it by it's Indian name."

"Well, next time you see Miss . . . er . . . Deer, give her my compliments, and speaking of the Cherokee, Ernest, when did you see all your friends up on the mountain last? Is the new settlement getting off the ground?"

"Yep, *Big Hair,* that's Malaki Messer, and *Man Who Hunts Himself,* that's Jesse McNabb have both been adopted into the Cherokee tribe and cabins and wattles are being built right now as we speak. I hope to start building my big trading post soon, where I'll sell everything from plows to beaver skins and Red Feather's people will sell their pottery and baskets and jewelry and such.

By the way, Stanley, I shore do thank you for loaning us back them gold nuggets. According to what I hear, they surely did do the trick. The saved some free slaves from gettin' killed and we didn't even have to cash 'em in. I'll get those back to you next week. I would've done it sooner except, until we figure how to build a road through them cliffs up there, there's only one little ole path leading in and out and it's a secret, a well kept secret, and until the army gets back to settle down all them miners, them that's inside can't get out."

"Huh?" Said Stanley.

Ernest laughed, "Just know that your nuggets are safe and sound."

Tricha, who had been out in the kitchen with Melba cleaning up, came running out. "Daddy, are you . . ."

"Tricha," Said Ernest, gruffly, Can't you see we're talking?"

"Yes, daddy, but you better . . ."

"Tricha! Don't interrupt"

Melba stuck her head out of the kitchen. "I think she trying to ask you if you are expecting company, Ernest."

"Company?"

"Yes, Daddy," Said Tricha, running to the front door. "Ether the army is back and those are the biggest soldier in the world, or we are being invaded by a bunch of regular people riding itty-bitty horses!"

"Itty-bitty hor . . . ? What are you talking about. He flung open the screen door and went out on the porch. The sun was low, and the caravan was silhouetted black against yellow as they came up the road but Tricha's description had been pretty accurate. There were big people and big loads on what appeared to be little horses. Ernest went back in and got his shotgun and they all waited. The caravan stopped about forty yards out, and the lead person dismounted and called out.

"Hello, at the house! We are friends! May we approach?"

"Who are you," Yelled Ernest, "And what do you want?"

"We are friends of Malaki Messer, and we are looking for Ernest P. Holman. My name is Thornberry. Pastor Moses Thornberry!"

"Thornberry," Thought Ernest. "That's a name I recognize . . . I think. Come on in!" He called, "Slowly!"

As they approached, Ernest saw that they were all riding donkeys coincidentally noticed that Mr. Thornberry was the same color as Mal and Leolla with three men and a woman. One of the men was wearing a dress.

"I am Holman," Said Ernest.

"Mr. Holman, so nice to meet you. Your name was given me by my daughter Leolla as a person to contact if I ever needed to find her.

"Leolla? You mean Leolla Messer?" Asked Ernest.

"Yes," Said Moses as Fergus walked up. "And I would like to introduce you to The Honorable, Fergus McNabb."

Ernest looked down at his skirt. "He is from far away Scotland."

"Oh-o-o-oh" Said Ernest, remembering suddenly, a travel magazine he read once on Scotland and all the men wearing kilts. "Begging your pardon, sir, for staring. It's just that we don't get many folks dressed . . . I mean wearing a . . . .I mean . . ."

Fergus let out a loud laugh and grabbed Ernest's hand and started pumping.

"Ae, Laddie. e know jus wot ye kin."

"Huh?"

"He says that he knows just what you mean, and he is proud to meet you. If we could go inside, I will introduce you to the others and talk of our mission."

An hour later, Mia, B.J., Fergus, Moses and Otis had all been introduced to Ernest, Melba, Tricha and Mr. Dobson. Their herd of donkeys, Henry, Lightening, Red-Head Rusty, Phyllis, Sunshine, Bobby and Big Boy had all been given fresh hay and were resting comfortably in the barn. Fergus had Tricha on his knee singing Scottish songs.

After a round of cold elderberry wine, Pastor Thornberry told the whole story as he knew it, about a British soldier who was wounded in the Battle of New Orleans and lost his memory. Mia and BJ picked it up and described their search through the years to find that soldier and how the recurring vision of a shining, white mule led them to this mountain. Then Fergus picked it up with a boisterous "Aye! Twas an Angel from God, 'ye kin. whas brought us here, d'ye know."

"So, when you put it all together," Mia summed up, "We strongly believe that the man known as Jesse

Lafayette McNabb or *The Man Who Hunts Himself,* may really be The Honorable *Duncan McNabb,* heir to all holdings, territories, titles and privileges that make up, what is known as, *The McNabb Clan* and if it is so, we are here to perhaps escort him back to his destiny."

"If I may," Said BJ as he stood, "It may not be as easy as that, Mia."

"Oh?"

"Well, I'm no psychic or psychiatrist, but if Jesse, or Duncan if you will, were standing here now, listening to you all, I'm sure her would be fascinated and complimented that you all came to find him and take him back to his real life, but I feel I should point out, that in his head, his real life started the second he opened his eyes in that medical tent in New Orleans. Everything that has happened since that time is what makes up his life now. A life that includes you, Ernest and Melba and little Tricha, Reverend Thornberry and your son-in-law, Malaki and your daughter Leolla, the Quabalaka Mountains, the Cherokee Indians and, from what I hear, Wings of Ivy, whom he loves very much. I dare say, if he did accept the life you all are offering, the only thing he could do with it, in his condition, is hook it onto the end of the life he has now.

"Ae, Laddie," Said Fergus, "Wha ye say be true, but e dinnae kin wit to do! d'ye?"

"No, Sir," Said BJ, smiling. "It's hard to say what a brother should do to convince a brother that his life in Scotland will be better than his life here, short of restoring his memory."

"How would you go about doing that?" Asked Moses.

"I would think," Said BJ, looking off into nowhere, That meeting you again, Fergus, and you Mia, and you Otis and listening to what you tell him about his beginnings, would ring some bells and go far in getting him back with us, but something else has to happen, in my opinion, something emotional or tragic, something that would shock him back."

"You mean like a fall or gittn' hit on his head agin?" Asked Ernest.

"Maybe." Said BJ. Tell me about this white mule spirit or angel. How big a part has she played in this whole drama?

"Malaki said he first saw her on the battlefield in New Orleans." Said Pastor Thornberryy. "When she saved Jesse's life."

"Doc DuPhol, over on Galveston Island says he saw her amongst the blue coat at the medical tent, in New Orleans, when the Feds came after Jesse for being a spy." Said Mia.

"Leolla wrote me a letter," Said Pastor Thornberry, "About her and Malaki and Ivy and Jesse and Running Deer seeing her when a bear attacked them up on the mountain.

"That's right," Ernest chimed in again. Ivy told that whole story to that injun prophet . . . Yeller Owl, about how . . . ."

"Yellow Owl?"

"Yeah, he was the one the army shot. He was one of the first that saw the Spirit Horse. In was in one of his visions, you know, them dreams that is sent down by the Great Spirit? Well, he told the whole tribe about seeing a White Spirit Horse with ears like the wings of Angels, leading what was left of the Cherokees to a new beginning."

"And, did she?" Asked Mr. Dobson.

"She shorely did!" Said Ernest. That's when Jesse saw her for the first time."

"Ae, un A see her in me dreams, gud, ye kin . . . twice!" Blurted Fergus.

"And I saw her, for real, on the side lawn of the McNabb homestead before I came to America. I know I did," Said Mia and BJ and I would never have met Dr.

DuPhol if reports of a white mule vision hadn't popped up in all those newspaper articles. It can't all be coincidence. It's almost like it was she who led us all here."

"And Running Deer, who is the wife of Red Feather," Said Ernest, "Tells me that the white spirit horse is recorded in Cherokee history and shows up several times on their legend skins leading their people toward the sun.".

Pastor Thornberry's mouth dropped open. "Dogged if I don't think I'm the only one in this family that *ain't* seen that Mule."

BJ, who had been listening quietly with his eyes closed, opened them and asked, "Has it occurred to anyone else that Mia could be right? That, maybe, the white Mule has led us all here and, in fact, is leading us now as we speak? I feel, that somehow, she is going to answer the question of what to do about Jesse's . . . or Duncan's loss of memory."

"I think yer right as rain, Mr. BJ." Said Ernest, pouring another round of elderberry wine, "I suggest we all get a good night's sleep and start up the mountain tomorrow."

Chapter 36
❀

Strong Eagle, the second son of Tall Trees was not to be seen in his "nest" atop a giant long needle pine, overlooking the deer path leading down the mountain. Even before he heard it, he sensed it. Something un-forest like was wafting up from below. He readied and arrow in his bow. The plan, if he suspected movement, was to shoot and arrow into a dead log that had fallen at the base of the cliffs. The sentry there would, in turn, send an arrow over the cliffs that would land in the level grassland above, where another guard would immediately send an arrow painted red, into the base of a live oak growing in the center of the settlement. A runner would then warn the Chief.

To Strong Eagle, the sound was coming from a number of people and animals who were trying to be anything but quiet. There was talk and laughter coming from both men and women, there were twigs and sticks cracking underfoot. There was the sound of horses hooves that clattered when they struck the stones along the trail. Strong Eagle let an arrow fly.

Red Feather and ten braves slipped silently through the Glory Door, one by one, keeping low under the bushes, careful not to be seen. They planned a rendezvous just short of the long-needled pine. Strong Eagle looked down and pointed to his ear at the same time he pointed down the deer path. The braves hid themselves and waited.

As the noisy column came into the clear, Red Feather recognized his friend Ernest Holman immediately and motioned to his braves to hold their fire.

When they came into the open, Ernest was on foot leading a red donkey with Furgus, replete in kilt and tam, gesturing to the wonders of nature, while Mia and BJ rode abreast of each other holding hands and Otis bringing up the rear on *Lightening*. He was holding on to his stubby mane with both hands, to keep from falling off. Red Feather stepped out into the open.

"My friend!" Said Ernest with the greatest of smiles on his face. "How good to see you."

Red Feather came forward, smiled and the two men grasped each other's forearms in a brotherly fashion.

"Ernest, my friend!" Said Red Feather. "I ask you to excuse the armed reception. From the thunder of your approach, we thought, perhaps, the buffalo had returned to our hunting grounds."

"Oh, I guess we were a little noisy, but . . ."

"Let us just say, my friend, when both our lives are normal again, remind me to fashion you a pair of moccasins and show you the Indian way of not being seen."

"Ha!" Laughed Ernest. "You got it, Chief." Now come and meet some people that you want to know.

"I have heard the thunder voice of the one who rides the little horse of fire since he first crossed the river of stones," Red Feather smiled, "Perhaps I should meet him first."

Fergus, who had spent the last three minutes getting down off of Red-Head Rusty without tilting his kilt, heard everything and gave the Chief his best smile, pulled his tam down over his left ear and held out his hand. "I canna say how guud e tis ti meet ye, Chief."

Ernest jumped in, "He said that he can't say . . ."

"I recognize his tongue from *Man Who Hunts Himself.* I have learned to listen." Said Red Feather, looking down at Fergus' knees.

"Ay!" Said Fergus, "Me name is Fergus, n e see ye wonder boot me kilt, well . . ."

"I know that as well," Said Red Feather, "I have heard about your hunting ground across the sea and what you wear when you hunt. That is where our tribes are quite similar, don't you know?"

"Ay? Similar? How ye say?"

"Yes," Said Red Feather. When you hunt, you wear, how you say, kil . . . k . . . kilts, I believe."

"Ay,"

"Well, we are the same, only the Cherokee word for kilts, is loin cloths."

It took about a second for Fergus to get it, then he laughed so loud you could hear it bouncing off the mountain tops for miles.

"And this is his great granddaughter Mia McNabb. She and Mr Barnwell Jackson, have been leading a search for over three years now and it's them that's brung us here." Said Ernest.

The Chief welcomed them.

"And this is Pastor Moses Thornberry, a holy man from the Island of Little Majorca and the father of Leolla, wife of Big Hair."

"Ah, yes," Said Red feather. "She has made slaves out of us all with her little sweet cakes that we cannot stop eating."

They all laughed just as Otis got his foot caught in Lightening's reigns and fell head over heels into a pile of leaves.

"Ay, we nae furget me nephew, ye kin. Last but not least, this magnificent horseman be Otis, Otis McNabb. Along with his ability to fall off of any animal you put him on," Said Fergus, "He can also add two and two and make them come out five every time.

"We are here, Chief, because we suspect that *Man Who Hunts Himself* is the one we have been searching, for many years." Said BJ. "In fact, we strongly believe that he is the long lost brother of Mr. Fergus McNabb here, whose life he saved in a mighty battle fought back in 1812."

Red Feather held up his hand. "I want to hear all, my friend," He said, "But first my braves will show you, one by one, through the secret Glory Door."

"The Glory Door?" Quizzed BJ. "That's what you call your entrance?"

"Yes, it is named after the white Mule spirit horse who first led us through. Come, we must hurry before we are discovered."

Fergus was the first to be led through the fault and he was in awe. He stood dumfounded on the overlook and couldn't believe his eyes. Here, completely hidden from the rest of the world, was one of the most beautiful, enchanted valleys he had ever seen. It reminded him of the green, plush hills and valleys that surround his beloved Loch Ness in Scotland.

Red Feather walked up beside him. "Does it please you, my friend from across the sea?"

"Ay, Chief. It be the most bonnie Lea me eyes hav niver see! Wi yon Lochs an linns it be . . . whit ye call ye white mule?? Glory! Aye, It be Glory-us!"

All Red Feather could do was laugh. "That it is, my friend."

Ivy and Running Deer walked up behind them, unnoticed.

"Could it be, my father, that you did not tell your new friend that he forgot his pants?"

Fergus turned and stopped in his tracks. He in all his life had never seen such beauty. "An who . . . wad dis bonnie lass be wha jus stole me heart?"

Red Feather laughed again at the expression on Ivy's face. "Mr. Fergus McNabb from the land of Scotland, I would like you to meet my daughter Wings of Ivy from the land of paradise and my wife and life's companion Running Deer."

Fergus fell all over himself saying hello. Running Deer was very gracious, but Ivy, whose hand he was holding, just stood and stared at him and said nothing.

"Can you not say hello to our new friend, daughter?"

"Oh!" Ivy woke up and smiled. "I apologize, sir . . . it's just that . . ."

"Jus wha, me lass?" Said Fergus.

"It's just that you look so much like my Jesse."

Fergus looked confused.

"Her . . . Jesse she speaks of," Said Red Feather, is *Man Who Hunts Himself*, perhaps, the same one you seek."

"Ay," Said Fergus, understanding, "An wha be the lad who's handsome as me?"

"Unfortunately." Said Red Feather, "He, Big Hair and Little Fox are on a mission below to find a brother, whom they fear is hurt or killed. They should return tonight, when they can slip through the door unseen."

Ernest, BJ, Mia, Reverend Thornberry and Otis were now through the door. A squeal came from the lean-to as Leolla came running across the compound.

"Daddy! You're here! I thought you would never make it!"

Moses flipped his old hat off and ran to her and they embraced. After a quick introduction to the others, Moses excused himself and Leolla and they quickly disappeared.

The others gathered around Red Feather and Fergus. After introductions all around, Ernest stayed behind to talk to Red Feather about what he had heard from the miners, while Ivy and Running Deer took all the others to the shade of their lean-to for rest, refreshments and above all . . . talk.

Ivy was all aflutter. Mia had shown her the flintlock pistol that was identical to the one Jesse . . . or Duncan . . . fired at the bear when he saved her life. She couldn't wait for him to come face to face with Fergus. She just knew that it would be the end of his lost memory an could answer the question of who he really is an where he came from. What she did not say to the others, was that it could also be the beginning of their life together. She just knew that his loss of memory was all that was standing in his way to asking her to marry him. She just knew it!

BJ, however, did explain that Jesse's recognition of his brother was not guaranteed and that the life Jesse has been living, may have filled his head with new memories and experiences that he might not willingly give up. He said that it might take more that just coming face to face with his brother to bring him back.

Ivy didn't want to hear that. To her, there was no doubt and she was living the longest day of her life. It crept by just a little slower than two snails going up-hill.

After what seemed like forever, the sun finally started to sink down behind the timberline running along an adjacent mountain top. It was the same mountain top where, just minutes ago, word had come through from the lookout, that the miners had placed their mighty cannon on the opposite slope and it was facing the cliffs.

Ernest and Red Feather were sitting near the live oak, deep into their plans and observations when a red arrow thunked into it.

"What was that, Chief?" Asked Ernest.

"It is most likely the arrival of *Man Who Hunts Himself*, *Big Hair* and Little Fox. They will wait until the dark of night before they come in.

The sun finally completed it's journey and soon the only light that could be seen were the fires outside the wattles and the ever burning council fire. Fergus and Otis were catching some well deserved sleep while Ivy, Leolla and Moses were still talking up in the lean-to.

The first to come through the Glory Door was a tired and worn out Jesse who was leading Fur-Ball who had an ominous, black draped load across his back Malaki was silently walking beside it and Little Fox was bringing up the rear. Ivy was the first to see them and ran and threw her arms around Jesse's neck. She wanted to be the first to tell him about the people from Scotland who were there to see him along with Leolla's Daddy.

Jesse did smile, but the only thing he heard was "Leolla's Daddy" and asked where the good Reverend could be found.

"He's in the lean-to with Leolla, but can we . . ."

"Good," Said Jesse, "I need to see him. I'm afraid we have bad news.

Chapter 37

When they reached the lean-to, Pastor Thornberry ran out to say hello and help wherever he could as Jesse and Mal carried the body of Longfeller Posy in and laid him on a bed of leaves. Leolla lit a candle and held it so they could see. A great gaping hole was all that was left where his stomach should have been. Jesse said they found him pinned against a large tree with a sharp stone half buried into his mid section.

"The pain must have been unbearable," Said Mal, "But look at him, in spite of it all, there is a smile on his face! Can you believe that?"

"He was holding a pencil in the fingers of his right hand," Said Mal, "And in his left hand, he held this."

Mal held out a piece of ledger paper like they used at the saw mill to count the number of boards they sawed. It was smeared with blood around the edges, but in the middle, there were crude, shaky letters written, so faint, one could hardly read them.

"I didn't know slaves could write." Said Leolla.

"Oh yes," Said Moses. "Mrs. Posy taught all three of them boys to write, 'n read too, least some. As I remember young Oglethorp, he wrote in rhyme. He said it was because, sometime you have to write things that ain't happy, but if you write unhappy things in rhyme, ain't nobody going to notice."

Ivy lit another candle and moved in close for all to see the words.

TO PaT
aN PAUL . . .
I SeeD HER!! ME eYES
DUN SEED MIZ GLORY!!!
SHE CUM TO BE WITH ME.
SHE SAID I AINT a SLaVE NO MORe,
SHE CUM TO SET ME FREE . . .
AN WHILEST I Lay IN ALL DIS DIRT
SHE TURNED DE NITe To DaY!
Au ALL AT ONCE, I DIDN'T HURT!
ME PAIN DONE GONE AWAY!

GLORY! GLORY! HALLaLOOYa!!!

GUD BI . . .
MY BROTHERS . . . .

Great tears welled up in Leolla's eyes and Moses put his arm around her. "At least, now, we know why there was a smile on Longfellers face. Someday, my darling daughter you must introduce me to the elusive Miss Glory. She and I work for the same boss, you know. She is everywhere she needs to be at the right time." He went over to Jesse and Malaki and gave them both a somber hug. "I best go find Pat and Paul." Said Moses. They will want to say goodbye to their brother. We will make preparation for the funeral tomorrow. He looked at Jesse, Malaki and Little Fox. "In the meantime, you boys go get some rest. The miners and their cannon are still out there and we have lots to talk about and there are people who want to meet you, Jesse but that can also wait until morning."

The next morning, Mia was up with the sun, standing in front of the lean-to when a sleepy BJ finally came out yawning. "BJ, has it yet dawned on ye that the laddie we have been searching, for over three years, is possibly sleeping in the next lean-to . . . and, any minute now, me Grand Uncle Fergus is going to charge out in this compound, bellowing like a bloody bull and insisting that he be taken to his long-lost brother and we don't even know if Jesse really is Duncan or not."

"Oh, did Jesse get in last night?"

"Aye, he an Malaki an Little Wolf bring in wi the deid body of the slave lad, Longfeller, dat is de slave lad's name, jus afor gloamin dis morn, they did. He had been crushed by a rock, he was, and not only that, our white mule, spirit horse hae shown up again, She has!"

"Really? Where?"

"I am told it was doon de brae in a place called a *Raven's Wing*. The Cherokee call it that, fer tis da steepest slope of all the slopes on the mountain, it is, and it lay directly below the cliffs which overhangs it and shades it from the moon at nicht and the pines have grown thegither so thick, they say, one can look oot in any direction at night and see only black. A black de Great Spirit made blacker than black, He did. It is, as the Cherokees say, 'black as a Raven's Wing.' I am sure you will hear them use dis phrase."

'If that's so," Said BJ, rubbing his chin, "How did . . . ."

"Little Wolf was leading above the Wing and knew they canna go doon thar at nicht an dinna stop. Then he see a glow far below. Malaki had a roll o rope on de cuddie, Furball, and they sclim down an go toward the glow. When they were most there, de glow wi oot. Jesse lit a torch an de see Longfeller there wi a rock in his chest, it was an the lad looked happy wi a smile on his face, it was. an in his hand he held a note to his brothers to say good-bye. It was in the note dat he told of the White Mule Angel. It was a beautiful note an was written in verse, it was. I dinna stop crying all nicht."

"That's fantastic, my love." Said BJ.

Mia's eyes rolled up, she did three quick blinks and stared into his.

"Who has the note now? . . . Mia . . . . Who has the note now?"

Mia said nothing. "What? Oh . . . Leolla, Leolla has it. She is taking it to the Posy brithers to preserve atween da pages o thair auld Gullah Bible. Wad ye like to read it?"

"For sure, honey."

Mia's eyes started to blink again.

"Would you ask them not to press it until I have a chance to make a copy."

"Yes, but . . . ?"

"It's just a thought, honey, I want to send it to someone who I know will love to read it and . . . ."

❀

Pepper Jean Salt sat quietly with big alligator tears running down her face.

"I am so sorry," Said President, elect Ernest H. McNabb, holding out the tissue box, "I certainly didn't want to upset you."

"I'm s-sorry too, Sir," Said PJ, sniffing and blowing her nose. "I'm not being very professional, I realize. It's jus . . . well it's just such a sad story. I think I loved Longfeller. Why did BJ want a copy of Longfeller's words?"

"Oh, well now . . . that's an interesting story all it's own. You see, while at Oxford, BJ met a lady named Julia Ward. They both loved to write and after graduation, Julia went back to New York State where she became a well known writer and poet. Her married name was Julia Ward Howe and she was an active abolitionist and wrote many articles and poems on the subject.

She and BJ kept in touch and when he read Longfellers words, he became more than just emotional. and realized that it was not enough for just their little group to read them, they needed to be read by the world and the first name that popped into his mind at that moment was Julia Ward Howe."

"Did he send them to her?"

"That's exactly what he did. Fort Sumter hadn't been fired upon yet, but the country was already starting to split themselves apart over the question of slavery and Julia wrote back that *Longfellers* life as a slave and his incredible words could be just the inspiration she needed to write a song for our Union troops to sing when, and if, they marched off to fight and make men free."

"Wow! Did she?"

"She sure did. At the peak of the country's anger, on the front page of *The Atlantic Monthly*, the title and lyrics to a new patriotic marching song was introduced. It was written to the tune of another popular abolitionist song entitled *John Brown's Body* but this one was called *The Battle Hymn Of The Republic*. It became the most popular patriotic marching of any sung by our armed forces as the marched off to war. You certainly must know it."

"I surely do!" Said Pepper. I've heard it all my life. I even remember most of the words. We even sang it in my church. Listen . . ." She closed her eyes and sang, giving every word what it needed to raise goosebumps on one's arm.

Mine eyes have seen the glory
Of the coming of the Lord
He is trampling out the vintage
Where the grapes of wrath are stored
He has loosed the fateful lightening
Of His terible swift sword
His truth is marching on.

Glory, glory, hallelujah
Glory, glory hallelujah
Glory, glory, hallelujah
Our God is marching on.

In the beauty of the lilles
Christ was born across the sea
With a glory in his bosom
That transfigures you and me
As he died to make men holy
Let us live to make men free
While God is marching on

Glory, glory, hallelujah
Glory, glory hallelujah
Glory, glory hallelujah
Our ... God ... is ... marching ... on.

"That was beautiful, Pepper. You have a beautiful voice."

"Well, it's a wonderful song and I just noticed that it gets even better when you know where all the *Glories* came from." Said Pepper, wiping the lsat tear from her eye.

"What church do you go to?

"You must know it, Sir. It's Saint Lucy, the great tabernacle in Sweetgum."

"Ah yes," Said the President Elect, "Reverend William Bledsoe and the Church of the White Mule. I was just a little boy when they built that church and I was so in love with that white mule."

"I wasn't even born yet!" Said Pepper. "But as I remember the story, after the church was finished, Lucy wouldn't stay and came home with you and your family."

"Ah yes," Said the President. She stayed with me through all my growing up years and, as I mentioned, after I was elected Governor, she dissappeared. I suppose she figured I didn't need her any more and went away. I still miss her."

"Well," Pepper said sternly. "It's getting late and this is probably the only interview you are going to grant me, so I have to make sure we're not leaving anything out. After you're sworn in, you probably won't have time for *little* people like me and since you're agreeable to not holding me to that one *question issue*, I do have a couple more. OK?"

"Pepper, you are anything but little people. Fire away."

"OK, ... In one of your speeches to the Council of Churches in Washington, you mentioned the Cherokee

Trail of Tears as the most regrettable episode in American History and it begs for an apology from the American people. You went on to mention how very good we are at patting ourselves on the back when we do something good, but when the time comes when we should stand together, bow our heads and apologize for something we've done wrong, we're miserable at it."

"Yes, I remember"

"You asked the Council to hold up their hand if they were aware of a formal apology for the Trail of Tears, that was written and passed by Congress and voted into law during President Obama's tenure. When no one raised their hand, you said you weren't surprised, because when it came time to post and publicise it, you found it *buried*, and you repeated the word *buried* in the middle of the mammouth and highly criticized 2010 Appropriations Bill and has not been heard from since. Do you remember?" Said Pepper.

"I remember," Said President Elect. I said that one of the first things I would do as President would be to go to that unfortunate Appropriations Bill in the file room and retrieve the apology, reprint it in every major newspaper in the country and take the *meat* of it and engrave it in gold and post it permanently by the right hand of Abe, in the Lincoln Memorial."

Pepper said nothing. She was staring directly into Ernest's eyes. One of those stares that remained a little too long to be just casual. "I was so proud of you that day . . . . Sir." Then she blinked, shook her head and asked, "Why?"

"Why? . . ." Well, Wings of Ivy that we have been talking about, was my Great, Great Grandmother. My little sister, Ivy, carries her name. I am the name sake of Ernest P. Holman who, with Chief Red Feather, not only showed us that red, white and black men can live together for the good of them all but went on to established the town now known as Glory Door and I am proud of every drop of Cherokee blood that courses through my veins. Is that enough?"

"I would say so, Sir" Said Pepper, who was starting to stare again. "Now, speaking of the Cherokees, we need to get back to the compound. Have Fergus and Jesse gotten together again? Did he get his memory back?"

Chapter 38

It was morning and the sun seemed to just pop up from behind a neighboring hillside. Longfeller Posy had been laid to rest on "Posy Hill", the newly designated cemetery named after him, since he was first.

BJ and Mia were sitting down by the water watching a school of minnows work their way around a lazy sunfish. He brushed a stray lock of hair out of her eyes and took her hand.

"Mia, I have . . ."

"Yes, BJ?"

"Mia, I . . . ?

"Mia!" Screamed a sleepy Fergus, squinting at the bright sun. "Guid morn ta ye! Wad ye n ye laddy cum up?"

"What were you going to say, BJ?"

"Mia!" Fergus yelled again.

"First things first my dear, Big Brother is watching now."

As they walked up, they caught Fergus awkwardly trimming his great mustache while half sitting on his cane and stretching to look into a shard of mirror hanging on a tree. Otis was feeding Furball.

"Da me brither get in las nicht?

"Aye," Said Mia, "Jus afor gloamin dis morn, he did, Sir.

"Guid! Guid! A canna wait. A think A will throw me arms aboot his neck an nae let go."

"Er, yes sir . . . but . . ." BJ tried to interrupt.

"A canna believe it, me wee brither alive! We mus tak em hame, we will!"

"Please, Mr. McNabb . . ." Said BJ.

"Fergus, e tis."

"Yes, Fergus it is." Said BJ. "Mia and I think we need to talk about some things we agreed on, before we see the man that you are so sure is your brother, for the good of everyone involved."

"Talk?" Said Fergus with a frown. "A talk, aye, but a wee talk. It's passed time fer me to o tak me brither, get on me cuddie an gae!"

"Do you remember, Fergus, when we were talking down in Mr Holman's house and we discussed the fact that we are going to have to give Jesse . . . or Duncan, a chance to recognize us, or you, before we start throwing our arms around his neck an yelling welcome home?"

"Aye, a remember, but . . ."

"We talked about what is in Duncan's head now and the fact that he is already living a life, a life that he found for himself away from Scotland. One that involves Ivy, the woman he loves and Malaki and Leolla and Reverend Thornberry and Ernest and Red Feather and all the Cherokees.

What do you think will happen if a bunch such as we came charging him like a herd of buffalo saying we have come to bring you back to your old life. A life, if you will, that you can't remember and you will live it in a country far away from here across the sea. What do you think he will say?"

"He dinna want to gae?" Asked Fergus thoughtfully.

"It is a real possibility." Said BJ, putting his hand on Fergus' arm. It could turn him away from you . . . forever.

Fergus buried his face in his hands and sat there silently for a moment, then raised his head, looked up at the sun, and over to Mia. "What dae ye think Mia? Ye, who is more like meself den meself, what dae ye think?"

Mia sat with her eyes closed and her chin resting on her fingers, like she was praying. Then she opened her eyes and looked up at Fergus.

"It appears to me, Gran PaPa, thae be twa options an only Gran Uncle Duncan will ken whit wey ta go, but atween de twa, de nae be guid nor bad. Thair both be guid! So, me Gran Uncle Duncan mus decide wha be de guid-er! He canna do that if we all speak at him all at once.

"Whit be ye say, Mia?" Queried Fergus

"A propose we tak Ivy, Malaki, Leolla, Pastor Thornberry, Little Wolf and Ernest, together ta one side. Thay be his present life. Then we put ye, Gran PaPa, Otis, BJ, meself and our whole herd of cuddies, if ye like, together on tother side. Thay be his forgotten life. Then we put Red Feather atween de twa.

Red Feather be de Chief of all the Cherokee and hae much wisdom and Grand Uncle Dun . . . or Jesse, whit ever, haes much respect for him and wad sit wi him. We ask Red Feather ta be de middle man an explain ta Grand Uncle Duncan wha brings us here to this meeting today. He be a great Chief who rules with fairness and wisdom. It could be that when he talk to the McNabb named Jesse, the McNabb named Duncan wil hear as well. Then, we sit quiet and wait to see what will happen. If the shock of meeting us all brings Jesse's and Duncan's memory together, then all is well and there would be much happiness an we all would be Grand Uncle Duncan McNabb's third life, which will be the one he and we live from here on oot."

"And, If that does not bring his memory back?" Asked Ernest?

"Then Jesse wi go on wi his present life." Said Mia and wi canna question it. He wi maybe marry Wings of Ivy and as they say in the wee books, live happily ever after and we all go back to Scotland wi the knowledge o knowing that our beloved Duncan is, at least, still alive and well and we will count our blessings also, we will."

"That is true," Said BJ. "Then, I suppose that if something did happen, like a shock or an accident, that *would* restore his memory, we could all get together again and start all over."

"Aye," Said Fergus, brooding over in the corner. "Tha is, if A am still on de earth ta see it and, if tha still be a McNabb clan fer him to come back to.

"One thing more," Said BJ, "Fergus you have never seen this man face to face. You will tonight. If, when you do, and you are sure that he is indeed your brother, I feel strongly that you do not let him know that . . . yet. If you do, and he does not regain his memory, it will question the very life he is living now and may become an issue he can't deal with. If the word "brother" is spoken, it must come from him. That way, we will all know that he is back among us."

Fergus said nothing, he just looked, one by one, at each face around him. When no one flinched, he reluctantly agreed.

Chapter 39

❧

Word was sent to *Man Who Hunts Himself* and *Big Hair*
from Red Feather that there would be a great council
fire . . .in the partly constructed council wattle house
that evening and that their presence would be required.
The area was cleared and a stone circle was built in the
center and wood was collected for the fire itself. Another
stone was rolled to the top of the circle and covered with
doeskin and a peace pipe was carefully placed on it. A
blanket was placed beside it for Red Feather, and another
on the other side for Jesse.

As dusk came on, everyone started filing in and
seating themselves. There had been a whole new council
elected since the attack, and Little Fox was elected it's
head. They seated themselves first. Jesse then came in
with Malaki, followed by Leolla, Reverend Thornberry,
Ernest, and Wings of Ivy. Jesse thought it strange that all
were invited, and as he started to sit down with them all
anyway. Little Fox caught him by the arm, said something
in his ear and led him to the blanket beside the pipe. Red
Feather then appeared and took his place on the other
blanket. Jesse is surprised that he was sitting beside the
Chief and when Red Feather lit the pipe, drew on it,
swirled the smoke and handed it to him, he was honored.

When the pipe had been passed and the council had
smoked and when the fire got to it's brightest point, Red
Feather held up his hands for attention. "My friends,"
He said, "We have summoned ourselves together this
night to see if we can be of help as we summon the Great

Spirit to help us answer a question that has forever gone unanswered."

Jesse looked down at his friends for a clue. None returned his gaze.

"On my right," Said Red Feather, "Is one you all know as *Man Who Hunts Himself.* We, the Cherokee gave him this name when we learned that his real name was separated from his soul when an explosion all but killed him in a mighty battle. *Jesse McNabb* was the name given him by the white eye medicine man but through all the years since then, he has never known who he really is.

I will introduce you now to those who claim they *do* know who he really is. They are from far off Scotland where their tribes are called Clans. They honor and respect their clans, as we honor and respect out tribes.

They claim that the same White Mule Spirit with ears like the wings of Angels that our beloved Yellow Owl saw in his vision and the same who led us here to this beautiful place, after the white eye army attacked, is the same mule spirit who made herself seen in the land of Scotland and led them through many countries and many years in a search to find their lost brave. Meet them now.

Mia, BJ and Otis and Fergus, replete in his plaid kilt, mustache and red bunnet, appeared to their right. Jesse was curiously interested and had a warm smile on his suntanned face and twinkle in his eyes, until the fire flared up brightly and illuminated both of their faces. Fergus looked at Jesse and stopped in his tracks. His eyes were wide open and locked on him. Fergus held out his hand and started to say something when Jesse, who was getting his first sight of a man that he knew he knew, but his brain wouldn't cooperate, grabbed his head and leaped to his feet. His eyes were agape and his fingers were buried in his long, blond hair as visions and sounds and aromas started racing though him one on top of the other.

He squinted at visions of sun shining on fields of purple thistle and snow capped mountains and golden eagles sailing to-an-fro to the perpetual bleat of bagpipes and the baaa's of sheep and giggle of red haired lassies and ho-ho ha's coming from under bushy, turned up mustaches, fiddles and flutes and meerschaum pipes and the sound of barking hounds on the hunt and castles and loch's wi monsters and . . . a great explosion . . . Jesse collapsed.

Ivy rushed toward him, but even before she got there he was back on his feet, a little shaky and a whole lot embarrassed. After a drink of water and a quick apologetic smile over to Fergus who had taken his seat, Jesse brushed the hair out of his face, sat down on his blanket again and the council went on.

Each person took turns telling their relationship to the McNabb Clan and how they came to know the person they call Duncan.

Fergus told the story of him and another boy who lived high in the mountains of Scotland and how they both went off to battle at the same time but he was the only one who came back. He described the battle, the charge, the explosion and how the boy saved his life and then just disappeared and after a year without word, he was presumed dead.

Then he paused, and with a tear in his eye, looked over to Jesse and said, "That boy wa never seen again, . . . until now . . . maybe? We be wondering, laddie, if ye, after all these years, could be him."

"Jesse had his arms crossed and his fingers dug into his own flesh as he looked up into Fergus' eyes, The visions were started again.

Mia noticed his discomfort and quickly stood up. She was relieved and happy that Fergus never used the word "Brother". He did well at portraying Jesse as more of a friend than relative.

She put her hand on Fergus' shoulder and introduced herself as his granddaughter and then described the dream her Grand PaPa had, where a white, shining mule came forward and said "He who saved your life, lives." Grand PaPa could not believe that the boy of which he spoke, was still alive, but he woke up convinced and vowed to find him.

"So convinced, he was," She said, "He called for me, his Granddaughter, and sent me here to America to find him, and it has been the greatest and most challenging journey of all me life.

It started in New Orleans, Louisiana, wha I met Mr. Barnwell Jackson, here, (he winked) wh . . . who joined me in me search . . . an what a search it be! Thegither, we left New Orleans an went to Little Majorca, one of the Sea Islands it be, wha tak us on ta Galveston Island, whaur we met others who hae seen them, they did."

Little Fox smiled as he looked at the faces of the council trying hard to keep up with her Scottish yarn.

"Each stop," She went on, "Had twa things in common. Each ha a sighting of a White Mule Spirit named Glory, it did, and each knew aboot a man named McNabb. So, we say, whar we find a white mule named Glory, we find a man named McNabb.

Tha trail led us over to tha mainland, an up into the Quabalaka Mountain Range to the town of Sideways, wha ye know, and then . . . up the brae . . . to this, ye very own Cherokee village.

She folded her hands together, propped her chin on them and looked lovingly at Jesse. "They led us here to you, Mr. McNabb, whaever ye sur name may be."

For just a moment, everything was quiet . . . too quiet.

Without a word, Jesse jumped to his feet, grabbed his hat and ran out the door into the darkness. Ivy rushed out behind him but stumbled over a lodge pole protruding from a lean-to and before she could get up . . . he was gone.

Red Feather looked at the puzzled faces of the council. They were puzzled and talking wildly among themselves. He held his hand up for silence.

"I thank you, my brothers, for being here tonight. Our intentions were to let you hear the story of *Man Who Hunts Himself* from those who have sought him for so long and hope that the combined inner power of us all, combined with his own will, would be enough to re-connect him to his own memory. Perhaps we did, I do not know. Before we leave, there is yet another to reach."

He raised his arms to Heaven.

"We came here tonight, Oh Great Spirit, in search of a name. A name that was lost in war. We know when you created us all and gave us Mother Earth and Her bounty on which to live and hunt and feed our young, but you gave us no names for which to call ourselves. You simply called us your children. You did not call us your white children or your red children or your black children, You just called us your children and left it up to us to be as one.

It was us, Dear Lord, who gave ourselves names and for that we ask your forgiveness. Little did we know that such a simple act could lead to such pain.

Little did we know that the very names we gave ourselves did not bring us closer together. Instead, they underlined our differences

We are thankful, this night, even as we watch the world around us enslave and kill and torture, that you sent your Angel to lead us inside this place with God's walls around us to shield us from the evils outside. Here, your white children, your black children, your children from across the sea and the Cherokee will learn to live together and may the names we give ourselves be as ropes, woven of doeskin to bind us together, not as fences with barbs to keep us apart.

A dark cloud hovered over the compound. Jesse had just disappeared. Strong Eagle, who was on century duty at the Glory Door, reported that he saw someone or something slip in and out of the moonlight just before daybreak but when he came down to investigate, it was gone.

Ivy thought she had broken her leg when she fell while running after Jesse, but Running Bear saw that it was only bruised and wrapped it tightly and gave her a wooden fork crutch to help her walk.

Fergus was holding court in the next wattle, with Otis, Ernest, Reverend Thornberry, Red Feather and Furball, trying to sort out what their next steps should be. Did Jesse's memory come back? Will Jesse come back . . . or won't he? If he does come back . . . when? If he doesn't come back . . . where will he go?

Ivy listened until she coldn't stand it any longer. Her life had just hit a wall. "Why does it matter if Jesse gets his memory, or dosen't get his memory?" She thought. "He remembers me! They say he needs to remember the Scotland that he loves so much. Why? If he can't remember it, he can't love it. He lives here now and he loves me, and I love him, that's all we need. He is Jesse either way, and Jesse is gone.

She hobbled back to her sleeping quarters to lay down. She hadn't been on her own mat for at least two days since the Council meeting and her fall. Running Deer had insisted she sleep close to her while she was treating her leg. Now, all she wanted to be was alone. As she pulled back the doe skin cover, she saw a package sticking out from under the pillow. It had *IVY* written on it and it was Jesse's writing. She quickly opened it. There, wrapped in oil cloth, was Jesse's flintlock pistol . . . and a letter.

Dear Ivy,

First off, I want you to know that I love you more than anything in the world . . . in my world, anyway, wherever it might be. I feel bad for running out the way I did, but it seemed like my whole life was being threatened by another life that cannot be mine to live.

I know that some of those people have been part of my past but I can't remember them and until I can, they are poor substitutes for you and Mal and Theolla and Reverend Moses and Earnest. How could I give up all of you for a life I do not know.

I pray tae God every night that He give me my memory back. No one could want that more than me, for a very, very good reason. I want you to be my wife, Wings Of Ivy, and I can't ask you until a have a proper name to give you.

I thought it had happen when I saw Mr. Fergus. My brain went crazy with sights an sounds and smells an music I had never heard nor seen before but yet I had. It was crazy. When it was all over an I opened my eyes, I was still in the same old world and it is not grand enough to ask anyone, especially an Indian Princess to share with me.

Tell Mr. McNabb that I hope he finds the boy of which he spoke and that I was sorry that I couldn't be him. It would have been a priveledge.

Inside this wrapper is my flintlock pistol. Give it to Mr. McNabb to give to the boy when he finds him . . .

I love you so very much, Ivy, and, God Willing, somehow I will get myself together enough to come back to you. I do believe in God, but I have seen no sign of Glory. I can't help thinking that she will be our salvation, somehow.

Tell everyone good bye for me and thank them for being my friend.

Love, Jesse

Chapter 40

❊

Mia, my darling, Our hearts are now one.
In light of our Glory, we've only begun,
I now have you, and you now have me,

And we sway with the Cher-o-kee

BJ sat with Mia in the dappled shade of a live oak
tree that marked the entrance to the Posy Hill cemetery.
Furball was silently munching the first appearance
of yellow oat grass that had popped up along a little
brook gurgling it's way downhill and the headstone on
Longfeller's lone grave glistened like a pearl in a coal
yard.

They had hardly said three words to each other in the
last half hour, and those were not about Jesse. His absence
hung over them like a heavy, dark fog that would not go
away. So, they talked about other things.

"I thought it be quite a surprise for Ernest an Red
Feather to declare this hill and the pond below as the first
cemetery for the town of Glory," Said BJ, "And then, to
go on and agree that all will be buried here whatever their
color or race is something our country's Fathers should
take note of."

"Ye right, me darlin'." Said Mia, "Just think,
Longfeller Posy was the first to die for our new town,
God rest his soul, and he be a Gullah slave! If ye or I were
to be killed, in whatever battle we fight in, we'd be put
right in beside him and be proud of it too. Would we not?"

BJ didn't answer.

"Would we not?" Mia repeated.

"What", Oh . . . Yes, you're right, Mia, it's just . . . ."

"What, me darling," Said Mia, sensing a problem and taking hold of his hand.

"Well, it's real hard for me to talk about dying when . . . well . . . when I'm right on the edge of . . . ." He lowered his head.

"Of . . . what . . . ? Mia said, cautiously.

"Of . . . ." He raised his head, and when he did, his eyes had a sparkle that wasn't there before. "Of confessing to you that I am hopelessly, head-over-heels in love with you and I want to ask you to spend the rest of your life with me and I want it to be a long, long life, not a short one."

"Are ye askin me to . . ."

"Yes, Mia," BJ said, looking straight and unblinking into Mia's eyes. Then he blinked and said, "And if you say no, I'll just shoot myself and go down and crawl in beside him!"

(Bingo! Did ye hear that, Diary?")

"I've known since I first met you at the train station in New Orleans that I'd finally met the girl of my dreams and . . ."

(Are ye still listening, Diary?")

. . . then we got so involved in our search, I didn't know how to tell you and no, well, it's just might be too late. I mean, here we sit and . . ."

Mia took both hands and held his face. "If I could, just for one minute, say that ye are mine, BJ Jackson, it would be all that I could ask of God. If I could have ye for another hundred years . . . it would be all gravy, it would." She whispered as she closed her eyes and drew him closer and closer to her until their lips met. She had never felt love like this before. It almost hurt.

Then she backed off, opened her eyes and they twinkled. "And, me answer be . . . aye . . . . Aye . . . . AYE!"

They kissed again.

"I do hope I'm disturbing you at just the right time," Said Ivy, who just walked up.

"Ivy! Oh, Ivy. Of course you're disturbing us, but whit ye dinna ken is, this handsome laddie jes asked me ta be his wife, he did!"

"O-Oh!" Stuttered Ivy, "Oh-Well, I . . . , congratul . . . . I mean . . . Oh heck, come here!" She ran up and threw her arms around both of them at the same time . . . "I'm so happy for you!" "Come on, let's tell everybody."

"Whoa!" Said BJ. "ASKING is one thing, GETTING is something else. This is hardly the time and place to get married!"

"Why not?" Said Ivy. "Cherokees do it all the time."

"Of course," Said BJ. "That was not a reflection on you or your people, but you've just come out of a terrible disaster at the hands of the army and we are now sitting here about to be attacked by a band of drunken miners and . . ."

"And what?" Said Ivy. Your news is exactly what I . . . . I mean, we need to pull us all together again. It could be a combination Cherokee, Scottish and Gullah ceremony and Leolla's daddy could . . ."

"That's true!" Said Mia. "But . . ."

"But what?" Asked Ivy.

"I was hoping that ye and Jesse . . ."

"Yes, I was too . . ." Said Ivy, pausing for a second and then coming out of it, "But, love has a head of her own, and she decides just when and where we will get married and it is clear to me that she has already decided about you two. What do you say?"

"Well," Mia said, taking a quick look down the front of herself and picking up BJ's hand. "This laddie wad look guid in any auld thing, but I . . ."

"You just leave that to me." Said Ivy, "I have been helping Indian maidens dress for their weddings since . . . well . . . since Indian maidens"

"Are you two ladies actually suggesting that we get married here? . . . Now?" Asked BJ, with his mouth open.

"YES! Oh, Yes!" Said Ivy. "It's just what we need. The white eyes, the Army, the attack, the time they held my father prisoner, Jesse not regaining his memory when he saw his brother and the death of poor Longfeller, don't you see? It's been bad news since I can't remember when! We need good news, and we need it now and your wedding is just the thing. The Cherokees LOVE weddings."

"Hm-m-m," Mused BJ. "It would be a good story to tell our Grand children."

"What's all the squealing' about over here?" Said Malaki, as he, Leolla, Jesse and Pastor Thornberry walked up.

"See?" Said Ivy, "It's fate! You needed a preacher, and look who just walked up. Now, all we need are lots of red feathers and two blue blankets."

———•———

Ivy was right. Even though they were still *under siege* and guards and lookouts were still posted in the rocks and the trees to report every movement made by the miners and Red feather had given strict orders that no one, would go in or out the Glory door until the second and third shot had been fired from the canon, but when the news got around the village center that there was going to be a wedding, the village center got as busy as a New Orleans train station.

Reverend Thornberry was beside himself. He, a Gullah, had married many a couple from different walks of life, but he was sure that he would never, ever, get the chance to marry a Scottish Lass to the Grandson of a President of the United States . . . in the middle of a Cherokee village again.

He hardly knew where to start, but he did know that the wedding had to be outside, because outside is the Cherokee's most sacred cathedral, with *Father Sky* as their roof and *Mother Earth* at their feet and everyone would come with gifts for them, such as corn and squash and sacred tobacco, for allowing the ceremony to happen in their space. He did, however have Little Wolf help him erect a cross made of timbers and placed directly behind the ceremonial fire.

He learned that both the bride and groom would wear a blue blanket over their shoulders, to be replaced by a large white one when they were one in the eyes of the *Great Spirit,* and that a special moment of the ceremony would be w the trading of baskets, with food and items that were symbolically special.

BJ tucked a locket with a picture of his Grandmother Jackson under some beef jerky, two potatoes and a mess of collard greens while Mia decorated hers with two of Leolla's sweeter than sweet pies, two red beets, a lock of her hair pinned to a red feather and, for good measure, she tossed in her diary.

Chapter 41
🌸

Mia peeked out. She had hardly slept a wink. It was her wedding day! Father Sky had done his part. It was a blue different than any blue she had ever seen, with just enough fluffy, white clouds to make it interesting. The sun had just broken over the mountaintops and was back lighting and blending a thousand different greens into the perfect backdrop for just such and occasion as this. Maybe it was just Mia's imagination, but there seemed to be more birds singing and more cool breezes blowing and more trees rustling than ever before. It's like all that grows and lives on Mother Earth had heard that there was going to be a wedding, and they all came to see for themselves. The ceremonial fire had been prepared and drums were lined up around the cross and the area where the actual wedding will happen was strewn thick with white dogwood blossoms.

Little Wolf had carved a beautiful, ornate ring out of a pine knot and, carefully embedded in it, was a fourth nugget of gold that he had been keeping for just such an occasion. BJ teared up when he gave it him to put on Mia's finger when the time came.

Malaki ceremoniously loaned BJ his precious white shirt. The same shirt he got married in but he accented it with a black, buckskin ribbon tie.

Mia, who never needed any help being beautiful, was resplendent in her bleached doeskin dress, with red and turquoise and yellow bead work forming an elaborate collar around her neck and with sides that were slit just enough to give a hint of her pretty legs. A playful buckskin fringe ran down either arm and the bottom of her gown was left natural to reflect it's origin but was kept high enough to frame her colorful beaded moccasins.

She carried a bouquet of daisies and bluebells, and in her long, silky black hair, she wore, of course, a red feather tiara.

Except for those posted on guard duty, the entire tribe of Cherokees of the *"New Beginning"* sat cross-legged in semicircles around the fire. Fergus stood out, again, in his plaid kilt and high stockings and his red *bunnet*. Malaki sat beside them looking to see if BJ had gotten any spots on his white shirt yet, and was holding Leolla on his lap, who wiping a tear from her eye. Ernest was beside her, with his slicked-down-parted-in-the-middle hair, trying to help Otis who kept fidgeting with the celluloid collar he always carried with him for just such occasions.

When the ceremony began, Chief Red Feather stood priestly, holding the white blanket under which they will begin their married life together and, beside him was Pastor Moses Thornberry, holding the same Gullah Bible he presented to Mal and Leolla after they were married on Little Majorca Island.

Red Feather held up his hands for quiet and motioned to his right, and then to his left.

BJ quietly approached from the south and Mia approached from the north, each wearing a blue blanket over their shoulders.

When the couple came together, Chief Red Feather welcomed everyone and choreographed the exchange of baskets. Running deer played a traditional melody on the flute with soft drums beating in the background. When she finished, Reverend Thornberry stepped forward and opened the huge leather bound, Gullah bible.

"Ladies and gentlemen, brothers and sisters, Father Sky and Mother Earth, we are gathered together here today to unite Miss Mia McNabb and Mr. Barnwell Jackson in holy matrimony. If . . . that is, with the exception of our friends outside with the cannon, anyone has reason why this marriage should not be, then speak now or forever hold your peace." The only voice heard was a lone papoose in the rear.

The ceremony went without incident. Pastor Mose presided throughout their vows and when they both had finished, BJ slipped the ring on Mia's finger. Then, Red Feather stepped forward and removed their blue blankets and covered them with the white one. Mia and BJ, holding hands, then came together and stood before the two of them. Red Feather raised his arms to Heaven and recited, in Cherokee, the wedding prayer. Pastor Mose then bowed his head, placed his right hand on the great bible and prayed for God's blessings on them, in Gullah.

The drums had started a soft slow beat. Red Feather held out his left hand and looked at Mia. Mia covered it with her right hand and the drums got a little louder and a bit faster and when BJ's covered their hands with his, the drums speeded up even more and got louder yet. They were building to a great crescendo and when Pastor Moses' hand came down on top of them all, they stopped.

Moses looked out and closed his eyes and raised his arms toward Heaven. "In the name of the Great Spirit and God Almighty, we now pronounce Barnwell . . . no, we now pronounce BJ Jackson and Mia McNabb husband and wife.

BJ stepped forward and took Mia's face in his hands and their lips met, and when they did, loud screams bounced of the cliffs. The drums went wild and dancers started stomping and the braves started screaming. This went on and on and just at the right time, it started to slow down and the drums were now maintaining a slow . . . soft . . . beat. Everyone in the center closed their eyes, held their loved ones and swayed to the beat. BJ was standing behind Mia with his arms around her waist. Tears rolled down her cheeks as she looked up at him.

That was about the last time she got to be alone with him. For the next hour and a half, lines formed and one after another the warmth of the Cherokee came out in force. There was more hugging and kissing and hand shaking than Mia could handle. Then, just as she thought she might rest, out came the food . . . and, food it was. Turkey and Venison right off the spit accompanied by everything from swamp potatoes, hominy, hoe cakes and hush puppies. Leolla's sweeter-than-sweet pies were the hit of the whole day.

Chapter 42

❁

Ferges and Malaki had just cornered BJ in a conversation about taking some of the Cherokee recipes and Leolla's sweetater pies back to Aberdeen and opening a restaurant, when he glanced back to see how Mia was doing and saw that she had moved over to a seat by herself and was deep in thought. He went over.

"What is it, honey?"

"Oh, nothing."

"It's got to be something." BJ said, sitting down beside her. "Come on, now, me bonny lass, this is no way to start our new life together."

"No, it's silly. You will just laugh at me.?"

"I promise, I won't."

"It was just something that . . . . well, something . . ."

"What?"

"OK, something that I promised my diary."

"Your diary?"

"Yes, you see, all my life I have dreamed about getting married, and the highlight of every dream was whirling around an around a great dance floor in the arms of me new husband . . . none as handsome as ye, o'course . . . and the orchestra had filled the air with violins and trumpets and bagpipes, playing a waltz as big and beautiful and Scotland itself. I could feel the magic throughout me whole body as ye, me husband, that is, gracefully guided me around and around through it all.

At tha moment . . ." She said with her eyes closed and her face raised to the sky, "We were completely unaware that there was anyone else in the whole of the world except . . .us."

266

So," She said, opening her eyes wide and blinking, "I promised me diary, I did, that whenever I get married, and where ever I get married, I would always bless me wedding with a magic waltz such as that."

"I see," Said BJ, rubbing his chin.

"I shouldn't have mentioned it honey." She said, holding his hand and looking into his eyes. "Please . . . don't get me wrong. I loved the ceremony and the drums, but . . . well, it's not a waltz . . . . an I'm afraid I'm not a stomper."

All of a sudden, something caught . . . . no . . . . grabbed BJ's attention. A thought, . . . well, not a thought exactly, it was more like a commandment coming from somewhere and it hit him like a canon ball. He said nothing. He just stood up, looked over the crowd and waved.

"BJ, have I hurt ye feelings?"

"Of course not, honey. I just need to talk to Ivy for a moment."

"Ivy saw him waving and came over. "Yes?" She said.

"Ivy, I want to talk to to the braves playing the drums and I may need you to interpret.

"Of course!" She said. "What do you want them to do?"

"Come with me, I'll show you."

They approached a brave sitting with a large drum and one large drum stick. Through Ivy, he asked if he could hear his drum. The drum went "*Boom! . . . Boom! . . . Boom!*" Then he spotted another brave with a tall, tom-tom drum which he beat with a much smaller stick wrapped in buckskin. The sound was higher and sharper. It went "*Tom!, Tom!*", . . . "*Tom!, Tom!*"

"Great!" Said BJ. "Now, Miss Ivy if you would ask the big drum to beat only once and let the little drum beat twice, the sound should come out something like "boom-tom-tom, boom-tom-tom."

Ivy spoke to the drummers and they were happy to oblige.

"*Boom-tom-tom, Boom-tom-tom, "Boom-tom-tom, Boom-tom-tom . . .*

"Oh, I see," Said Ivy, "Like a waltz!"

"Exactly." Said BJ. "Ask them to keep it up." And he walked back over to where Mia was sitting on their blanket.

"Excuse me, my bonny Lass, may I have the pleasure of this waltz?"

Mia looked up, and then she heard it.

Boom-tom-tom, Boom-tom-tom. Boom-tom-tom, Boom-tom-tom.

She stood and put her right hand in his left. He put his right arm around her waist and they both closed their eyes and swayed.

Boom-tom-tom, Boom-tom-tom. Boom-tom-tom, Boom-tom-tom.

As they swayed, a strange glow came over them and the B*oom-tom-tom, Boom-tom-tom* was joined by a pixie-like ocarina melody coming in from somewhere. It gave the impression of a beautiful bird floating in and out, and before they even opened their eyes, a violin joined the high pitch whistle and together, they joined the proud and majestic bag pipes that came in behind them.

Boom-tom-tom, Boom-tom-tom, Boom-tom-tom, Boom-tom-tom,

Then, softly at first, more violins and cellos and flutes joined the waltz-time magic and an oboe picked up the haunting melody and carried it up and up and up until, with the crash of the cymbols, a majestic crescendos commanded them. No more swaying, it is time.

With eyes still closed BJ stood proudly, and stepped out. Mia followed him as one. She felt a warm tingle over her entire body. Her feet were not even touching the ground. They dipped and they twirled and they glided and swirled. Around and around they went and as they did, the bigness of the orchestra gave way to the violins that seemed to be setting the stage for something else. The orchestra lessened and lessened until it came down to one long sustained note . . . then the ocarina came back in and carried them back to the start of the melody.

Then, she heard it. A voice! "Where was it coming from? Was BJ singing?" That thought took only a fraction of a second before she closed her eyes and completely dissolved into it's meaning. Mia didn't care. All she knew was that the voice was singing to her.

Oh, how we glide, like two feathers are we . . .
With love in our hearts, like slaves who are free
We know the Great Spirit—is in you and me,
As we sway . . . with the Cher—o—kee

"tom-tom boom—tom-tom"

We blush with the robin—who warms from our love
As we bask in the light—of miss Glory above
We wink at the stars—and the blooms on the trees
As we sway . . . with the Cher—o—kee

"tom-tom boom—tom-tom"

Then the music crescendoed and symbols crashed
again and more voices were added as they poured out
the essence of BJ's love.

> *Mia, my darling, Our hearts are now one.*
> *In light of miss Glory, we've only begun,*
> *I now have you . . . and you now have me,*
> *And we sway . . . with the Cher-o-kee*

> *And we sway . . . with the Cher-o-kee*

They swirled once again, the music started to retard, and
BJ slowly dipped and leaned his bride backward, and they
kissed. The music and the drums and the voices all faded
out together and left the two lovers quietly standing alone
in the center of the compound with their eyes closed and
their foreheads together.
They looked up at the mysterious glow. it too began to
fade and as it did . . .

BLAM!!!

A sudden, thunderous crash shook the earth. BJ
held her tight in his arms as they watched with wide,
unblinking eyes, as parts of the cliffs, far to the left of the
village, crumbled and rolled down the hill.
The second shot!

Chapter 43

Jesse awoke with the jolt. He shielded himself from the loose gravel and dust falling from the ceiling of his "man cave" and crawled toward the entrance to see what had just happened.

"Was it thunder?" He thought, "Or, could it be, that I've been asleep on the miners back porch all this time and didn't even know it? If so, Mr *Man who hunts himself*, That was their second shot?"

His goal, the night before had been to climb above the overlook high on the adjacent mountain, where he knew the mob of angry, drunken and misled miners had set up their cannon, and somehow creep down from above and booby trap their weapon. The one direction he knew they would not be looking was up. He remembered, somewhere back in his foggy past, someone telling him that the best way to destroy a cannon was to stuff it's barrel with mud so that, when it was fired, it would blow itself up. A good plan, but, if that was a shot he just heard, it's probably too late.

He reached the entrance to his cave, looked up and discovered immediately that he hadn't climbed far enough. Black powder smoke was still hanging around the pine boughs about two to three hundred feet above him. He listened. He could actually hear them talking and cursing to each other. He looked across to the next summit and saw the dust where their shell had exploded. He saw that several large trees had been blown away and bare rock showed where they stood and a small avalanche was crashing down harmlessly into the valley below. A lot of noise and a big mess, but they were far left and many yards above where he knew the Cherokees had settled and further yet from the Glory door.

He collected what he had with him, took a wide berth and started up again. "Why," He thought, "Dae I be doing this? Suicide, me thinks. Here I be crawling up a mountain atween the guid fowks I love and the blokes that wad kill em deid, they wad. Thair guid fowks on yon mountain wha have their whole lives afore em, they do, they deserve to live. Me? . . . it dinna matter. I didna have a name, I canna remember where I come from an I dinna know where ta gae. Except fer Ivy . . . I wad dee for me Ivy, I wad . . ."

He reached a spot several yards above the miner encampment, and quietly snaked down into a depression behind a rock where he could see, without being seen. He could hear Sergeant splinter yelling and cursing someone.

"You idiot! You couldn't hit the red side of a green barn on a sunny day.! Look out there, that was our second shell and all we have to show fer it is four logs and pile of rocks.!"

"It ain't my fault, Sarge!" Said someone else. "I done hit what you said for me to shoot at. I can't help it if there war't nobody there!

"Weren't nobody there! Why you four-eyed possom, you didn't . . . ."

"Sarge!" Another miner yelled. "Millard Perkins is coming in. He's calling your name. Seem like to be in a powerful hurry!"

"Perkins? The lookout? What's he want."

"I don't know, Sarge but . . ."

"Sarge!" Puffed Millard Perkins, rubbing his face with a dirty red handkerchief. "You . . . *puff, puff,* You way too high!"

"What you talkin' about, Perkins. Here, sit down n' get your breath.

"Perkins held his head in his hands for just a minute and looked up. "Sarge, the door to them cliffs ain't up here, it's clean down in the valley at the foot of them rocks.

"What? How you know that?" Said Sergeant Splinter.

"A twelve pointed buck told me, Sarge. I seen him."

"A twelve point . . . ." Deers don't talk, ye idiot!" The Sergeant handed him a jug. "Here, have a swig and start at the beginning."

After three swigs, Perkins took a deep breath and started. "Well, I was up in my tree with the spy glass ye gave, looking all around. I hadn't seen nothing atall in the four days I been up there until yesterday and I noticed the bushes moving and looked. It was the purtyest twelve point buck I ever seed. If I'd had me thirty ought, I could've picked him off easy, but I didn't, all I had was this here spy glass, so I jes watched him. He seemed to be going somewhere in a hury and all of a sudden, he turned dead into them rocks and dissappeared!"

"Dissappeared? A deer can't just dissappear!"

"He did, Sarge. Somewhere behind them bushes. I kept looking at the bushes and then I noticed something moving up higher and I raised up my spy glass and what ye think I saw?"

"What! I don't have time for no guessing games, dumbbell. We're down to our last shell and we ain't even seen no Indians yet, much less kill em. NOW WHAT DID YOU SEE?"

"Geese, Sarge, don't bust a corpuscle! It was the deer, Sarge. He had gone through that cliff somehow and showed up on the landing on the tother side. I knowed it was the same deer, I mean, how many twelve points can a body see in one day?"

"Can you take us there?" Asked Sarge.

"I can get you close, Sarge. but not plumb. Them Cherokee has got lookout guards in ever one of them trees with bows and arrows and they ain't aftaid to use em neither."

"OK! All you men gather around. We got work to do!" Sarge yelled.

Jesse had inched himself down behind a moss encrusted log laying in such a was that he could not only hear every word they were saying, he could almost feel the heat of their bodies, and heat there was.

"I want two of you men to dismantle this cannon and, Perkins, you fetch the horse team yonder, and the rest of ye gather everything up, check your guns and ammo.

Sludge! You go down and rouse that army of drunks and tell em' to brush the moss off their backsides and clean their guns. Before we lose our light I want this entire army to be re-assembled down at the bottom of the valley, ready to attack, the minute our third shot opens the door for us. By daybreak tomorrow, we are going to be standing proud over a bunch of dead injuns and a bunch of dead injun lovers looking at the headwaters of the crick that's gonna make us all rich!" A great cheer arose.

Jesse waited until they all walked down the slope raising their fist to the sky and patting each other on the back, before he sneaked silently down the mountain. He knew that, alone, he would beat them to the bottom by at least two hours, which should give him enough daylight for Strong Eagle and the others to recognize him and get him back through the Glory Door undetected. He had to get this news to Red Feather and the others in time to prepare.

With only one shell left, Red Feather ordered all traffic through the Glory door to cease. They had enough supplies and provisions to last for at least a month and he had talked it over with Ernest, Malaki and Little Fox and once again, agreed that the location of the Glory Door is still their greatest secret weapon. The miner army outnumbered their braves at least two to one, but if they can't get in, there would be no issue. The newly named town of *Glory Door* will simply wait. in silence until they fire the third and last shell.

"If it does not find our door," Said Red Feather, "We have won. With our armour around us and our bellies full, they cannot out wait us. If necessary, we will attack, but I am sure they realize by now, that without their cannon, one Cherokee in the forrest is worth twelve white eyes on the plains.

It was getting dark, all fires were out or hidden back under rocks and caves. Red Feather and Ernest asked all to speak in low tones so the enemy could not see nor hear that they were actually in there.

There was no moon expected and there was an overcast, which meant that not so much as a star's twinkle would shine. Soon, it will not just be dark, it will be another night, black as the raven's wing.

Malaki, Leolla, Fergus, Ivy, BJ, Mia and Pastor Mose sat in semi darkness around a single candle, talking about Jesse.

Fergus was holding Ivy's hand and talking at her. "Dinna ye worry yeself lassie. Amnesia or nae, Duncan or Jesse, now or later, he be me brither, an a canna believe no brither o mine wad ever lea his lassie in danger. He heard the shot, he did, as well as we. He knows the rabble will attack tonight nor never, and he will be here wi ye. A dinna ken how, but it's the way of a McNabb, it is.

Rubbing his chin, with his brows a-furrow, BJ rolled his eyes over to Ivy and said thoughtfully. I agree . . . "I think."

All the others patted Fergus on the shoulder and laughed until Running Deer popped her head in and shushed them.

She came in and put her arms around her daughter. "Be at peace, my Angel of Ivy. I know that . . ."

THUNK!!

An arrow with red feathers buried itself into the trunk of the live oak growing in the center of the village. A young boy ran to fetch it and take it to Red Feather. It had a note from Strong Eagle on it. Written in charcoal, it said, "*Man Who Hunts Himself is Here. Must come in.*"

Red Feather read the note and without a word, brought it to Ivy and gave it to her and went immediately to make arrangements. Ivy watched her father leave and read the note. It's impact hit like a bolt of lightening and released what had been building up inside Ivy since she Jesse left. She looked up into her mother's eyes, buried her head in her lap and broke into uncontrollable sobs.

Chapter 44

"It was right over there, Sarge,' Said Millard Perkins. "Sommers behind them bushes yonder."

Sarge looked, then looked back over shoulder, back to the bushes and said, "OK, get some men and haul ole Napoleon there, over to that flat rock, level her up and tie her down. From there, we can hit any target that shows itself, forty feet either side of them bushes."

"Got ye, Sarge. Said Millard.

"Are you sure they're in there? I can't see or hear a blasted thing."

"They's in there alright," Said Millard. When I was on lookout, I could even hear em."

"Hmm-m-m," Muttered the Sergeant, rubbing his ear. "I'd hate it if I found out later that we been sitting out here waiting for a sign while all that time them injuns slipped out some back door that we don't know nothing about."

He saw Sludge walking by. "Hey Sludge!"

"Yeah, Sarge, what's up?"

"See that line of bushes over there along the foot of them cliffs"

"Yeah, Sarge."

"Why don't you slip over there real quiet like and walk along behind them and see if you see any signs of people or cracks in the rocks."

"Got ye, Sarge." Sludge then crouched down, squinted his eyes, and looked both ways. Slowly and carefully, he started toward the bushes. About mid way, his foot came down on a dead twig and it snapped. He stopped quick, looked both ways again, back at Sarge and took another step forward. He was about to turn and wave to Sarge, when an arrow with red feathers caught him square in the heart. He grabbed his chest, twisted around and looked at Sarge with eyes as big as could be before they rolled back into his head and he fell.

Both Millard and Sergeant Splinter stood agape with their mouths wide open. "Where did that arrow come from?" Sarge said pointing his rifle up at the trees.

"I don't know," Millard said under his breath with eyes rolled up. "It shorley told us one thing though."

"What" Asked the Sergeant.

"They's in there."

Jesse slipped through the Glory Door as invisible as a man can be without being invisible. Red Feather met him at the top of the landing and they embraced, Indian style.

"I have much to tell you Chief but I must see Ivy afore we talk."

Red Feather hesitated.

Jesse looked at the reluctant expression on Red Feather's face and smiled. "Don't worry, sir, a dinna think yer fowks is going nowhere."

Ivy saw Jesse at the bottom of the slope. She came running. Darkness was starting to set in. All Jesse could see at first was some movement and then the movement became what he wanted more than life itself. They grabbed each other and hugged and kissed and hugged some more.

Jesse came up for air. "No matter wha happens tonight, Wings of Ivy, princess of the Cherokee, I wad hae somthin ye need to know

"What is that, my *Man Who Hunts Himself?*

"A wad hav ye know that a love ye more than life itself, a do, an wha ever we do . . . whar ere we go . . . an wha ere me name be . . . a ask ye tae tak it an be wi me tegither . . . fae now til forever . . . a do!

A giant tear formed in the corner of Ivy's eye and started it's journey down her cheek when she said, "If all of that is Scotch for *Will You Marry Me*, my darling, all I can say is *a wi . . . a wi!*"

He started to yell, but Ivy quickly shushed him, kissed him once again and sent him on his way.

The night of the raven's wing had arrived. It was pitch black. The human eye could see nothing. To make matters worse, Red Feather had doused every fire and blown out every candle. There, in complete darkness, with spears and arrows and knives and guns, red man and white man together . . . waited.

On the other side, after the arrow to sludge's heart, two hundred, plus, bloodthirsty miners, armed with rifles, sidearms, shotguns and knives split their forces and are now lined up on either side of the bushes ready to charge through the hole in the wall that *Napoleon* will give them. The cannon was locked down and loaded with the third shot ready to fire in an instant.

"Tonight, Red Feather, you will die!" Thought Splinter, "Sooner or later you will make a sound or show a light or make a movement and give me what I need. A target . . . and then . . ." He too waited.

Standing on the landing, just behind the Glory Door, Malaki and Jesse stood watching the dense black for something to shoot at when Fergus came up and started pumping Jesse's hand.

"Duncan! Me brither!" He whispered, "It be God Hiself wha brought ye back to us, laddie. A canna say how guid it be to see ye!

"Sh-h-h" Whispered Jesse, holding his finger to his lips. "It be guid ta see ye too, Mr. McNabb but a am nae the one ye search for . . . . Me name is . . . ."

"What are they waiting for?" Whispered Malaki impatiently.

"A target," Jesse whispered back. They dinna take a chance and fire their third shot at something they just think they see."

"Me brither's right." Said Fergus, "We fought tegither in New Or . . . ."

"What was that?" Mal broke in.

"What?"

"I thought I saw a light."

"A light? Where?"

"There, right in the center of the Glory Door." Said Malaki. "It's gone now. I guess it . . . No! There it is again! It's getting brighter!"

"It be Glory!" Whispered Jesse . . . then he screamed! "Glory get down!"

They were all screaming now. "Glory! Get out! They will fir . . . !"

BOOM!

They heard the thunder of *Napoleon's* voice, followed by the distinct whistle of an explosive shell coming at them.

Something snapped in Jesse's head! It was the same whistle he heard at the Battle of New Orleans! The same shell that was headed straight for . . . !

"FER-G-U-S-SS!" Screamed Jesse, running as fast as he could, grabbing his brother on the fly, and shoving him and Malaki as hard as he could back behind the huge boulder sitting in the center of the fault . . . . then all went black . . . . The shell exploded right on target.

The night came alive as hundreds of screaming miners came pouring through the hole. The flashes from their gunfire, like a million fire flies, lit up the dark. They were so loud and the smoke was so heavy, no one saw nor heard the low rumble at first and then the sharp CRACK as the fault running up the cliffs started to widen. Up and up it went until it reached the very top and when it did, the ground shook.

The bewildered miners started to fall all over themselves as they looked up to see the peaks falling forward, crashing into the great blue pond above them and destroying the earthen bowl that held it intact. When it gave way, billions and billions of gallons of water poured downward, widening the fault another eighty feet.

The invasion ended as quickly as it began as water, boulders and silt crashed down the mountainside unchecked, taking the entire army of miners, to a man, down and out the Glory Door to their deaths.

Chief Red Feather and Ernest stood, with the entire village, wide eyed on their vantage point above. They couldn't believe what they had just seen. The whole village had been steeled for a battle that never came and in it's place, was a miracle.

BJ and Mia came out of their *honeymoon lean-to* and joined Running Deer, Leolla and Ivy waiting for the dense smoke to clear and the dust to settle. Little by little the tree tops started to come into view. The sun had just peeked over the cliffs that were still intact and was now spreading it's beams down through a wide gracious opening. An opening that had never been there before.

"Good. Golly, Moses!" Ernest said as he and Reverend Thornberry looked down. "It looks like to me, Pastor, that our Glory Door has just become the most wide and welcome Glory Door-way we been dreaming about. Glory had it under control right from the git-go."

As the last of the smoke cleared away, Mia screamed, "Look!" And pointed. There she was . . . Glory, glowing through the last of the smoke as bright as anyone had ever seen her glow. She seemed to be looking up at her work. She looked to the right, then to her left, and up to those looking down. Then, as if she were completely satisfied with her work, her ears stood straight up and she slowly and proudly walked behind the rubble and disappeared.

———•———

Down at ground level, under what seemed like a ton of rock and mud, Malaki slowly opened his eyes. He saw that he had been slammed down by the explosion, into a crevice behind the fault rock which shielded him from everything, which was good. He moved all the parts of himself that are supposed to move and, with the exception of his great head of hair that was now hanging, wet, down around his face and neck like black spaghetti and a left leg that wouldn't work, he seemed to be fine. He managed to move enough of the landscape to sit up. As he parted his hair to see, he discovered that the reason his left leg wouldn't work, was because Fergus was laying on it.

He heard a groan. "Ye still with us, Ferg, ole boy?"

"Aye, that I be," Fergus mumbled from under somewhere, "But, a hae tae tell ye, twas a walk in tha park, it were. Now back in the battle of New Orleans, that wer a . . . ."

"Yes, yes . . . ye told me," Said Malaki respectably. Right now, If you can dig your way out of there, we . . . we have to find Jesse."

"Ye mean Duncan dae ye? Asked Fergus.

"Have it your way . . ." Said Mal, shaking his head. "Duncan or Jesse! If we can pull you out of there, we'll . . . well, we'll go find 'em both.

Ten minutes later, they were on their feet. Malaki found Fergus' cane about forty yards from where he was laying and it was still intact. They searched the immediate area from head to toe and finally decided that Jesse, or, they hated to think, his body had been swept out the Glory Door with everything else, so they continued their search outside. There were dead bodies everywhere and it took time to examine every one.

Leolla and Ivy came running up. Leolla leaped into Mal's arms. She hugged his neck and planted kisses all over his face and whispered in his ear. "I love you Malaki Messer, but you have to do something about that hair of yours."

"You ladies should not be here!" Mal said forcibly, sorta, "It ain't a purty sight!"

Leolla said nothing, but Ivy went ahead of them, frantically going from one body to the nest.

They went in the direction of where they suspected the cannon had been positioned. The rushing water had made a swamp out of the whole area and the going was slow.

When they reached the big, flat rock, sure enough, the cannon was there. Malaki crawled up to it and saw an arm in a blue uniform. He crawled closer, stopped and yelled for Leolla to go back.

There, half buried, was Sergeant Burt Splinter. His eyes were bulging and wider open in death than they ever were in life. They were eyes that were not looking at you but through you to some other world unknown, and jutting out from where his chest used to be, was the twelve pounder. *Napoleon.* The cannon that was his key to fame, fortune . . . and revenge.

Ivy came back in near panic. "He's nowhere." She said, tearing up. "I've checked every one of those poor devils out there and Jesse is not here!" She all but collapsed at their feet and started sobbing.

Fergus walked up and saw her pain and sat down beside her. "A say, me lassie, mae a sit doon wi ye a bit? A want tae find our laddie mair den ye, an a wad think tha ye an me tegither mae can dae it quicker."

"How?" Asked Ivy though her tears.

"Love." Said Fergus. "A dinna know who loves him more, ye or me, but it be love whit will lead us. Love is strang. It be love tha sae me brither lives an brait me here fae Scotland ta find him, it was . . . an It be love that sae ta me now, that he still lives . . . here."

Ivy raised her head and looked into his kind eyes. Fergus took her hand and his eyes locked onto hers. "If a put me love fer him . . . wi ye love fer him, atween the twa o us . . ." He smiled, "He lives!"

Ivy stood, her eyes were still locked on Fergus' eyes as they went back into the swampy battlefield, hand in hand.

They knew that when the cliffs crumbled and the basin gave way, the wall of water had rushed straight down collecting everything or person with it until it hit the valley floor, then it broke and went in two directions. One direction went through heavy underbrush and it was pretty clear that whatever the water washed in that direction could be seen, but the opposite direction was deeper and might possible support debris, so Fergus and Ivy went that way. As they walked, Ivy could not help but be impressed at how the rushing water had washed all of natures colors together. It was a veritable rainbow and then some. There were, at least, a dozen shades of green highlighted with red berries and whites and purple blossoms and yellow things and . . .

"Yellow! Fergus! Go back!" Screamed Ivy, as she went to her knees by a sunlit mound of sand.

Fergus came running up. "Wha be it Lass?"

"Yellow! There's something yellow here!"

"Yellow?" Said Fergus, puzzled. "It be mos likely a . . ."

"It's hair!" She had brushed some of the sand away and saw . . . it was hair . . . yellow hair, turned bright under the hot sun. They dug carefully, and sure enough, a head appeared. They dug more and when it was clear, turned the body over. There was mud caked all over the face and blood from a wound on his forehead had run down into it, but it was clear enough for them to know, it was . . .

"JESSE!" Screamed Ivy. Then she stood quickly, put her clenched hands to her mouth, as if praying and closed her eyes. "tell me he's alive, Fergus. Please tell me he is alive."

"Gae fetch some water, Lass. We hae tae get a bit of mud off him"

When Ivy returned, Fergus had the body sitting up and had shaded it with two pine boughs. He washed away the mud ad blood and examinaed the wound on his head.

"Is he . . . ?

"A don nae yet, lassie. I . . .

"FERGUS!

Fergus' head shot around. Duncan's eyes were open, blinking, but clear and looking straight at him. His left arm grabbed Fergus and pulled him close.

Fergus, it is you. Your are safe! Ye are not deid! My brither! MY brither!" Then he took his arms away and got serious. "Tell me, Fergus did we dae it?"

"Dae what?"

"WIN! Said Duncan. A remember, the twa o us were running an when a heard the shell, a . . ."

"In a minute, me boy, first a mus tell ye, thar be someone else here. He leaned back so Duncan could see. There, lit by a single ray of sun that suddenly broke through the sycamores, wrapped in hope and love and all the beauty God had given her was . . . Ivy.

Duncan looked at Fergus, then Jesse looked at Ivy. She rushed to him, put her arms around his neck and started kissing him madly.

When she slowed down a bit, he whispered in her ear. "It's over, me darlin'. Now we can be married and . . . . wait!" He looked up at Fergus. "Ivy, me love an future wife, hav ye met me big brither, Fergus?

They were dumbstruck. Fergus looked at Ivy. Ivy looked at Fergus. Then they both looked at Duncan . . . and all broke out in uncontrollable laughter.

Chapter 45

❦

*"I'll let you be in my dreams
if I can be in yours . . ."*

BOB DYLAN

285

The next year saw the culmination of a million dreams. Ivy and Jesse McNabb, were married in what Moses called his second greatest Cherokee, Scottish, Gullah wedding ever performed. (He even had them jump the broom.)

Fergus reluctantly agreed to allow *Duncan* to be *Jesse* while he is living in America, but the other half of their lives spent in their great manor in Scotland, *Jesse* had to be *Duncan.*

A wide, red clay and gravel road was built from the two-way fork above Sideways, up through the Glory Door, where it was deliberately wound around the lake and up and over an arched bridge just below the waterfall just to show off. Then it headed straight through the majestic pines, sycamores and dogwoods that frame the compound that will become the center of town.

Since the two-way fork is now a three-way fork, there is a new sign post. One arrow points to *Sweetgum, South,* 14 *miles.* The second arrow points to *Sideways, North* 6.8 *miles.* The third sign points to *Glory Door,* 1200 *Feet, Straight up.*

Ernest P. Holman designed and supervised the building of the town's first *Watt-bin* ever built. (That's the architectural mixture of a Wattle house and a log cabin") for the McNabb's to live in and named it *"The Wing . . . Of Ivy"*

Fergus and Otis stayed while all this was happening. He was fascinated and wanted to be part of the new world home of *The Clan McNabb* and financed the future building of the two center structures that will be built around a natural stone fountain and patio. One side will house the council Lodge of *The Eastern Quabalaka Mountain Cherokees,* and will have it's own stone circle in the middle for council fires, above which will be a round opening that will let the smoke out, and the light of the sun and the twinkle of the stars in. Around it all will be the pictorial history of the Cherokee, as they lived it, from the time they came to the beautiful mountain, through the tragedy of the Trail of

Tears and their salvation led and guided by the light of the spirit horse with ears like the wings of Angels.

On the other side will be Ernest P. Holman's *Glory Door General Store and Trading Post*, where he will feature outside stands for fresh produce, in season, a barn and corral for horses and donkeys and inside, he will reign like a king amid food for any kind of fixin'. Jerky, flour, candy, jaw breakers, chewing gum, brooms, blankets, pillows, n' wash tubs n' Indian sweet grass baskets, clay bowls n' pots in all the color of the rainbow and more, will be featured daily.

His haberdashery section is going to feature buckskin pants n' store-bought dresses, shoes, moccasins, cowboy hats, war bonnets, coon-skin caps and, for the hunters, bows and arrows, twelve gauge double barrel shotguns, thirty ought lever actions rifles, side guns, chew-baccer, fishin' poles, bait, and hunting knives. And, at Fergus's insistence, a counter of kilts, tams, bag pipes, flint locks and red bunnets.

Malaki and Leolla have staked out claim on a corner that is going to have a brick oven and fireplace and room for tables and chairs to sell her sweetater pies. Mal is already working on their sign, in spite of the fact that it will be at least six month afore it's built. The sign is going to say

LEOLLA'S SWEETATER PIES!
"Ye don't know sweet, till ye meet . . . Leolla."

Jesse and Fergus smiled as they watched Malaki trying to nail it to a post with Leolla directing.

"So far," Said Fergus, "He hing it too high . . . he hing it too low . . . and nau, tha bonnie lass say he hing it crooked, he has. A think it wad wark better to gie her tha hammer."

Jesse laughed. "Tha wad tak aw tha fun oot o it, it wad. Thay could go on lik tha ferever, thay nae care. Thay still be on thair honeymoon, they are.

"A been meanin ta talk to ye aboot tha." Said Fergus.

"Aboot wha?"

"Aboot a honeymoon." Whaur ye plan tae tak yer?"

"Honeymoon? Me, masel?"

"Aye, I be thinkin how pretty tha fall be in Inverness."

"Inverness? Ye mean . . . ?

"Aye, Ye need ta get home to Bridget, ye do, 'n tell her ye forgive her fer marrin up wi me. She wa jump oot o her skin, she wa, when she see ye an she wa fall in luv wi Ivy . . . nae to mention the fact tha ye need to show yesel to tha Clan. Tha still thinks ye dee'd!"

"Tha be true," Said Jesse, looking off into nowhere, "A'll tawk ta Ivy aboot it the nicht.

"Gud!" Said Fergus. Otis an me is needin to ga hame, wi do, an A cud nae think o naethin better tha ye twa be wi us."

That night, Leolla, Melba, Mia and Ivy cooked a "job-well-done super supper for Jesse, Malaki, Ernest, BJ and Reverend Thornberry.

Melba fixed another great iron-pot *wapiti*, with fried grits and Leolla's sweetater pies. It was a magic meal and when it was over, they all went out and sat under Leolla's sign, which was beautifully hung, by the way, and looked at the harvest moon while they all un-wound, sipping gooseberry wine.

Jess thought this would be the perfect time to tell them about his conversation he had wi Fergus.

"A wa tawk'n ta Fergus, today, aboot honeymoons." Jesse said under his breath, without looking up from his wine glass.

"Honeymoons?" Leolla said, overhearing Jesse and looking at Mal.

"Aye", said Jesse, looking over at Ivy. "He say tha Scotland in tha fall be pretty an tha Clan wa to see A nae dee'd an . . ."

"Aye!" Said Mia, jumping into the conversation and looking at BJ, Tha be a verra guid idea! Scotland be verra pretty 'n da fall! BJ, can we gae?"

"Whoa!" Said Jesse, "A wis talkin aboot . . . ."

"You deserve a trip like this too, pretty lady!" Mal said to Leolla. "Them Scots will flip their kilts when they see how beautiful ye are, and when they taste your . . . ."

"Nae, wyet!" Said Jesse, losing more and more control of the conversation. "A diddna say . . . ."

"Melba n' me would love to make it, Jesse but somebody's got to stay here and see after the buildin. Thanks fer askin, tho." Said Ernest.

"Yes" Said Moses. "You kids go on," That's a little far for this old man and I got to get back to Majorca."

"I think it's a wonderful idea, my handsome hero." Said Ivy, looking deep into Jesse's eyes. "Tell him we all love the idea, and when can we leave?"

The next morning, Jesse met Fergus down by the water washing his face. "Guid Morn" Said Fergus. "Di ye tawk ta Ivy aboot tha honeymoon?"

"Aye"

"Well, whit de she say?

"She thinks it be a guid idea, but . . ."

"Guid!, Da be guid!" Said Fergus, "Now wi mus pick a day ta . . . ."

"All o them think it be a guid idea." Said Jesse, without turning his head.

"All-o-them?"

"Aye, Mal 'n Leolla, Mia 'n BJ 'n Ivy . . . all think it be a verra guid idea." Said Jesse, looking up at Fergus, meekly.

"Tha all want ta . . . ?

"Aye," Said Jesse, "Earnest n' Melba n' Reverend Thornberry say thank ye much but tha need ta be sumwha else."

Fergus' eyes stared out at the water. He said nothing.

"A know ye was tawkn' aboot jes me an Ivy, but A didnae know . . . ?"

Fergus' head jerked around suddenly. "Guid! It be settled! We all go!" Then his eyes took on an impish look and he giggled. "Me dear Bridgett wi nae know wa ta do whin she see wha Da brung home."

The departure date was set for one week away and there was lots to do. However, a trip to Scotland was exciting and just the thing to get everybody's mind going in the same direction. Even those who were not going were just as excited as those who were. All the squaws in the village had to know what Ivy was going to wear and what she was going to do. A bunch of braves took a piece of buckskin and painted it red and green and made it into a kilt for Jesse to wear. The whole village was a-buzz.

News was also starting to get around about the new town that was happening atop High Mountain where whites and Indians and blacks will live together and share their skills, their food and their heritages with one another. It was an unbelievable concept and a steady stream of settlers, ex slaves and down-on-their-luck miners started coming up for a look.

Ernest and Red Feather decided, until the building is done, to have Running Deer paint a sign and post it out in front to greet them all, so Ernest had the Posy boys cross cut a slab off an old live oak that fell in a storm last year and plane it down smooth. One day later, a beautiful four foot by eight foot piece of oak was given to Running Deer to paint.

Mia and BJ took Ivy and Leolla down to the general store in Sideways to try on their latest store bought dresses. They bought six, plus two hats, walking shoes, toilet water, three different size suitcases and a steamer trunk to put it all in. BJ bought a camera and flash powder from the hardware store to take a picture of the whole town, to show their Scottish counterparts.

On the evening before their departure, Ivy and Jesse went to say goodbye to Red Feather and Running Deer.

"If we had not met you, my son, Running Deer, my daughter Ivy and I would not be here." Said Red Feather.

"Aye . . . well, aye, but if mi God, 'n ye Great Spirit, had not sent Glory, the white spirit horse to me on the battle field, a wad nae be here.?" He looked at Ivy and took her hand. "A wad nae meet Ivy.

"Now," Said Red Feather, "We sit here in peace as one family bound together by trust in each other. Never before has this been the way of our people." He then took the hand of Running Deer, looked into her tired old eyes and said something in Cherokee.

Jesse sat and waited. No one spoke. He looked at Ivy. "What did he say?"

"He simply said, *The world is changing.*"

Jesse smiled, got up and walked around the fire and knelt between Running Deer and Red Feather and put his arms around them both. "Ye richt, me friends. Tha wurld do be changin, it do, n' a hope we do naw to stop it." He gave them both a hug. "A thank ye both fer being me family, a do."

It was departure day. The entire village was up with the sun. Stacks of suit cases, boxes and backpacks were piling up on the green grass by the road. Ernest had arranged for a stage from Sideways to pick them up and take them to Sweetgum, where they could get a stern wheeler to take them down the mighty Quabalaka River to the coast where they could board a ship.

Fergus was pacing back and forth with a clipboard in his hand holding the list of everything and everyone making the trip. Running Deer had finished the sign and it was standing, proudly, by the front gate. It was now just a matter of getting everyone in the whole, entire village seated under it . . . and smiling.

"OK!" Said Fergus. "Wi seem ta be all here. Wi best gettin ta . . ."

"Fergus!" Yelled Ivy.

"Wha, Lassie?"

"Otis!"

"Otis? Wha aboot him? He jes . . ." He looks around. "Oh no, he nae here. Wi canna forget Otis!"

"Ain't nobody gonna ferget Otis, Mr. Ferg." Said Malaki, looking down the road. Look!"

Fergus turned and froze. There was Otis with Jesse's old miner hat pulled down around his ears, smoking the corn-cob pipe, and riding Furball.

"Otis!" Screamed Fergus, "Ge rid of that animal and come over here."

"A come over, Mr. McNabb, but a nae get rid o me friend, here. I bought her an mean to tak her home wi me."

"Tak her home?" Fergus' eyes were as big as saucers and his mouth was hanging open. "Wha ye think ye wife will say when ye walk in wi tha cuddie?"

"Tha be easy, sir. A jes tell her tha cuddie follow mi hame, she did."

Everyone was in place. The stage arrived. Time stood still. There they were, Scots, Gullahas, ex-slaves, Cherokees, six dogs and a flock of free-range chickens, all together, under a beautiful sign with a stately white mule figure at the top with big exeragatted ears and glow marks all around her. She was standing heroic, like a guardian Angel over words that read . . .

Welcome to
GLORY DOOR
The halo that shines over God's most beautiful mountain
Elevation 7,200 feet.

(FLASH!!!)

*The
Senate Office buildings,
January 18, 2024
Capitol Hill, Washington, DC*

10:00 *P.M.*
*41 1/2 hours
Before Inauguration:*

"Wow!" Said Pepper, with her head back and her eyes closed. "I can almost see it. Glory Be!" Then her eyes popped open suddenly and she looked at her watch.

"Oh' My Gosh!" Look at the time!" She said collecting all her papers, "I had no idea it was this late! I'm so sorry. Your story just completely carried me off to somewhere else."

"It was a mite long in the telling, I suppose, " Said Ernest, "But I just hope it answered your question."

"It answered a heck of a lot more than that, Sir!" She said. "It told me who you are, I mean who you really are, and why you will not go down in history as just a president, Sir, you will be known as a *people* who knows how to talk to *people* and more than that, she stopped and showed an embarrassed smile. "It told me why I voted for you. I did, you know."

"Thank you, young lady." He said, helping her pick up her things. "I'm sure that it was your vote that put me over the top. "And, you're right. If I do nothing else as president, I would like to point out to the world that long before we were white, black, Scotch, German, French, Eskimo or Ubangi . . . we were all people. Now, I . . ."

"I know, Sir, I'm on my way."

"Well, I do have to get my pants pressed and dust off the old bible, but before you go, I . . . ."

Pepper stopped what she was doing and did a double take. She closed one eye and looked suspiciously at Ernest with the other.

"Bible? . . . What Bible?"

"Oh! Didn't I mention that? Little Wren Messer dropped it by here yesterday." Ernest said. "You might know Wren, she would be . . . Malaki's and Leolla's . . . now let me think, great, great, great, grand child, I suppose. The family wanted me to use the old Gullah Translation bible in the swearing-in ceremony tomorrow. Here let me show you."

He reached down into the bottom, left drawer of his desk and brought out a large something wrapped in oilcloth. "This Gullah Bible, dates all the way back to 1823."

When he pulled off the wrapper, Pepper gasped. "I can almost hear the Angels singing," She said, running her fingers over the gold embossed letters on the old worn leather cover. It is so beautiful. Then she opened it to all the front pages that had been written on throughout the years.

"There," Said Ernest is the hand written proof that all we have talked about here today, really happened. I am sure that I will be the first person in the world, who has been sworn into the office of President of the United States of America, with his left hand on a Gullah bible. Old Abe would have been proud of me."

"I'm sure he would" Pepper said, grabbing her jacket. "I thank you for . . . .

"Pepper, do you have just a minute more?

"Sure," She said cheerfully. "Why?"

"I have a question too," Said Ernest. "Only one question."

Pepper giggled, "I think I've heard that before.

"Well, as you know, Inauguration Day will start Saturday and it's going to be a *Watch-Out-Katie-The-Did's-at-the-Door!* kind of day! I mean, it will be attended by everybody whose anybody. There will be Senators, Representatives, member of Congress, Supreme Justices, High Ranking Military officers, former Presidents, medal of Honor recipients and even a few important people."

Pepper giggled.

"Then the swearing in ceremony itself will happen on the Capital building's west front and like ever gathering in the history of Washington, DC, there will be speech making and more speech making. But, if we're lucky, they will commence to run out of steam after an hour or so and that's when the Chief Justice of the Supreme Court will have me place my left hand on that bible over there, and swear me in."

"Wow," Whispered Pepper. "Then you will really be President, at last. Now what was? . . .

"Then" Said Ernest, waving both hands up in the air at one time, "The Marine Band is going to break loose with *Hail to The Chief*!!. Can you believe that? Me? Ernest Holman McNabb . . . the Chief? And that's when . . ."

"And your question is, Sir?" Asked Pepper, cautiously.

Ernest stopped with his hands still up in the air. "Oh, yes, I'm coming to that. You see, this year, for some reason, the Joint Congressional Committee on Inaugural Ceremonies has seen fit to plan a ball that will take place in the rotunda of the Capitol building. You know, those kind of balls with a full orchestra with whole sections of violins and a grand piano and caviar and champagne and balloons and, out on the dance floor, couples from all over the world, with men dressed in black suits and beautiful ladies is long flowing gowns will glide around and around to the Blue Danube Waltz.

"Um-m-m." Said Pepper with her eyes closed again.

"Now don't get me wrong, I'm really looking forward to it. I know it will be magnificent and there's nothing I would love better than going around and around with a beautiful lady in my arms also, but . . . there is one little thing that the committee didn't take into consideration.

"And . . . . what was that, Sir?". Pepper said softly.

"I'm not married!"

"Oh . . .", Pepper's eyes looked into his, and she blinked, slowly. "And . . . your . . . question . . . is?"

"Would you . . ."

". . . Yes?"

"Would you be my beautiful lady?"

Epilogue

The swearing in of Ernest H. McNabb, to the office of The 46th president of the United States of America went flawlessly. The ancient Gullah Bible used in the ceremony was so big and bulky, it took the aid of two page boys to hold it on the podium.

It was reported later, that the Bible had been used in eighty six marriage ceremonies, four hundred twenty two baptisms, one hundred twenty six funerals and six hundred thirty eight births. Two hundred and twenty three boys and six hundred thirty eighty girls, with twelve sets of twins. All the names and dates were penned in the front twelve pages.

At the gala ball that same evening, America got their first look at *MS Mary Jean Salt* on the arm of the newly elected *President Ernest H. McNabb*. She soon became *First Lady* Mary Jean Salt, but the country loved her as *Pepper*.

B.J. and Mia Jackson moved to Scotland where B.J. joined *The Press and Journal* of Aberdeen and soon became their Editor in Chief.

Mia gave birth to three children. Two girls and a boy, Melba, Mary and Bagwell Jr. and went on to become one of Scotland's leading writers of children adventure stories, many of which took place among the Native American tribes of North America.

Pastor Thornberry stayed in *Glory Door* and started the *Second Gullah Church and Tabernacle* but divided his time with the church on *Little Majorca Island*. The Gullah population in Glory Door grew steadily each year as newly freed slaves sought homes. Their talent and gifted hands soon turned *Glory Door* into one of the country's most prestigious folk arts center. Pastor Moses lived to be ninety six years old.

❦

Malaki Messer fought for the North during the War Between the States while Leolla stayed in Glory Door during that time and gave birth to the baby boy, Moses, named after his Grandfather.

After the war, towns along inland waterways, such as Sweetgum flourished. The smell of black powder and the thunder of cannons was gone and cotton and tobacco grew, once again in the fields where Blue and Gray soldiers fought and died. Sweetgum's population all but doubled and Mal, Leolla and little Moses found a piece of land atop Floyd's Knobs, just outside of Sweetgum, with soil that was perfect for growing Leolla's hybrid "sweet-sweet taters. By the time Moses was four, there was a crop, a barn, a house and a brick oven big enough to keep up with the town's growing demand for "those magic pies.

Just after little Moses turned eighteen, he came home with his new wife Jaleen. The former Jaleen Jasper, who was now Jaleen Messer. One year later, Jaleen gave birth to Leolla, which immediately became Little Leolla until she was eight, then she grew. By the time little Leolla was twelve, Big Leolla had taught her everything about baking and selling *Leolla's Sweetater Pies*. By the time she was seventeen, she and Moses were running the bakery all by themselves.

Malaki and Big Leolla had been talking for years, about going to Scotland to find Jesse and Ivy and knew it was now or never. With tears in their eyes, they waved goodbye and started down off the knobs . . . and were never seen again. They never arrived in Scotland.

Little Leolla and Moses ran the bakery for the next fifteen years and when Leolla was just turning forty, she gave birth to a strapping baby girl and they named her *Eulanda Mae* which was later southern-ized to *Eula Mae* who carried the "sweeter that sweet" secret well into the twentieth century. She lived to a ripe old age of one hundred and five.

※

For Ernest P. Holman and Chief Red Feather, the epiphany they had called *Glory Door,* showed the whole world that it can actually keep turning without war or hatred or deceit. Peace and prosperity prevailed. The red man created from his heritage and sold it to the white man. The white man did the same and sold it to the red man. The outside world heard about it and started coming up the mountain to buy from them both. In spite of all who fought it and said it could not be done, Glory Door, today is the bright and shiny gem in the diverse history of America.

※

While threats of civil war were rumbling through the states, Duncan and Ivy stayed in Scotland for the next three years and Ivy gave birth to a whopping nine pound baby boy with curly blond hair and brown eyes. His name was kept a secret until his baptism. The whole clan gathered in the stone sanctuary of *The Kings Church of God* as the priest, in full robes, came forth with the baby. A hush fell over the multitude of Clan members. It was completely silent when the Priest touched the baby's forehead with the holy water and said, "I now baptise you . . ." You could hear a pin drop . . . *"Jesse Lafayette McNabb,"* A cheer ran through the hall.

The next day, announcements were sent out to all the Scottish domains. It was a simple embossed card that said *Mr. and Mrs. Duncan McNabb Announce the birth of their son, Jesse Lafayette McNabb. May 28, 1865.*

The same announcement was also sent to Ernest, Melba, Red Feather, Running Deer, Pastor Thornberry, Little Fox and all, back in *Glory Door.* The only difference was that under the embossed lettering was a hand written phrase in Cherokee that those in the tribe could read, For all others, there was an asterisk with a translation. It said *"The Man who Found Himself."*

Young Jesse stayed in America after the passing of his parents and married Sarah Leigh Tinsley, daughter of Howard Tinsley, of *Tinsley Farms.* They had eight children, the oldest of which was *Jesse Lafayette McNabb, Junior,* better known as *JL* who eventually inherited the Farms.

At the age of 19, while unloading grain sacks at the mill in Sideways, JL met, courted and wed *Orah Mae Berrong,* the daughter of Ben Berrong, proprietor of the BB Berrong Milling Company.

Orah and JL made their home in Glory Door and had two children. A daughter with long, straight black hair, and named after her Great, Great, Great Grandmother Ivy, and a son who inherited the curly blond hair and blue eyes of his Scottish ancestor and was named after an old, old friend of the family, Ernest Holman. Both Ernest and Ivy rode in on the dust clouds of the worst depression the country had ever seen, but the flamboyant and cheerful Ernest saw light through it all.